895.609
Ueda, Makoto,
Modern Japanese wri literature
A   ocm02372166

19019200033 0935

N
OF EASTON AREA
PUBLIC LIBRARY

W9-BYV-573

MISHIMA

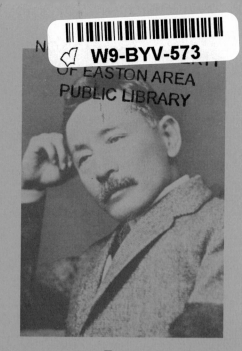

SŌSEKI

KAWABATA

SHIGA

Modern Japanese Writers

AND THE NATURE OF LITERATURE

895.609
U22m

Ueda.

Modern Japanese writers and the
nature of literature.

October 1976

MAKOTO UEDA

Modern Japanese Writers

AND THE NATURE OF LITERATURE

STANFORD UNIVERSITY PRESS

STANFORD, CALIFORNIA

1976

EASTON PUBLIC LIBRARY
EASTON PA

895.609
U 22 m

Stanford University Press
Stanford, California
© 1976 by the Board of Trustees of the
Leland Stanford Junior University
Printed in the United States of America
ISBN 0-8047-0904-1   LC 75-39336

The photographs on the endpapers appear with
the kind permission of the following:
Sōseki, Kōchō Shorin; Kafū, Mozumi Hideshi; Tanizaki,
Higuchi Susumu, courtesy of Mrs. Tanizaki and
Bungei Shunjū Ltd.; Shiga, Irie Taikichi,
from *Shiga Naoya zenshū* (Iwanami Shoten), XIII;
Akutagawa, Museum of Modern Japanese Literature;
Dazai, Kyodō News Service; Kawabata, Mozumi Hideshi;
and Mishima, Mozumi Hideshi.

EASTON PUBLIC LIBRARY
EASTON PA

SEP 2 4 1976

Preface

❀

THIS BOOK is a study of eight major writers of modern Japan, eight writers whose novels and stories constitute the great bulk of modern Japanese fiction available in English. Because the book seeks in particular to identify the literary concepts of these eight writers, it should be of interest to two broad groups of readers. For those interested in general and comparative literature, it will serve as an introduction to some of the major literary theories informing contemporary Japanese writing. As in the premodern period, literary aesthetics in modern Japan have been dominated not by philosophers or rhetoricians but by poets and writers. By looking into the literary thought of these eight writers, then, we acquire at once a fairly good grasp of the forces at work in Japanese letters during the last one hundred years. In this respect, the book can be considered something of a sequel to my previous book, *Literary and Art Theories in Japan* (Cleveland, 1967), which stopped short of the modern period.

The book will also interest those who read the novels and stories of these eight writers. The Western reader is of course free to interpret a Japanese novel from a Western point of view; to be sure, such a view sometimes results in a refreshingly original interpretation. But coming to the novel with a knowledge of the novelist's concept of literature unquestionably adds a dimension to the understanding of his work, and perhaps conveys the key to the meaning of his novel. This method is especially helpful in studying a writer like Kawabata, whose purposes are often exasperatingly elusive. To some degree a literary work is a manifestation of the author's concept of literature; understanding something of that concept should help the reader to understand the work.

To grasp one's literary concept, however, is no easy task, and obviously some kind of comprehensive scheme is needed. In this study, therefore, I have discussed each writer's concept of literature under five headings, each taking up a major issue in literary theory. These issues are (1) art versus nature, (2) the literary work and the author, (3) the literary work and the reader, (4) structure and style, and (5) the purpose of literature. These are issues so basic that any writer has to confront them in order to write at all. By making a systematic survey of the way in which each writer confronted them, I have tried to illuminate his approach to literature in general.

I found plenty of material to support such an undertaking. These eight writers all expressed their views on the nature of literature through literary essays, critical reviews, prefaces, postscripts, and so forth. Indeed, some were first-rate critics, and several even published books on the art of writing. Though less direct or systematic, their autobiographical essays, diaries, and letters also contain clues to the secrets of their craft. And, of course, their novels and stories reflect their concepts of literature. A scene or an incident described in the novel sometimes reveals a great deal about the author's idea of a novel.

A comment on the treatment of names is in order. Throughout this book Japanese names appear in the Japanese order, the surname preceding the given name. I have also followed the Japanese custom of calling a writer by his surname unless he took a *gagō*, that is, an "elegant name" used professionally by an artist or scholar in place of his given name; thus Tanizaki and Kawabata, not Jun'ichirō or Yasunari, but Sōseki and Kafū rather than Natsume or Nagai. As for the titles of Japanese works, I have in most cases employed the ones used for the standard English translations, where such translations exist; hence Tanizaki's *Sasameyuki* is *The Makioka Sisters*, not *Thin Snow*. Otherwise I have translated the titles myself, although I did not hesitate to borrow extant English titles if they seemed excellent. An explanation of sources and where to locate them can be found in the Source Notes, pp. 261–67. The original Japanese titles will be found in the index, where they both follow the translated titles and supply cross-references to them.

In preparing this book I have incurred a number of debts to individuals and institutions. My thanks are due to the University of Toronto, which supported my research for several years through its summer grant program. Stanford University helped me through the later stages by granting an early sabbatical leave, as well as by awarding a research fellowship through its School of Humanities and Sciences. The typing of the final manuscript was done with the assistance of a grant from the Center for East Asian Studies at Stanford. I am also grateful to the members of the Asian Library staffs at Stanford, the University of Toronto, and the University of California, Berkeley, for their assistance in securing materials necessary for my research. Mr. J. M. B. Edwards helped me not only as an expert editor but as a well-informed reader of world literature while I worked on the final draft. Mr. William W. Carver also read parts of the manuscript and offered me valuable suggestions. Last but not least, I thank my wife, who took various sacrifices in stride on our family's behalf during the long period of research and writing.

M.U.

Contents

Modern Japanese Writers

AND THE NATURE OF LITERATURE

CHAPTER ONE

Natsume Sōseki

❀

M ORE EARNESTLY than most Japanese writers of his time, Natsume Sōseki (1867–1916) sought answers to questions on the nature of literature. Before becoming a novelist he had been a professor of English deeply interested in Western literary theory. He had read extensively in this subject while studying in London, and upon his return home he offered a course in it at Tokyo University. Later, in a course on eighteenth-century English writers at the same university, he applied his views on literature to literary criticism. Even after taking up writing as a profession, he gave several public lectures on aesthetic problems. His novels themselves reflect his interest in the subject: *I Am a Cat* abounds in philosophical discussions of literature and the arts; *The Red Poppy* closes with an argument on tragedy; and *The Three-Cornered World* can almost be called an essay on aesthetics written in novelistic form.

Life Without Form Is Meaningless

Sōseki's view of the relationship between art and nature is well summed up in a preface he wrote to a book reproducing the works of a certain Japanese painter. Entitled "Art That Tries to Depart from Nature," the preface identifies three different types of art. In the first type, the artist faithfully copies nature and thereby creates a "second nature" that resembles the original. The copy differs from the original in that it is insulated from all nonartistic, and therefore perishable, elements of reality. In the second type, he is more individualistic and deliberately tries to display unique color

added by his mind. "He endeavors," Sōseki explained, "not to reproduce nature but to depict the image of it that his mind has
projected." In the third type of art, the artist moves even farther
away from nature. "Yet another step in this direction," wrote
Sōseki, "and the artist finds himself depicting neither nature nor
the mind that projects nature, but rather his own interpretation
of it. By 'his own interpretation' I mean the way in which he gives
meaning to nature, the way in which he views nature."*

Sōseki thought well enough of this classification of art to use it
in a scene of his novel *The Three-Cornered World*. The hero, a
painter, is seated at his desk in a resort inn, trying to produce a
work. Unable to do so, he muses on the general nature of art and
classifies paintings into three main types. The first type is the one
in which "a flower looks like a flower." In the second type of painting, the artist's "personal viewpoint is manifest in every single
brush stroke." The third type presents the painter's "inspiration,"
which is independent of any material object. The hero of the novel,
being a Japanese painter, cannot help preferring the third type
over the other two.

These three types of art conceived by Sōseki can be termed
"realistic," "impressionistic," and "expressive," respectively. The
idea was no doubt of Western origin. In a well-known passage of
Poetics, Aristotle wrote that the poet must imitate one of three
objects: "things as they were or are, things as they are said or
thought to be, or things as they ought to be." Basically, Sōseki's
scheme differs little from Aristotle's. And yet, a study of Sōseki's
scheme in the light of his other writings reveals several noteworthy
facts.

To begin with, we should note the fact that Sōseki actually wrote
three different types of novels, and with fair success in each, too.
Normally a novelist, or any artist for that matter, tends to work
in one type only, or two at most. Sōseki tried his hand in all three
during his relatively short career as a novelist. *Grass on the Wayside* can be cited as the best example of the first type. The hero, a
college professor, is unmistakably Sōseki himself. The heroine, the

---

* Sources of quotations will be found in the Source Notes, on pp. 261–67.

professor's wife, can be easily identified as Mrs. Natsume. The novel realistically describes the unhappy relationship between this couple as they live a dreary family life day by day, with no sensational incident ever breaking the monotony. Making a sharp contrast is *The Red Poppy*, which can be considered the third type of novel. It presents no character resembling Sōseki. The protagonist is a beautiful young woman who, confident in her charms, tries to dominate each and every person who comes near her. Most of the incidents in the novel, leading up to the sudden death of the heroine, take place within a few days that are replete with coincidences. The novel is far from being realistic, but it expresses the author's moral philosophy in a dramatic manner. Sōseki's first novel, *I Am a Cat*, falls midway between *Grass on the Wayside* and *The Red Poppy* as far as its proximity to real life is concerned. The main character, called Kushami Sensei ("Mr. Sneeze"), is a teacher of English, as Sōseki was, but he is consistently caricatured by the novel's narrator, a cat. Undoubtedly this is the second type of novel, with the narrator's viewpoint manifesting itself throughout the narrative. All other novels by Sōseki can be placed along with or between these three novels. One of the main charms of reading Sōseki, as has often been pointed out, is his versatility as a storyteller, his ability to give his readers an illusion that they are seeing a wide variety of human life, when, in fact, all are variations on the same major theme. This versatility can be attributed, at least in part, to Sōseki's theory of literature, which readily accepted three different types of relationship between nature and art.

More intrinsically, Sōseki's thought on the question of nature versus art is distinguished by its emphasis on the autonomy of art. In his opinion, there is always a certain distance between art and nature. Even when the artist is of the first type and copies nature faithfully, the work produced is a "second nature" distinct from nature itself. "It is for this reason," Sōseki observed, "that the artist, even when he imitates nature, always feels himself to be not a slave but a demigod." No artist can, or should, reproduce nature exactly as it is. Sōseki thought of two reasons why this has to be so. One, influenced by Buddhism, is that nature as such is "all too fleeting." The other, more Western, is that whatever the artist takes from nature cannot ultimately be freed from "the way in which he views nature." Both have profound implications for Sōseki's concept of art.

Sōseki was always painfully aware that nature is fleeting, that life is in a state of flux. Among his earliest surviving writings is his translation into English of a thirteenth-century Japanese classic, *An Account of My Hut*, which begins with a sentence comparing human life to an eternally flowing river. His last complete novel, *Grass on the Wayside*, ends with the hero's bitter observation that nothing in life is settled, that things that happened once will keep on happening. One of his university lectures makes the same point. "Some say that life has no form, that it is extremely diffuse. I think I can agree with them. . . . A life without conclusions is painful." Sōseki's answer was to reduce the pain by observing life from a definite viewpoint. To such an observer, life would yield a pattern that might be put down in writing and become a novel. The artist had to impose a pattern in this way because life as it is is formless. Life as such is painful, frightening, uncanny—or else it is monotonous, tedious, unbearable. Literature gives it form, and therefore meaning.

Accordingly, Sōseki showed a distaste for the kind of literature that seemed to him to fail in this respect. For instance, he was quite impatient with Defoe's novels, which he felt were too rambling. He compared them to a diary which dutifully begins on January 1 and ends on December 31. Similarly, he remarked of Swift's *Tale of a Tub* that it was less successful than *Gulliver's Travels* because the material (the history of the Church) to some extent dictated its form, curbing the author's artistic freedom. Sōseki also censured Japanese naturalist writers, saying that they wrote about specific people and events for the sole reason that they actually existed. In his opinion, these writers either lacked a philosophy of life or, if they had one, failed to apply it. As a result, their work exhibited the same lack of discrimination between good and bad men or important and unimportant events that made everyday life so lacking in form and significance.

This idea that literature gives form and significance to the chaos of life was further reinforced by Sōseki's philosophical point of view, for which he drew on contemporary psychology. "In the final analysis," he said in one of his lectures, "neither you nor I exist. What exists—what truly exists—is nothing but consciousness." He went on to make the "stream of consciousness" one of his theory's central features. Things in life, he maintained, appear and disappear in the stream of consciousness largely without order or pattern. The individual, in his effort to understand reality, automatically accepts or rejects them, instant by instant, as they come into his consciousness and occupy his attention at that instant. Next moment, as his mind flows on, they are replaced by something else. Life, in Sōseki's view, is nothing other than this flow of consciousness, and is therefore what the artist has before him when he says he is imitating life. Life as it really is cannot be perceived; what is recorded is its "semblance."*

In sum, Sōseki's view of the relationship between literature and life is remarkable for its emphasis on form and clarity. It derived from his fear of the chaotic and the unknown, a fear that amounted to deep pessimism over life as it is. It also suggests, however, that he was rather optimistic about the human capacity for dealing with chaos and ignorance. He thought that artists, in particular, were peculiarly gifted in this regard, since they could shape the fluid and chaotic material of life into an orderly structure. Life thus transformed was "insulated" in an unchanging artistic sphere that terrestrial and unartistic influences could not reach. Presiding over this sphere were the artists, demigods who gave it eternal life.

The Artist as Taster

The artist, according to Sōseki, is a person especially gifted in creating, through his mind, a structured semblance of external reality that gives meaning to an otherwise meaningless life. But there are others—philosophers, for example, or historians—who might appear to perform essentially the same function. A more precise definition is needed to distinguish the artist from them. In

---

* For these ideas Sōseki was indebted chiefly to the works of William James, especially to *The Principles of Psychology*. Another major influence on his theory was *Essay on the Creative Imagination* by Théodule Ribot.

a lecture entitled "The Philosophical Basis of Literature and Art," Sōseki gave such a definition. He first established that people have three main faculties—intellect, emotion, and will—and that they can be classified according to the ways in which they apply these faculties to external reality. He then went on to say: "Now, those who apply intellect [in the main] are people who *elucidate* the interrelationships of things; they are labeled philosophers and scientists. Those who apply emotion are people who *taste* the interrelationships of things; they are known as artists and men of letters. Those who apply will are people who *improve* the interrelationships of things; they are called warriors, statesmen, beancake makers, carpenters, and so forth."

Obviously the key term in this definition of the artist is "taste," a word Sōseki was especially fond of both as a verb and as a noun. It appears time and again in his writings on literature. What he seems to have meant by it was a subjective feeling of like or dislike as against either intellectual or practical judgment. An artist neither abstracts from things in life, like a scientist, nor tries to improve on them, like a statesman; rather, he leaves them where they are and tries to understand them through his sensibility. This enables him to represent them in a way that involves emotion. As Sōseki observed elsewhere, the artist specializes in a type of perception that incites emotion.

Characteristic of Sōseki was the fact that he considered taste an integral part of consciousness. In his opinion, one's likes and dislikes, far from being innate, are acquired *a posteriori*. They are therefore largely the product of the time and place one happens to live in. "Taste may be universal in part, but on the whole it is local (you need not ask why this is so; it is a fact no one can deny)," Sōseki declared. "When I say taste is local, I mean it is formed in close connection with the history, the tradition, the institutions, and the manners peculiar to the society." One unfortunate victim of this fact, according to Sōseki, was Alexander Pope. Though sufficiently endowed with poetic passion, as can be seen from some of his shorter, more lyrical works, he expended his chief energy in writing such passionless, contrived verse as "An Essay on Man" because the taste of the time commanded him to do so.

Although he recognized emotion as the mark of artistic genius, Sōseki unknowingly limited its range and depth by linking it so closely to taste. Indeed, he placed emotion on the same plane as intellect and will, thus confining it to the sphere of consciousness. Because emotion was rooted in the conscious self, it was conditioned by historical, social, and moral factors. From today's point of view, this approach is defective; for instance, it omits the role of the subconscious. But Sōseki should not be blamed too harshly for this; after all, he lived in the pre-Freudian age. Rather, we should see his approach as explaining some of the characteristics of his own novels: the persistent social and moral concern, the wealth of references to his cultural heritage, the stream-of-consciousness technique—and the failure to confront sexual problems.

Sōseki's location of intellect and will in the same sphere of consciousness as emotion causes him, ironically, to minimize the differences between writer, scholar, and statesman—the very differences that Sōseki emphasized in his definition of the artist. Since emotion, to Sōseki, was part of consciousness, and therefore open to analysis, he thought that the novelist both could and should be an analyst—a kind of scholar in human psychology. Likewise, since consciousness is conditioned by the external environment, he saw the writer as a historian, a sociologist, an anthropologist, or at any rate a man of learning. It is no accident that Sōseki, when listing the essential ingredients of a modern novel, put "character analysis" and "psychological analysis" in first and second place. He is also reported to have said that the most important qualification for being a modern writer was to possess a firm viewpoint from which to interpret people's behavior. When asked how one could acquire such a viewpoint, he is said to have answered that the easiest way was to acquire learning, and that many Japanese writers in the past lacked proper education and therefore a proper viewpoint. But Sōseki's idea of emotion also made the writer a sort of statesman. By presenting a political or moral viewpoint, the novelist could move his readers to act in conformity with it. "What we call an ideal," Sōseki once said, "is simply an answer to the question: What is the best way to live? Painters' paintings and writers' writings are all answers of this kind."

Sōseki's definition of the artist, then, has much to do with psychology and ethics, despite its overt emphasis on emotion. True, the artist is a person who perceives life chiefly through the medium of his emotions. But since these can be analyzed, he might want to turn psychologist. Moreover, since his emotions affect the reader's, he might want to write for the purpose of moral education. Sōseki himself did all these things. His strength and weakness as a writer are both due in no small part to the consistency with which he followed his own theories.

Kokoro, probably the best of Sōseki's later novels, will provide as good a test case as any other. The main character is a middle-aged intellectual whom the narrator reverently calls Sensei. As a young student, Sensei fell in love with his landlady's daughter, but in his shyness he kept his feelings to himself. Then his close friend came to lodge in the same house and, unaware of his feelings, began to love the same girl. Sensei was quick to act when he discovered this. He immediately talked to the landlady and obtained her consent for his marriage to her daughter. He had hardly had time to celebrate his victory, however, before his friend committed suicide a few days later. Sensei was never the same man after that time. He had a lovely wife, was financially well-off, and lived as comfortable a life as any man could wish for, and yet he was never able to free himself from the sense of betrayal. Finally, when he heard the news of a certain famous general's having committed suicide to follow the late Emperor Meiji (1852–1912), he decided to kill himself and thereby end his prolonged agony.

The strength of the novel lies in the range, depth, and intensity with which psychological and moral issues are probed. Especially in the last third of the novel, which consists entirely of a letter written by Sensei, Sōseki penetrates deep into the mind of a man faced with stark human reality: egoism. The novel is a psychological study of basic human egoism, and a very moving one. And, as such, it serves as an effective means of moral education. Young people who read the novel learn how deep-rooted egoism is, how destructive it can be, and how seriously they should try to cope with it. As a matter of fact, Sensei's letter is addressed to the novel's narrator, a young student who befriended Sensei because he felt Sensei had something important to teach him.

Kokoro, however, has at least three weaknesses, all of which are related to Sōseki's concept of art discussed above. The first is Sensei's apparent inability to see that his wife, an innocent woman, is deeply disturbed because he never confides to her the cause of his agony. Granted that Sensei, with his gentle affection toward her, does not want to involve her in his problem, it is obvious that he is incapable of communicating with her at the deepest level of human relationship. Indeed, he seems to communicate better with the young student than with his wife. The reason is simple: she is a woman. She incites emotions at a level deeper than the conscious mind, and Sensei is afraid of that. He has an unusually pessimistic view of heterosexual relationship. This limitation of Sensei's viewpoint reflects that of Sōseki, who confined emotion to the sphere of consciousness.

The second shortcoming of the novel has to do with Sensei's suicide. The timing of his decision to die is not convincing. To put it crudely, Emperor Meiji died, then the famous general died, and therefore Sensei is going to die, too. Sensei himself is aware that young people may not understand the motive of his suicide, and he talks about the lack of understanding between the generations. Our knowledge of Sōseki's view of literature, especially of emotion, clarifies the issue. As we have seen, Sōseki thought that one's emotions are affected by the time and place one lives in. Sensei's emotions at the time of his decision to die were, therefore, those of a man who lived in Meiji Japan. Sōseki left the issue at that.

The third problem with *Kokoro* is about the wisdom of Sensei's decision to die, regardless of his motives. Suicide is an escape, not a solution. We wonder whether he could not have taken a more positive attitude in coping with his predicament. In fact, one possible solution is suggested toward the end of the novel, where Sensei does all he can to care for his ailing mother-in-law. Eventually she dies, but for the first time since his friend's death Sensei is able to feel that he has been of use to others. Could he not have lived on, then, to do things that help his fellow men? From Sōseki's point

of view, he could not have. This was so because Sensei was someone
like Sōseki, a man of letters who is basically a "taster." A taster is
not a man of action.

The Beautiful, the True, the Good, and the Heroic

Sōseki's thoughts on the relationship between the literary work
and the reader are embodied in "The Philosophical Basis of Literature and Art." In his opinion, there are four kinds of effects that
works of art produce in the mind of reader or spectator. They are
"the beautiful," "the true," "the good," and "the heroic."

The effect that he called "the beautiful" is produced by a work
of art that embodies the artist's perception of an ideal interrela-
tionship among things in life or nature. Being artistic, this perception has to be of a predominantly emotional kind. Accordingly,
the things in question are full of sensuous appeal. Among the examples cited by Sōseki are Chinese-style landscape paintings, Western-style paintings of the nude, and Japanese haiku. However, he
made no attempt to enumerate the different types of beauty produced by such works; indeed, he professed bewilderment at the
proliferation of aesthetic categories in Western discussions of the
topic.

Nevertheless, it appears from other sources that Sōseki had his
favorite type of beauty. For instance, a typical passage in *The
Three-Cornered World*, a novel that he says he wrote with the sole
aim of producing a beautiful effect, describes how the hero, taking
a bath in the public bathroom of an inn at a hot-springs resort,
unexpectedly encountered the heroine in the nude.* Barely able
to discern her lovely contours amid the steam, he was moved to
reflect:

Her figure was not that of a naked body fully disclosed before one's eyes.
Looming in a strangely mysterious atmosphere that made everything look
ethereal, it yielded only a few modest hints of its ripe beauty. The figure
had an air, warmth, and ineffable rhythm that were artistically impeccable, like some black-ink drawing of a dragon's scale done with such

---

* Most Japanese inns at a hot-springs resort have a large bathroom open to
all guests. In Sōseki's day, mixed bathing was usually allowed in this type of
bathroom.

verve that the spectator can imagine everything the artist's brush has omitted.* If a minute depiction of a dragon with all its thirty-six scales produces a ludicrous effect, then the appeal of a great artistic masterpiece surely lies in the artist's refusal to observe every last detail of the naked body. When I saw her figure outlined there, I wondered if I was not looking at that celestial lady Ch'ang-e, momentarily hesitating amid the beautiful rainbow fairies who had come in pursuit of her when she fled from the palace of the moon.†

The passage has the verbosity characteristic of Sōseki's early writings, but it perfectly illustrates his ideal of beauty. It was a distinctly Oriental ideal, especially valued by medieval Japanese aestheticians, who gave it an almost mystical value. The taste of the hero, as revealed elsewhere in the novel, is undoubtedly that of a traditional Japanese: he likes the poetry of T'ao Ch'ien (365–427) and Wang Wei (701?–61), the haiku of Matsuo Bashō (1644–94) and Yosa Buson (1716–84), the calligraphy of the Zen priest Kōsen (1633–95), the landscape painting of Wen T'ung (1018–79) and Ike Taiga (1723–76).‡ Common to the works of all these artists are an otherworldly mystery and depth. They feature the ethereal beauty of some object only dimly visible to the naked eye—an effect that defies critical analysis. The term that medieval Japanese gave to this effect was *yūgen*, and it became standard. In fact, the word appears in the second sentence of the passage quoted above.

The same effect predominates in Sōseki's haiku poetry, a literary genre that he thought existed for expressing ideal beauty.§ He also seems to have invented the term *haikuteki shōsetsu* ("haiku-like novel"), referring to a novel that, like *The Three-Cornered World*,

---

* The dragon referred to is a mythological serpent-shaped creature with four legs and a horn. That it had 36 scales seems to have been Sōseki's own idea.

† Ch'ang-e, according to an ancient Chinese legend, is a beautiful fairy living on the moon.

‡ T'ao Ch'ien and Wang Wei were Chinese poet-recluses noted for the beauty of their nature poems. Yosa Buson, along with Bashō, was one of the two most influential haiku poets. Kōsen, a native of China, came to Japan in 1661 and headed one of the largest Zen temples there. Wen T'ung was especially known for his painting of bamboos. Ike Taiga, a friend of Buson's, excelled in a style of painting known as nanga.

§ Sōseki said: "Those who want to express their concept of ideal beauty by relating it to objects in nature become painters specializing in landscapes, or writers of Chinese-style verse predominantly singing about scenes of nature, or poets writing in the haiku form."

had a primarily aesthetic purpose. Here are three examples from
his haiku:

> Plum blossoms fall:
> turning in the moonlit night,
> a water wheel.

> The piercing cold—
> I marry a plum blossom
> in a dream.

> I take my leave:
> in my dream there is a flow of light—
> the River of Heaven.

All these haiku have an unreal, dreamlike atmosphere in which
certain beautiful objects are softly enveloped. In the first poem
both the falling plum blossoms and the turning water wheel are
as soundless as the moonlight. But the only obvious feature of the
second and third poems is that they describe dreams; everything
else about them is mysterious. Sōseki himself confessed that he did
not know the exact meaning of the third one. Nevertheless, its
ambiguity adds to, rather than detracts from, its ethereal beauty.

Sōseki's predilection for the yūgen ideal of beauty may seem inconsistent with his fear of the formless, his love of clarity, and his
generally analytic approach toward life and literature. In reality,
it is not at all inconsistent. Sōseki prized yūgen precisely because
he found it beyond the reach of intellectual analysis; beauty dis-
sected, he seems to have thought, is beauty lost. His case is rather
like that of Swift, who harbored deep reverence for the mystery
of religion because of (and not despite) his extraordinary intellectual gifts.*

In time, Sōseki became less interested in beautiful literary effects
and more interested in true ones. He did not write a novel like
The Three-Cornered World again. Even before he wrote it, his

---

* Incidentally, Sōseki, who in general respected Swift more highly than
Addison, Steele, Pope, or Defoe, criticized *Gulliver's Travels* for its lack of
poetic beauty. He wrote that a world traveler like Gulliver should have enjoyed
the colors of the ocean, the sound of the waves, the sight of flying birds, etc.,
which Swift hardly portrayed at all. Here, Sōseki seems to be unconsciously
comparing Gulliver to such Oriental poet-wanderers as Tu Fu and Bashō.

productivity in the haiku form had already declined markedly. He wanted to write novels that would create an impression of truth, and he did.

According to Sōseki, a literary work that rings true is one that expresses a universal law of nature through the representation of tangible objects. In the main, the author deduces the law intellectually, as a philosopher or a scientist would do. Unlike the latter, however, he has to win the reader's emotional involvement, and therefore has to make a greater emotional investment in the deductive process. Abstractions tend not to incite emotion, so this law has to be conceived and presented in particular rather than universal terms. In one example cited by Sōseki, a novel describes how a starving husband, who used to love his wife dearly, snatches away her share of gruel and eats it himself. Here, the law that imparts a sense of "the true" is the law of universal egoism: in the final analysis, we are all hungry husbands and wives engaged in desperate battle over a bowl of porridge. Elsewhere Sōseki wrote: "Man cuts man with knives and cruel words, never suspecting his turn for being cut will follow. Nature abhors a vacuum. Either love or hatred! Nature likes compensation. Tit for tat! Nature likes a fight. Death or independence!" He expressed this view of society on many other occasions, even in a haiku:

> On a charcoal kiln
> a vine keeps climbing, while
> being burnt to death.

The clash of interests—a plant that wants to live and a kiln that wants to burn—though aesthetically striking, has obvious social overtones. A similar kind of struggle is found in Sōseki's later novels. In *Mon*, the hero shamelessly betrays a close friend, at once robbing him of his beautiful wife and ruining his promising career. In *Kokoro*, Sensei does a similar thing with a more tragic result: his friend is driven to kill himself. *Grass on the Wayside*, a more autobiographical and less sensational novel, presents a strained relationship between the hero and his wife, both of whom seek more independence, as well as a series of small clashes between him and his relatives and acquaintances who try to exploit him for his money. All these novels produce an impression more truthful than beautiful.

While maintaining that modern writers should aim at the truth, Sōseki warned that they should not pursue it at the expense of other values. In this connection he expressed his dissatisfaction with the works of some Western realist writers, notably Maupassant, Ibsen, and Zola, who he thought were often so concerned with the bare facts that they failed to give the reader moral satisfaction. For instance, he criticized Maupassant's "The Necklace" for its harsh ending: the heroine was a morally admirable person, and the reader could not help but feel that she suffered unfairly. For similar reasons, Sōseki did not like *Othello*; he admired the verisimilitude of Shakespeare's plot and characterization, but found the conclusion depressing. A literary work, he seems to be saying, should not wantonly violate the reader's sense of justice even when truth is its main concern.

The impression of "the good," Sōseki's third type of literary effect, can be described as a feeling that satisfies this very sense. Such an impression is produced by works that reflect the various types of human emotion manifesting themselves in life in the highest forms of which they are capable. The types of emotion that can be transformed into literature are, of course, numerous. Partly following the French psychologist Théodule Ribot (1839–1916), Sōseki mentioned love (romantic love, that is), loyalty, filial piety, nobility, friendship, fear, anger, sympathy, pride, patience, jealousy, among others. In many cases he cited appropriate examples from English literature. Sōseki considered love the most frequent source of literary inspiration, and professed himself astonished at the fact. "It may even be said," he wrote, "that all literature at all times—almost 90 percent of it in the Western world in particular—has centered on material that falls into this category." His reservations, when he reviewed some representative examples of love in Western literature, were considerable. For instance, he did not like the presentation of Phoebe's love in Keats's *Endymion*; indeed, he thought that its effect on a Japanese reader, at least, was far from "the good." A Japanese, he argued, would feel a sense of guilt—not unmixed with pleasure, to be sure—if he pursued romantic love to the same extent as Keats. "While we make much of love," he wrote, "we always try to restrain it. As educated men we feel ashamed of ourselves if we fall victim to it. We cannot help being haunted by a sense of guilt if we blindly follow wherever our heart leads us."

Sōseki's concept of love as such is latent in many of his later novels. It has its most direct expression in *Mon*. The hero of the novel is Sōsuke, a civil servant in his early thirties who had some years earlier fallen in love with a married woman and taken her away from her husband, a close friend of his. He and the woman, now married to each other, lead a secluded life together. He loves her tenderly, yet he is increasingly tormented by the memory of his past behavior. As a result, Sōsuke's love for his wife never burns as passionately as it might otherwise. He does not kill himself as Sensei does in *Kokoro*, but it is obvious that he is living in a kind of hell.

Mon is an appealing novel, mainly because Sōsuke and his wife are gentle, intelligent, sympathetic characters. Yet, reading the novel, we cannot help wondering if Sōsuke could not have been more courageous in loving his wife. We get the impression that he has not fathomed the deepest depth of conjugal love, the kind of love that might have provided him with the courage to face the outside world. His love is more mental than physical. But, from Sōseki's point of view, that was the way it should be. An educated man should not "fall victim" to romantic love; otherwise he will be forever haunted by a sense of guilt, as Sōsuke is.

One may well imagine what emotion Sōseki valued most as a subject for literary creation. It was a sense of guilt. If a literary work presents a hero suffering from a deep sense of guilt, Sōseki thought, it will give the reader a good deal of moral satisfaction, because the ability to feel guilt is the very mark of man's integrity. All men are egoistic and therefore guilty: the conscientious know this and suffer, but the unscrupulous do not know it (or pretend they do not know it), and therefore do not suffer.* Many of the protagonists in Sōseki's later novels suffer because they are aware of the evil in themselves. Thus Sōsuke in *Mon*, suffering the torments of conscience, eventually seeks salvation through religion, but in vain. Sensei in *Kokoro*, painfully aware that he betrayed his friend, refuses to seek happiness in life; he eventually commits suicide. A main character in *Until After the Vernal Equinox* finds himself incapable of loving a woman after he learns of his illicit birth. Even the hero of *And Then*, a lazy, almost frivolous person, goes into a frenzy at the end of the novel; tormented by guilty conscience, he has been trying to make amends to the woman he wronged.

Sōseki's fourth and final type of literary effect is "the heroic." As he saw it, this effect is produced by literature that illustrates the workings of human will power, as when one reads about a man who dared to climb a high mountain in winter, or swim a broad channel, or cross a vast expanse of desert. The sense of the heroic will increase even more if the person performed this heroic act for a worthy cause. Among the examples given by Sōseki were the medieval warrior called Kusunoki Masashige (1294–1336), who willingly sacrificed his life for the emperor, and the Buddhist priest Myōchō (1282–1337), who deliberately broke his misshapen leg so that he could be seated in the proper pose for Zen meditation.† To Sōseki, these acts produced a heroic effect because they transcended egoism. True heroism always demanded both self-sacrifice and a strong will.

In general, Sōseki seems to have preferred the literature of the heroic to that of the beautiful or the true. "A writer who holds literature as dear as life," he once wrote in a letter to a friend, "would not be able to content himself with the creation of beauty alone. He would not be satisfied, I think, unless he had the kind of

* "A man cannot be called mature unless he knows, through some profound experience, that he is a terrible villain," observes the narrator in *I Am a Cat*.

† Sōseki seems to have held Kusunoki Masashige in high admiration since childhood; at the age of seven he wrote a short composition praising Masashige's loyalty to the emperor. Myōchō, better known as Daitō Kokushi, was another hero of Sōseki's; his name appears in *I Am a Cat*, *The Red Poppy*, and elsewhere in Sōseki's writings.

determination with which those pro-emperor revolutionaries endured hardship at the time of the Meiji Restoration." The revolutionaries referred to were young, idealistic radicals who worked for the Restoration of 1868 at the risk of their lives. Sōseki also much admired Captain Sakuma Tsutomu (1879–1910), who, when his submarine sank during maneuvers, recorded its last moments calmly and accurately while facing certain death. Sōseki, all the more impressed with the incident because it happened in his own day, praised the captain's log as a deeply moving document and compared it with contemporary naturalist writings to the disadvantage of the latter. In an article called "Literature and the Heroic," he attacked the naturalists for their obsession with the baser human instincts and for despising heroic literature as fanciful and untrue. He pointed out that man is just as capable of heroic acts as base ones, and that the writer of fiction is therefore amply justified in presenting heroic characters.

Sōseki himself, however, did not write many novels in a heroic vein. Captain Sakuma's example notwithstanding, he claimed that no age had been so lacking in heroism as his own and that no literature was so lacking in heroism as contemporary literature. Of his own novels, the one that comes closest to creating a heroic impression is probably *Autumn Wind,* in which the main character is a destitute journalist who keeps fighting for his ideals in the face of pressure. Probably in the same category is a rather different sort of novel, *Botchan,* in which the hero is a comically naïve schoolteacher who follows his own convictions at all costs. This anti-hero of Sōseki's is remarkably convincing, more so than a conventionally heroic character would have been.

With his classification of literary effects, Sōseki established, for practically the first time in Japanese aesthetics, a causal relationship between the content of a literary work and its psychological impact. Its most notable feature was its tolerance: Sōseki emerges as a fair-minded theorist who could look on various types of literature without prejudice. This tolerance helps to explain the versatility that enabled him to write *Botchan, The Three-Cornered World, The Red Poppy,* and *The Miner* within a span of two years.

How to "Fabricate" a Novel

On questions of structure and style, Sōseki had a good deal to say. He had to ponder these questions for his lectures at the university, and, as always, his approach was a methodical one. Indeed, he had conceived some very definite ideas on the art of the novel before he ever became a novelist.

Sōseki demanded of a novel that it have a tightly knit structure in order to produce a unity of interest. If it was literature that gave form to life, then the structure of a novel had to be organic. The right kind of unity could be provided, Sōseki thought, by means of psychological causality. Starting from these premises, Sōseki worked out three ways in which a novelist could build an organic structure. First, he could make all the events in the novel relate to certain mental traits of the *dramatis personae*. When an event happens—a fire, an earthquake, or a murder—it deeply affects and changes the characters in the novel. Second, the novelist could make the events relate to the characters' general personalities rather than to their specific traits. In this instance, the connection between events would be looser, and the growth of characters slower. Third, the leading character would not change at all, but would simply encounter various events occasioned either by chance or by his own personality. In this case, the plot would serve merely to reveal the character more fully.

Sōseki stressed that these three types were very general and would be freely combined in an average novel. The classification is nevertheless a convenient one, and especially applicable to Sōseki's own novels. *Botchan*, for example, clearly has the third type of structure, as the young hero meets various comic events and reveals his reckless but righteous nature more fully each time. *The Red Poppy* can be considered to have the first type of plot. All the events in the novel, such as a visit to Kyoto, the Tokyo exposition, and the old scholar's illness, are laid out so as to affect and change one or more of the four main characters in a dramatic way. For the second type of plot, *Sanshirō* can be cited as an example. Its hero is a young student from a country town just introduced to the brave new world that is Tokyo. As he meets various events in the metropolis, he slowly begins to change, not in reference to any specific mental trait but as a whole human being.

Sōseki had little use for a novel that lacked a tightly knit structure. He attacked Defoe's novels for not being any of the three structural types, and therefore for not producing a unity of interest. He showed obvious distaste for the kabuki because of its episodic structure. But he seems to have been rather ambivalent about a new genre of Japanese literature called *shaseibun* ("sketches"), which offered little plot and sketched nature or life objectively and at random. Apparently he liked the genre, but was somewhat at a loss to defend it theoretically (he tried a defense by implying that shaseibun was not really a novel but a development of haiku). He also mentioned certain masterpieces of English literature, including *Cranford*, *Pickwick Papers*, and *Tom Jones*, as showing a viewpoint "somewhat like" that of shaseibun writers. Elsewhere, he expressed a high regard for *Tristram Shandy* despite its lack of coherent structure (he compared the novel to a sea slug because of its sluggish progression). He himself wrote one episodic novel, *Until After the Vernal Equinox*.

Finally, Sōseki attached great importance to the way in which a novel ends. "The profundity of a creative work," he wrote, "lies in the degree to which its contents can be summarized in one sentence—a sentence that penetrates human reality." In other words, a novel must have a clear, summarizable message that can be placed at the end of it. Sōseki considered this technique one of the chief things a beginning novelist should study. He himself employed it in many of his novels, and probably overdid it on occasion.

In dealing with questions of style, Sōseki distinguished nine principal literary devices: (1) projective association (description of external reality in emotive words); (2) introjective association (description of internal reality by means of concrete images); (3) association detached from the self (description of external reality by strikingly associational images); (4) humorous association (pun, parody, wit); (5) the method of harmony (harmonious juxtaposition of objects or moods); (6) mitigation (deliberate relief of tension); (7) acceleration (deliberate increase of tension); (8) pseudo-contrast (deliberate contrast that neither accelerates nor mitigates tension, yet adds something to the mood; Sōseki quoted as an example the monologue of the porter after Macbeth's murder of Duncan); (9) noncontrast (deliberate contrast of two objects or moods that do not harmonize with one another; Sōseki's example was Fielding's pseudo-epic description of Molly's fight in *Tom Jones*). Added to these nine is the method of realistic description, which is not a purely literary device but is used a great deal in literature.

Some interesting facts emerge from this list and the comments by Sōseki that accompany it. First, it is clear from the first four items that Sōseki must have had a high regard for associational language. To be sure, association has been central to the language of literature at all times and in all places. But even so, this emphasis is highly unusual for a novelist. It is, however, what one would expect from Sōseki's own style of writing: his works of fiction are full of richly associational passages, most of which rely on introjective association. However, he preferred simple, natural associations to complex or forced ones. He thought this was because he was a Japanese: he could not appreciate a Homeric simile, he said, because of the impression it made on him of length and verbosity. He criticized Matthew Arnold's similes in "Balder Dead" and *Sohrab and Rustum* for being too long. Sōseki also disliked pedantic associations and attacked some of his contemporary Japanese writers for being guilty on this account. He himself, however, was far from innocent of this fault.

The fact that Sōseki had humorous association on his list is interesting because humor is not usually thought of as a purely stylistic device. But he seems to have conceived humor as arising from whimsical association, that is, from the juxtaposition of things that are not ordinarily associated. He therefore disliked puns or wit for wit's sake. Instead, he prized the kind of humor that reveals the hidden interrelationships of things. Similarly, he laid great store by the method of harmony, which consists in juxtaposing two objects, usually one in nature and the other in human life, to create an atmosphere harmonious with the context. In his opinion,

Japanese literature, especially nō and haiku, was rich in examples of this method; in fact, he was afraid that Japanese readers were so used to it that they might be dissatisfied with any novel that was not full of it. Sōseki then went on to cite examples in English literature that he thought would please Japanese readers. Among them were the following:

> 'Tis thought the king is dead. We will not stay.
> The bay trees in our country are all wither'd,
> And meteors fright the fixed stars of heaven.
> The pale-fac'd moon looks bloody on the earth.
> —*Richard II*, 2:iv:7–10

> The wan moon is setting behind the white wave,
> And time is setting with me, Oh!
> —Burns, "Open the Door to Me, Oh!"

Sōseki himself often used the method of harmony, though not to the same extent as some other Japanese writers who also loved nature. The fair heroine of *The Three-Cornered World* is introduced to the hero (and to the reader) in beautiful surroundings, as moonlight falls peacefully on a bush smothered in white blossom. When the proud heroine of *The Red Poppy* meets sudden death, it is a day of gusty wind and pouring rain. There is also a rainstorm in a climactic scene of *The Wayfarer*, when the central character has a roaring fit of bad temper. He regains his calm when he takes up residence in a small mountain cottage amid idyllic surroundings.

Mitigation and acceleration are common techniques in drama. Sōseki, a novelist with much dramatic talent, often made conscious use of them. Sometimes he tells the reader directly that he is about to change the scene or mood. "My pen does not like this damp air," he says in *The Red Poppy*. "It must move into a sunny scene and get away from the dampness." Pseudo-contrast and noncontrast, which are akin to what later critics were to call "ambiguity" and "the grotesque," are not so common in Sōseki's works, but he does make use of them. A good example of pseudo-contrast is the madman's letter that the hero of *I Am a Cat* reads after he has read two politely formal letters from a nobleman and a school principal. Mr. Kushami takes the letter very seriously, but the cat, who reads the letter with him, thinks it quite absurd. The reader of the novel is left wondering whether he should take the letter seriously or not. A typical example of noncontrast can be found in the same novel. It is an incongruous scene in which a young, handsome physicist, dressed in a frock coat, delivers a well-prepared, carefully documented speech—on "The Dynamics of Strangulation."

On the whole, Sōseki's list of characteristic elements that constitute the language of literature seems quite a sensible one. Of course, one might argue there is little that is new or original about it; one might even say that all literary artists use these techniques without being aware of them. Japanese critics of the period certainly tended to value a literary technique more highly when the writer made use of it without premeditation, and they often attacked Sōseki for being too obsessed with technique. But Sōseki had prepared a reply to that charge, even before he wrote his first novel. He observed that the language of a novel need not conform to ordinary usage; more important, it should be readily acceptable to the reader. In his opinion, technique as such did not matter, but the results of technique did. He compared this fact to the making of an inkwell, which in Japan was more an *objet d'art* than a mere item of stationery. Some inkwells, he said, are beautiful because the original material is beautiful, while others are made beautiful by inkwell makers; art critics cannot say which kind of inkwell is artistically superior. This comment anticipates the later, more famous one that he directed at the naturalist school: "You complain about a novel that is 'fabricated.' But shouldn't you rather worry about 'fabricating' a character that cannot but be felt as alive, or a plot than cannot but be felt as natural?" To Sōseki, it was not fabrication that was bad. It was bad fabrication that was bad.

Toward a Neo-Romantic Ideal

Sōseki recognized that literature has both hedonistic and didactic functions. Of the two, however, he considered the latter far more important. Indeed, few Japanese writers of modern times have been more concerned with the edifying effects of their writings. It may even be surmised that part of the reason Sōseki became a professional novelist and wrote for a wide range of readers (most of his later novels and essays were serialized in Japan's largest daily newspaper) was his urge to teach the general public. Certainly Sōseki was more interested in reaching this public than in lecturing on Shakespeare's folios to a small class.

Yet Sōseki was keenly aware that what the general public sought in works of literature was entertainment, not edification. "No fine is charged if one does not read or buy a literary work," he said in a lecture. "Who would want to read it unless it was entertaining?" He went on to analyze the kind of pleasure that only literature can give. After observing how some of Swift's satirical works leave the reader with an unpleasant feeling, he went on:

Yet the author says this is the truth about men. There is neither a sign-board saying "We Sell Truths" nor a band of hired musicians advertising truths with fanfare. Still, truth gradually reveals itself, moves, struts, and marches, pushing aside everything else without hesitation, as calmly as Heaven's will. The reader first rubs his eyes and watches with pleasure the fresh, stimulating sight. He then nods his head, for what he sees is an undisputable fact: he has the pleasure of hearing something within him answer the call from the outside. Third, the reader realizes he has made a discovery, and thereby he gains the pleasure of having unearthed a fact that had been buried. Fourth, he is pleasantly surprised, for now he finds out that his discovery was a truth about human nature, though it was made in an unlikely place.

Beneath the playful tone, Sōseki makes clear why a novel like *Gulliver's Travels* makes delightful reading. In his view, it provides four kinds of pleasure in combination: the pleasure of being exposed to a fresh stimulus; the pleasure of hearing what one has subconsciously wanted to hear; the pleasure of discovering things that have been hidden; and the pleasure of knowing more about human reality. In short, the discovery of truth is a pleasure, and literature enables one to discover truth in an entertaining way. And this applies to all literary works that have the hallmark of truth. This explanation by Sōseki of the pleasures of literature could be extended to cover other types of literary works. For example, since it is pleasant to encounter people and things that are beautiful, good, or heroic, a novel dealing with them should give the reader the same sort of pleasurable feeling.

It was in this sense that Sōseki viewed the didactic function of literature. From the pleasure of reading a novel, he thought, there emerges new knowledge that in one way or another affects the reader's future life. Knowing more about life and about himself, the reader will automatically modify his future plans, for, consciously or unconsciously, he would like to approach closer to the ideals of truth, beauty, goodness, or heroism expressed in the novel he has just read. Thus, in the final analysis, literature teaches one how to live.

Holding the view of literature that he did, Sōseki was disturbed by the belief so widespread among his contemporaries that literature and morality were incompatible. He considered this belief an overreaction on the part of the naturalists to the more romantic literature of Japan's recent past. The literature of the period immediately preceding Sōseki's was "romantic" in the sense that it presented a number of faultlessly noble figures, so much so that the reader felt they were remote and inimitable, that their behavior was too good to be real. On the other hand, literature in Sōseki's time was in the main "naturalistic" in the sense that it omitted no ugly aspect of human nature, and was devoid of idealism. In consequence, the Japanese reader had come to believe that literature presented either an unearthly paragon of virtue or a slave of earthly passions, but never a realistic model for his own conduct.

Sōseki had a solution to this dilemma. It was "neo-romantic" literature, a dialectical transcendence of romanticism and naturalism. The romantic writers of early nineteenth-century Japan had created incredibly idealistic characters—characters who were only too willing to sacrifice their lives for their lords, for their parents, for their children, or for any other cause the feudal society considered worthy. The writers in the ensuing naturalistic period went to the other extreme and depicted people as blindly following their impulses and freely ignoring traditional morals. Neo-romantic literature, Sōseki thought, would pursue the middle way: it would present people who knew what their impulses were, but who tried to control them and aim at something more attainable. Such people would know that man is not a god but not a devil either, that he is capable of doing good as a human being with a human being's limitations. The ideal at which Sōseki was aiming here can be found in a public lecture that he entitled "Literature and Morality." Toward the end, Sōseki said: "In summing up, I will tell you what sort of person I consider most desirable as a Japanese of the future. He is the type of person who holds a high but attainable ideal and who seeks to live harmoniously with his neighbors—a person who, having ample generosity and understanding, can forgive human frailties and make that forgiveness the lubricant between himself and other individuals." The neo-romantic novel of the future would have such a person for its protagonist. And that, in Sōseki's view, was the kind of novel that would prove most useful for society. Literature, ultimately, would be most useful when it presented an image of an ideal but believable human being.

CHAPTER TWO

Nagai Kafū

❁

N AGAI KAFŪ (1879–1959) was not a systematic literary theorist like Sōseki. Yet there is plenty of evidence to show that he had some very definite ideas about the nature of literature. By the age of thirty he was already a professor of French literature at Keiō University and had become known as one of the leading Japanese experts on Western naturalistic realism. He spent six years as the editor of an important literary magazine, in which he published a number of talented new writers, including Tanizaki Jun'ichirō. Among his numerous literary essays we find such titles as "How to Write a Novel," "The Work of Art and the Artist's Duties," and "The Tone and Color of Language." He was also a theater critic with expert knowledge of the kabuki, and an art critic with a book on woodblock prints to his credit. Some of his fictional works also contain passages in which his own views on art are presented in unvarnished form.

Art and Selective Imitation

Kafū's thoughts on the question of art versus nature are well expressed in "The Work of Art and the Artist's Duties." In its very first sentence he asserts, as a matter of course, that a writer should be "true to the facts." But then he goes on to demonstrate how impossible it is to report all the facts as they are in life. A writer, Kafū says, must "select what he is going to describe." He explains why this is so:

An incident in real life has no protagonist or deuteragonist; each person involved in it behaves as if he were playing the lead. Yet when a writer sketches the same incident in a novel, a protagonist, deuteragonist, etc., naturally emerge from the throng. Nature as it is—nature with nothing selected or discarded from it—cannot become a work of art. A writer who tries to include all the facts will find himself launched on an impossible task. Even if he should succeed, the end result will be a piece of writing that is extremely ambiguous. . . . Therefore, when I write, I first decide what to emphasize and what to deemphasize. I take up my pen only after I have conceived a scene for which I feel a great deal of empathy. By that time I know where the focus of the scene is going to be.

Kafū's conception of art and nature, then, includes three basic elements: factuality, selection, and empathy.

To Kafū, who began writing fiction under the influence of Maupassant and Zola, the idea that literature should be "true to the facts" must have come naturally. More than anything else he loathed falsification; the novelist's first duty, he once wrote, was to "grasp the truth about life and transmit it to his readers, forcing them to form some kind of awareness of it." "A novel," he wrote on another occasion, "depicts the ways of the world and the feelings of men," and on another: "All we wish to do is to take a good look at life's realities, to show that such-and-such a form of life exists under such-and-such circumstances." These remarks are commonplace enough, but beneath them lies something that is peculiarly Kafū's: a marked preference for observable facts. He was more interested in "the truth about life," "the ways of the world," and "life's realities . . . under such-and-such circumstances," than in life as it ought to be, or the ways of the world as it once was, or life as it might have been. It was probably for this reason that Kafū, in his later years, came to like Maupassant more than Zola. He thought that Zola destroyed both life and nature under the pretext of presenting them truthfully, while Maupassant escaped this fault because he was free of all preconceived ideas about life. For the same reason he liked the works of Henri de Régnier, who sketched life realistically but nonchalantly and from a distance, without trying to impose his own prejudices on it.

It is no wonder, then, that Kafū urged beginning writers to observe nature carefully and present it faithfully. He advised that if they wanted to use a specific place for the setting of a novel, they should first pay a visit there and take down notes about the streets, houses, and gardens. Kafū followed his own advice. For instance, he once sketched certain back streets of Yoshi-chō in Tokyo and used them in *The River Sumida*. The novelist-hero of *A Strange Tale from East of the River*, who is obviously Kafū himself, visits a red-light district called Tamanoi before using it for the background of his novel. At the end of *Dwarf Bamboo*, Kafū put a note saying that the novel depicts life as it was around 1915, before retail prices soared and the people of Tokyo changed their ways. He kept a diary for over forty years; this industriousness was due in no small part to his desire to record facts for possible use in his fiction later on. Despite his expert knowledge of and nostalgia for Japanese town life in the Edo Period (1600–1867), Kafū wrote no full-length historical novel, whereas Tanizaki, who also had a good deal of nostalgia for old Japan, produced many works in this genre; part of the reason must have been that Kafū did not like to write about anything he could not observe personally.

As for the principle that the writer should "select what he is going to describe," Kafū mentioned two reasons for it. One was that the writer cannot write about everything in life, for life includes an infinite number of things. The other was that a novelist who presents people and events indiscriminately will create a novel that lacks meaning. Again, both principle and justification are commonplace enough. But Kafū's emphasis on deliberateness of selection is quite uncommon: he took up his pen, he says, only after he had conceived a specific scene. In other words, Kafū believed that when the writer was simply describing individual people and things, his master was nature, but when it came to working out their place in his novel, he became his own master. This explains one of the main characteristics of Kafū's novels: a realistic setting and vivid characterization are often found with a contrived plot and an artificial sequence of events. For instance, two characters, depicted with real flesh and blood immediacy, meet at a place described vividly and realistically, but their meeting is purely coincidental.

Take the celebrated scene in *A Strange Tale from East of the*

River in which the hero meets the heroine for the first time. The aging novelist is walking through the Tamanoi district of Tokyo, when suddenly a lashing thundershower comes up. All the passersby run for shelter, except the novelist, who, from lifelong habit, has brought an umbrella with him. He opens the umbrella and resumes his walk. "Sir!" A call comes from a young woman. "Could you let me walk with you? Just over to there." He shares his umbrella with the stranger, who turns out to be a local streetwalker. Kafū describes the setting beautifully; indeed, the scene is considered one of the most masterful descriptions of a red-light district in modern Japanese fiction. His depiction of the man and the woman is also impeccable. Yet one cannot but feel that the circumstances are too coincidental: without the sudden shower, they would never have met. This sort of thing happens far too frequently in Kafū's novels.

If the novelist is a "selector" from life and from nature, what kind of selector was Kafū as a writer? The answer must be that he was a very discriminating one, with strong likes and dislikes. To see what he preferred to choose from nature, the reader can do no better than consult an interesting book of essays he published under the title *Hiyori Geta* ("Walking Shoes"). As the title suggests (*hiyori geta* are actually wooden clogs designed to be worn for a long walk on a fine day), the book is the fruit of Kafū's own casual strolls over the years. It tells about various places in Tokyo that he visited and found interesting enough to write about. These places turn out to be markedly different from the ones that appear in an ordinary Tokyo tourist guide. The second chapter, for instance, is about unobtrusive little shrines popularly believed to help lovers. The third chapter is about trees, especially gingko trees, pine trees, and willow trees, that had been made famous by various episodes in the lives of townspeople during the Edo Period. The fifth chapter is about old temples that were not too well known—far less well known, for instance, than those in Kyoto or Nara. The seventh chapter is about backstreet alleys that were not on Tokyo maps. The eighth chapter is about vacant lots, the ninth chapter about cliffs, and the tenth chapter about hills. The book concludes with the eleventh chapter, which is about sunsets. From all the varying scenes of Tokyo, Kafū singled out these for the material of his book—a peculiar choice indeed. These places and things also frequently provide the background of his novels.

Just as he chose backgrounds that were forgotten places reminiscent of town life in earlier centuries, so he chose characters who were little, insignificant people barely managing to survive at the bottom or on the fringes of society as they clung to outmoded ways of life. There is no convenient book of essays to show this, but his novels are evidence enough. The main characters of *The River Sumida* are a disinherited heir to a large pawnshop, who earns a modest income by teaching haiku to amateurs; his widowed sister, who struggles to support her family by giving samisen lessons; her teenage son, who is reluctantly studying for his college entrance examination while longing to be a kabuki actor; and his girl friend, who is preparing to become a geisha. *Geisha in Rivalry* is about young women who, because of family misfortunes, have become geisha and are vying with each other for the male protectors who will give them financial security. *Dwarf Bamboo* not only presents young women who have been reduced to becoming geisha but focuses on their clients, who have dropped out of decent society; appropriately, the title of the novel refers to the short bamboo grass that grows on the roadside and is trampled by passersby. A barmaid is the heroine of *During the Rains*, a call girl that of *Flowers in the Shade*, and a streetwalker that of *A Strange Tale from East of the River.*

Kafū selected such people and lives for the material of his fiction because he felt in tune with them; they inspired him with a profound empathy that became the criterion of his choice. "Empathy is not merely the basic principle of artistic creation," he once said. "It is also the only path by which one can reach the truth about life and society." In other words, Kafū chose to write about geisha, prostitutes, and other downtrodden people because he thought they represented "the truth about life and society." They did so, in his opinion, precisely because they did not belong to respectable society, which he saw riddled with falsehood. In one of the stories

collected in *Night Tales from Shinbashi,* he explained the hero's
restless pursuit of pleasure as follows:

The indefatigable energy with which he frequented the brothel district
day in and day out, year after year, derived from his full awareness that
he was visiting a pit of immorality. Suppose that the values of society
were different: suppose that prodigals were generally considered paragons
of virtue. In that case, he would never have allowed himself to become
so depraved as to sell his house and spend the money for pleasure; he
never wanted to hear people's praise. It was his resentment at the vanity
and hypocrisy of legally married women, as well as at the fraudulent activities of illustrious members of society, that became the prime motive
for his running to the other extreme—to the place that he knew from the
beginning to be dark and immoral.

Kafū reused this passage in *A Strange Tale from East of the River*
to explain his fondness for women of dubious repute, and similar
observations recur again and again in his other works. It must have
been for the same reason that he liked lovers' shrines, crumbling
old temples, and vacant, grassy lots: they had been left behind by
what he considered the superficial progress of society. Of the backstreet shrines, for instance, he wrote that the superstitious folk who
worshiped at them might become robbers or sell their daughters
to geisha houses, but that they would never make use of such
"civilized" weapons as blackmail by threat of exposure in the newspapers or abuse in the name of social justice.

To sum up, then, Kafū's views on the relationship between
nature and art were colored by his ideas of selection as well as imitation. The artist tried to imitate nature as faithfully as possible,
but in so doing he selected from nature. This freedom of selection
gave him room to maneuver his characters and scenes, for he could
choose them according to his personal feelings. Individually, characters and scenes had to be lifelike; collectively, however, they
could be manipulated by the novelist through the process of selection and exclusion. What to choose or discard was up to the individual writer, but a good novelist would choose material that revealed hidden truths about life. Kafū found such truths among
downtrodden people living unobtrusive lives in the backstreets of
twentieth-century Tokyo.

The Outsider as Insider

Kafū's thoughts on the qualifications of an artist are inseparably related to his views of art. If art is selective imitation, it would naturally follow that a good artist must be a good observer and good selector. This is essentially what Kafū seems to be saying in "How to Write a Novel" and in other essays that touch on the nature of the artist.

The idea that a novelist must be a keen observer of actual life underlies much of his advice to would-be writers, as the following examples show. "Important in a novel is originality. It is safer, therefore, to avoid getting hints from other writers' works. Your novel should be made of what you personally experienced and what you actually felt. . . . The value of a novel depends on how well the characters are delineated. Whatever lofty ideal the writer may hold, he will fail as a novelist if his characterization is poor. Sketching a character is not a mere trick of the pen; it will be successful only when it is derived from actual observation, aided by the power of imagination." On another occasion he cited with approval the advice of Hirotsu Ryūrō (1861–1928), his one-time mentor, to the effect that a novelist should move his residence whenever possible in order to observe his neighbors with fresh eyes every now and then.* Kafū also told of his own unfortunate experience in having to leave a novel unfinished because he did not want to portray some of its characters from imagination alone. These characters were a new type of Japanese women, liberated and antitraditional (one was a graduate of an American college, another a woman writer). Kafū needed them for the plot of his novel, but felt that he himself had insufficient firsthand knowledge of such women. One of his acquaintances who heard of the dilemma urged him to go on with the novel, reminding him that art depicts the unreal anyway. Kafū answered: "But I just can't set my mind at rest unless I take a look at the actual model. I can't

---

* Hirotsu Ryūrō was an influential writer in the formative years of the modern Japanese novel. As a young student Kafū admired him and became his disciple for a time. This was during the last years of the nineteenth century.

visualize how the sort of woman who is eager to write a novel would be dressed." He went on to wonder if such a woman should be portrayed wearing low, rattan-faced clogs, whether some red clay should be seen sticking to the clogs, and whether the thongs of the clogs should appear loose.

Kafū also urged the novelist to observe everything from within. "To observe something from the outside and to delineate it, this is easy; to do the same from the inside, this is difficult. In his work Zola tends to delineate characters from the outside, and that is his weakness. Flaubert's *Madame Bovary*, Tolstoy's *Anna Karenina*, Anatole France's *The Red Lily*, Octave Mirbeau's *Father Jules*, Henri de Régnier's *The Libertines*—each is different in its style of writing, but each is a masterpiece in which the writer has tried to delineate his characters largely from within." The phrase "from within," ambiguous though it is, becomes somewhat clearer in the light of other remarks by Kafū. As we have seen, empathy was for Kafū both the basic principle of artistic creation and the indispensable source of knowledge about life and society. On another occasion he remarked: "Indispensable to every act of artistic creation are observation and sympathy." To observe something "from within," then, meant to observe it with empathy: the artist entered into the subject and perceived it from the inside, as it were. Without empathy he would not be able to do this, and his observation in consequence would remain superficial.

Kafū probably derived these ideas from certain contemporary French theories on the nature of literature and art. In an article summarizing part of Albert Antoine's *Art and Artist*, he argued that the artist "gains inspiration from reality and sets out to create a work of art, but can do so only after he has been closely united with reality." Kafū may also have been influenced by the premodern Japanese concept of a union between the artist and his subject. In traditional Japanese aesthetics, the artist was not expected to stand apart from the subject and observe it with detachment. Rather, he was to "enter into the subject, perceive its delicate life, and feel its feelings," as one poet put it. In any case, Kafū as a novelist really did show the empathy that he preached; except in his earliest works, which were written under Zola's influence, few of his major *dramatis personae* are wholly unsympathetic and most are far more favorably drawn.

Dwarf Bamboo provides a good example. Its main characters are all morally despicable people who make nothing of cheating, slandering, flattering, or intimidating. Heading the cast is a famous painter named Kaiseki, who has amassed a fortune by the help of a crafty art dealer. His widowed daughter is a homely woman who constantly boasts of her skill in poetry and calligraphy. His son is a selfish, irresponsible prodigal who wastes his days in drinking and visiting brothels. The son's bride is lazy, mean, temperamental, and abnormally hysterical. Usaki, Kaiseki's former student in painting, is practically the only main character without gross vice, but he is weak-willed, ineffectual, and petty. In reading the novel, however, one finds it hard to dismiss these characters with total contempt, because the novelist gets inside each character and shows why he behaves as he does. To attain this effect, the author frequently changes the narrative viewpoint in an arbitrary way. The abrupt change sometimes puzzles the reader who is used to the modern Western novel, but it allows Kafū to enter the mind of a character who is in dire need of the reader's understanding at that moment. Even when the character acts despicably, the reader knows the motives and is not repelled as strongly as he might otherwise be. It is obvious that Kafū felt no great love for Kaiseki and his clansmen, but he empathized with them. That comes through to the reader.

If empathy is crucial to the artist's perception of reality, it becomes important for him to select the sort of material he can empathize with, and to reject material he knows he can have no empathy for. Kafū was quite consistent in this respect. He once declared: "I am now seeking the kind of art that most befits my physique, my life, and my temperament"—and then proceeded to exclude everything political from his artistic frame of reference. He often did not even bother to read newspapers. Similarly, he advocated that a novelist change his subject matter with his age, or rather, that he let it change automatically, since his physical and mental conditions change as years go by. A novelist, Kafū said, should not hesitate to speak what he wants to speak at a particular juncture of his life; he should grow with age, or age should make him grow. For the same reason Kafū valued each novelist's individuality—his specific physical and mental traits, his inclination to empathize with certain things rather than others. Once a novelist has discovered his proper subject matter, he might as well look no further. All the great artists had done this. Young women were the favorite subject of Utamaro (1753–1806); plum blossoms of Baiitsu (1783–1856); tigers of Gan Ku (1756–1838); monkeys of Sosen (1749–1821);* cattle of Troyon; landscapes of Corot. The character in Kafū's *Sneers* who cites these examples also attacks those literary critics of contemporary Japan who criticize a writer for using the same subject matter again and again in his novels.

In Kafū's view, then, art is an expression of individuality: the artist expresses himself through his selection of subject matter. The artist's personality thus becomes a matter of great importance. Kafū stressed this point in "How to Write a Novel." "There are," he wrote, "many types of novels—lyrical, epical, objective, subjective, fanciful, realistic—indeed, too many to explain one by one. As for their literary merit, however, one sentence will suffice: The value of the novel lies in the writer's personality." Kafū used this as a criterion for screening plays when he served as one of the judges in a playwriting contest. He was quite disappointed with all the entries, which he invariably found to be imitations of well-known contemporary works. In summing up he said: "Whenever I read a new playwright's work, I try to see if it has something I don't know, if it has something that cannot be known except to a young man of today." It should be noted that Kafū was more concerned with content than with style: a good work of literature, he assumed,

---

* Kitagawa Utamaro was a leading ukiyoe artist of his time. He attained fame for the physical beauty and eroticism with which he depicted young women. Yamamoto Baiitsu was a painter especially famous for his skillful depiction of blossoms and birds. Gan Ku, founder of the Kishi school, was noted for his realistic paintings of tigers. Mori Sosen, another painter of the late Edo Period, is said to have spent many days at a mountain temple in Kyushu to sketch his favorite subject, wild monkeys.

should tell us something new about life. If it does, its manner of presentation—lyrical, epical, objective, subjective, etc.—does not much matter. And the writer acquires this "something new" through his personality, through the peculiar way in which his physique, temperament, and way of life combine to make him an individual. We have seen that Kafū considered the novelist a selector of subject matter from raw life. Clearly, the more individuality a writer had, the more valuable would be his insights into life.

But the writer was not only an observer; he had also to be a reader and thinker. In "How to Write a Novel," Kafū was quite firm on this point. "Reading, contemplation, and observation are the three things a novelist should not neglect at any time . . . ," he said. "A novelist who does nothing but read and contemplate by himself, neglecting to observe real men in the real world, will eventually be shackled by the example of past masterpieces and lose the sharpness of his own individual sensitivity. On the other hand, a writer who is confident of his talent and so works solely from his actual observations will, in most cases, reach a deadlock midway in his career, unless that talent is really an outstanding one." As for the question of what to read, Kafū recommended Chinese and Western classics while saying, "The reading of classical Japanese literature is not urgently needed." For this reason he urged beginning writers to become proficient in either classical Chinese or a Western language. His best-known remark in "How to Write a Novel" was made in this connection. "If you want to write a novel," he advised, "learn French at once, before you do anything else."

By "contemplation" Kafū obviously did not mean philosophical speculation or religious meditation. He simply meant that anyone who wanted to write a novel should, after reading a book or witnessing an incident, contemplate the experience and make it part of his outlook on life. It was this type of contemplation that finally resulted in a work of artistic creation. "Pleasure," a novelette by Kafū, contains an episode telling how a famous novelist came to write his first work of fiction. As a young student, this man fell deeply in love with a nurse, who, however, remained unaware of his feelings toward her and married someone else. In desperation, one evening he composed a long, passionate letter to her, but next morning decided not to mail it. He contemplated the experience throughout the winter vacation that followed, and then wrote a short story based on it. Kafū said the same thing more directly in "How to Write a Novel." "You can start working on your novel," he advised, "only when you have regained a contemplative state of mind after a period of intense emotional excitement."

Kafū's idea of a novelist, then, is basically of someone who observes rather than someone who participates. In observing his subject he should have a certain degree of empathy for it; otherwise he will not be able to penetrate beneath its surface. Since each person has his likes and dislikes, a novelist may sometimes find it difficult to empathize with certain people and things. In a case like that he should have no hesitation in ignoring them, both in actual life and in his work of fiction, for he is a selector from raw life and has freedom of selection. A good "selector" is a man who has something unique in his personality; through that uniqueness he selects and grasps truths about life, truths that his predecessors have not noticed. To increase his knowledge further, he should read the works of foreign writers and contemplate the lives of widely differing people. Reading and contemplation also help him to observe society with detached understanding. In brief, a novelist is a man of culture who has retired from the utilitarian world in order to observe with sympathy people and things that suit his taste, and who writes about them from a distance, with deep understanding but without losing objectivity. He is a recluse who observes mundane life from within.

Sorrow Veiled in Beauty

What is the nature of the impression produced by a work of art upon the reader's or spectator's mind? That it is an impression of beauty was Kafū's answer, but when he gave that answer he had a specific type of beauty in mind. That is evident, for instance, in a poem of his entitled "Mutterings on a Gloomy Day":

Knowing this to be a worthless life to live,
why do I keep living on?
Because this life contains something called beauty.
From where does beauty spring?
Beauty springs from poetry.
Poetry springs from artistic language.
From where does artistic language spring?
It springs from melody.
From where does melody spring?
It springs from sorrow.
Sorrow springs from the innermost nature of man.
That innermost nature springs from heritage.
From where does heritage spring?
Heritage springs from the undercurrents ceaselessly
    flowing in the world of men.
It is for this reason that I,
knowing this to be a worthless life to live,
still keep living on.
The winter day is cold,
the winter day is gloomy.
Give me
a bit of warmth,
a moment of light.

Almost devoid of imagery and lyricism, the poem bares his thoughts
unabashedly—too unabashedly, indeed, for it is not a good poem.
But it does serve to define the type of beauty that fascinated Kafū,
the beauty of sorrow expressed by means of melodious language.
He liked sorrowful beauty—or, more exactly, he thought that sorrow underlay every truly beautiful thing.

This idea is expressed again and again in Kafū's works. For
example, in *Sneers* a principal character named Kōu ponders the
nature of beauty. He confesses that even on a lovely day in autumn
he cannot but feel "strange gloom," that even in the warmth of his
sweetheart's lips he feels "inexplicable coldness." This strange
sorrow stems partly from his awareness that everything beautiful
and happy must soon fade. But that is not the whole reason, because he feels it even when he is not thinking consciously about
how time flies. Kōu concludes that perhaps this sorrow has its roots
in the universal agony of being human. The sorrow Kafū had in
mind was derived from the sad fact of human imperfectibility. Man

had aspired for perfection throughout the centuries, but to no avail; in the course of that endeavor man had written many a beautiful poem, but to no avail. Beauty was there, but man was left eternally imperfect; hence the sorrow. This sorrow was already an inseparable part of man's spiritual heritage; consequently, he instinctively felt it as if it were a natural part of him.

Recognizing that this existential sorrow underlies the beauty of poetry, and indeed of all types of art, Kafū went on to distinguish between the Eastern and Western versions of it. In the Orient, sorrow is tinged with resignation; in the Occident, it is mixed with the agony of effort. As Kōu notes in *Sneers*, there is an obvious difference between the gongs of a Buddhist temple and the bells of a Christian church, between the drooping roofs of the Buddhist structure and the sky-pointing pinnacles of the Christian one, between the awesome figure of Marīci* and the agonized posture of Laocoön, between the passive sentiments of eighteenth-century Japanese love songs and the dynamic passion of Wagnerian opera. Western artists express pain and agony in their works because they fight even when they are sure of eventual defeat; Eastern artists surrender, because they know the uselessness of fighting. In either case sorrow ensues, but with a difference in its quality.

It should go without saying which type of sorrow Kafū took more closely to his heart. After passing five years of his youth in the United States and France, he had become painfully aware that he was irredeemably Oriental in culture and outlook. To pretend otherwise would have been to deny his heritage, which had been nourished by the history and geography of Japan. Explaining his attitude as a writer, he once said:

Between the positive effort of self-assertion and the passive attitude of self-effacement, the latter choice seems far easier and more convenient for us to adopt now. The histories of China and Japan reveal that, since ancient times, all Orientals faced with an agonizing dilemma have chosen to strive for resignation and spiritual enlightenment. In the name of

---

* Marīci is a deification of the rays of the sun and usually takes the form of a heavenly woman. Sometimes, however, she is conceived as an awesome, wrathful figure with three faces, one of them a wild boar's. She was worshiped especially by Japanese warriors.

righteousness and humanity, Victor Hugo once railed at contemporary politicians and called them murderers, Neroes, wolves, and apes. But we can leave this type of seriousness, this courageous attitude, exclusively to Westerners. Oriental literature is different: we veil our true feelings and seclude ourselves from society, thereby making the reader feel an infinitely deep sorrow.

It was for the purpose of creating such "infinitely deep sorrow" that Kafū continued to write about geisha, call girls, prostitutes, and all the other downtrodden people to be found in his works. As an art critic he was fond of writing about *ukiyoe* because these paintings and prints were made by and for plain townsmen who were treated with contempt by their rulers.* As a theater critic he was strongly attached to kabuki, no doubt for the same reason. The authoritarian element in Japanese feudalism reached its peak during the Edo Period, and it was the townsmen, who had been placed at the bottom of the social hierarchy, who felt the pressures most. Resigned sorrow was nowhere more manifest than in their lives.

This sorrow, as defined by Kafū, might seem close to the "pathos," an aesthetic highly prized by premodern Japanese poets and playwrights. There is, however, an important difference: Kafū's sorrow owes little to the Buddhist implications that underlie pathos in the traditional Japanese sense. This type of resignation depended on belief in spiritual rebirth through the new order of Buddhism. No such belief was implied in Kafū's sorrow: after death, there was no Buddha—there was nothing. This lack of faith in a future gave his sorrow an epicurean tinge. Kōu, again speaking for Kafū in *Sneers*, clarifies the point: "In the face of approaching death, from which no one can escape, is there any consolation in this incomprehensible life other than to sing about this momentary pleasure?" To seek pleasure thus becomes a guiding principle in Kōu's life. "If I may speak with complete frankness," he says, "I believe that man was created to enjoy himself, indeed, that he can claim it as his legitimate right. In fact, as long as he lives, man

---

* Ukiyoe ("pictures of the floating world") designates a special type of Japanese paintings and woodblock prints that were particularly popular among the townsmen of the Edo Period. Their favorite subjects were popular actors, beautiful courtesans, and well-known places of interest.

cannot help enjoying himself even if he tries not to. As I just said, today the average person, when he hears the word pleasure, immediately thinks of something immoral. But nothing could be more wrong." Pleasure is infinitely more pleasurable to the man who is aware of the deep sorrow inherent in human life—who is aware, in short, of human imperfectibility. Pleasure, as conceived by Kafū, is such pleasure, and sorrow is such sorrow. It is an epicurean's sorrow, not a Buddhist's "pathos." Kafū was too much of a nihilist to believe in the possibility of religious salvation. It may be recalled that his poem "Mutterings on a Gloomy Day" displays no sign of hope in religion.

In this connection it is interesting to note that the masterpieces of Japanese literature admired by Kafū were, by and large, of the pre-Buddhist or post-Buddhist periods. He thought, for instance, that *The Tales of Ise* contained the "true essence" of Japanese literature. The claim is highly peculiar, but makes sense in view of his aesthetic ideal. *The Tales of Ise*, with an epicurean for its hero, does produce the kind of sorrow Kafū had in mind; written in an earlier time, it is less Buddhistic than *The Tale of Genji* or *The Tale of the Heike*. For the same reason Kafū admired Japanese writers of plebeian literature a century before his time, notably Ōta Shokusanjin (1749–1823) and Tamenaga Shunsui (1789–1843).* Living in an age long past the prime of Buddhism, these writers had much that was epicurean in them.

However, Kafū arrived at his ideal of beauty largely by means of East-West comparison. Ultimately, he preferred the passive, resigned Oriental ideal to the agonistic, Faustean Western one. Nevertheless, he owed much to Western culture because it gave him a clearer view of his own. But this view was in turn colored by his pessimistic view of humanity, which inclined him toward epicureanism and aestheticism. Beauty, in his mind, was necessarily short-lived and doomed to sorrow. For this very reason, it was to

* Ōta Shokusanjin, also called Yomo Akara, was a prolific writer of comic poetry and popular tales. Tamenaga Shunsui initiated a literary genre called the *ninjōbon*, a book narrating the amorous adventures of Edo townsmen. Kafū once took time out to study these two writers' lives and compile their chronologies.

be enjoyed all the more. The ingredients of Kafū's beauty are, in very general terms, human imperfectibility, Oriental passivity, and epicurean sensualism. And these seem to be the principal ingredients of his most successful novels, notably *The River Sumida*, *Geisha in Rivalry*, *During the Rains*, *Flowers in the Shade*, and *A Strange Tale from East of the River*. It was perhaps in these that he gained "a bit of warmth, a moment of light."

The Kabuki Style in Fiction

Kafū did not talk much about the structure of the novel. "How to Write a Novel," however, offers a couple of useful clues to his ideas on the subject. One is his comparison of a novel to a chat. The other is his observation that plot automatically emerges out of characterization. When seen in the light of his own fiction, these clues lead to interesting conclusions.

The comparison of a novel to a chat appears almost at the outset of "How to Write a Novel." "A novel is like a chat in daily life," he wrote, and went on to observe that there were many kinds of chat—"tenement housewives', country bumpkins', native Tokyoites', informed men's." From this observation one may infer that Kafū did not believe in the necessity of a well-thought-out, tightly knit plot. An ordinary chat has nothing like a plot: it wanders about, sometimes in a whimsical manner, as the speaker's or listener's interest develops. And indeed, some of Kafū's works do have a chatlike structure. Almost the whole of "Pleasure," for example, consists of a long after-dinner chat of a famous novelist with his young friend one spring evening. A large part of *Sneers* consists of a series of chats among a novelist, a kabuki writer, a globetrotter, a painter, and a bank executive—all "informed men." Many of the tales in *American Stories* are told by characters within the stories, often in the form of a chat. The narrator of *A Strange Tale from East of the River* is an aged novelist who chats about his recent experiences, so that the main story is preceded by his conversations with a bookseller and a policeman, is interrupted by excerpts from the novel he is writing, and is concluded by a lengthy postscript that looks almost like an independent essay.

If Kafū thought, as he seems to have, that a novel is primarily a chat and therefore does not have to proceed in a series of continuous episodes, it must have been largely because of his feeling that character is more important than plot. "A novel that emphasizes the colorfulness of story and neglects characterization," he observed, "belongs to so-called popular literature; it does not rate high as a novel. If character delineation is made the central principle of writing a novel, the plot automatically emerges as the writer proceeds with the work." Plot, Kafū is saying, develops out of character. If a character in the novel is given a specific personality, as he must be, then his actions will always be consistent with it, whatever he may do. Kafū may not have gone so far as to believe, categorically, that character is fate and that a man's actions are all predetermined. But it remains a fact that the characters in his novels seldom show noticeable growth. In some cases—the young student in *The River Sumida* or the three principal geisha in *Geisha in Rivalry*—they discover that they cannot but be themselves. In "Hydrangea" the heroine is murdered because she has been too true to her basic nature.

In Kafū's view, then, a plot would have to be so constructed as to reveal the personality of the novel's main character or characters. The novelist would set up a series of incidents in which characters dramatically clash, or a single character lyrically expresses himself. In either instance, the characters' mentality would be revealed. The writer would almost become a manipulator of puppets in a puppet theater; for instance, he would not hesitate to make frequent use of coincidence. And this is exactly what Kafū did in his novels and stories, which are full of coincidental happenings.

Kafū was fully aware of this, and once tried to defend himself. As we saw earlier, the hero of *A Strange Tale from East of the River* meets the heroine purely by chance: they happen to be walking along the same street when there is a sudden shower. Kafū, expecting the reader to complain that the shower came too opportunely, wrote: "But I have just written down what actually happened, without fictionalizing it. I had no intention of making it up. Noting that the action begins with a sudden thunderstorm, some may sneer and say this is a hackneyed way of beginning a story. Yet I did not want to invent another beginning just to avoid being sneered at." Kafū's defense, then, is that coincidences really happen —especially in Japan, where the weather is very unpredictable. In an essay, Kafū once listed a number of instances in which a sudden change of weather had been the starting point of a love affair between strangers or acquaintances. Moreover, Kafū's liking for coincidence was consistent with his nihilistic view of life. If in actual life men are manipulated by the fickle hand of fate, or the gods, or whatever, what is wrong with the novelist's manipulating his characters in his novel? If a person cannot change his inborn mental traits, Kafū would have argued, the sort of incident that matches his personality will occur sooner or later, anyway.

Kafū's deterministic view of personality is clearly expressed, interestingly enough, in *Geisha in Rivalry,* a novel whose main characters are free-minded, extravagant geisha in the Shinbashi district of Tokyo. They are all attractive girls, and wealthy men throng around them, ready to pay almost any sum of money for the right to monopolize them. Indeed, the heroine Komayo once did leave the demimonde and married a respectable gentleman in the north of Japan. Yet, when her husband died an untimely death, she simply could not continue living a widow's life in the country, despite the fact that she would have lifelong financial security there. She fled back to Tokyo, to the irresistible red-light district where she could feel at home, though that meant a good deal of debt and curtailment of freedom. Her being a geisha, then, is no accident. *Geisha in Rivalry* is replete with accidental happenings— in its very first page Komayo meets her former client by coincidence —but they are the kind of events that would have happened sooner or later to Komayo and her rivals, as long as these women continued their ways of life.

In passing we might also note that Kafū's characters, more than any other novelist's, like to have their fortunes told. Komayo, for example, goes to a Shinto shrine to consult the oracle when she has to decide whether or not to quit her profession. *During the Rains* opens with a scene in which the heroine Kimie, troubled by recent weird events, visits a professional fortune-teller to see what her future will be. In *Sinking and Swimming* the author in the opening pages also has his heroine buy a sacred fortune; later in the novel she and her friend try to foretell their future from cards. Even the samisen teacher in *The River Sumida*, a modern-thinking woman eager to send her son to the university, consults the oracle when the son fails his examinations. Obviously all these characters feel that their future has been determined by some force unknown to them.

Kafū's concept of a novel's structure, with its heavier emphasis on character than on plot, its characters that do not grow, and its deterministic implications, approaches close to the traditional concept of structure in the kabuki. And, indeed, the Kafū novels that do not have a chatlike quality—*Geisha in Rivalry, Dwarf Bamboo, During the Rains,* and *Flowers in the Shade* among others—have a kabuki-like structure: rather than narrating a story, they present a series of static scenes—one is tempted to say ukiyoe scenes—with a good deal of conversation being exchanged among the main characters. Reading this sort of novel is in fact rather like seeing a kabuki play performed on the stage, with its varied scenes coming in succession and each scene containing some moments when time stands still. This method of exposition may have been part of what Kafū had learned in his young days, when he was actually a trainee in kabuki writing. His lifelong admiration for Mokuami (1816–93), one of the greatest of all kabuki writers, is also a well-known fact.*

In the kabuki, backdrops and stage properties often have symbolic meanings. It therefore comes as no surprise that Kafū, too, attached great importance to the setting. In "How to Write a Novel" he advised:

Next to characterization, the greatest effort in writing a novel should be expended on the background (I do not mention dialogue here, because I regard it as part of characterization). In a novel, the background should always be closely related to the characters. There are cases in which a well-chosen background scene can reveal a character more effectively than ordinary explanation. Descriptions of a scholar's study or a garden, etc., which often appear in Anatole France's works, are cases in point.

---

* Kawatake Mokuami wrote a number of kabuki plays that became immensely successful among the Edo populace. One of them, *The Love of Izayoi and Seishin,* figures prominently in Kafū's *The River Sumida.*

Elsewhere in the same essay Kafū advised firmly against the use
of explanatory phrases. "In portraying a character or an event or
a scene," he wrote, "a novelist should not say anything explanatory.
The function of a novel is to induce the reader to imagine the characters and scenes vividly before he even knows he is doing it."
These are essentially dramatic values: plenty of characterization
and background, but no explanation as such.

Kafū practiced what he theorized—indeed, he overdid it at times.
Close correlation between character and background is a distinct
feature of Kafū's novels. Kimie in *During the Rains*, for instance,
is a sly, unclean, lustful barmaid who sleeps with anyone who can
be of profit to her. Kafū set her residence in a place most appropriate to her character: it is a cheap rooming house behind a fish store,
and a visitor has to dare mud and dogs' excrement to reach its
entrance. In sharp contrast Tsuruko, a clean, attractive, well-disciplined woman who serves as Kimie's foil in the novel, is introduced to the reader at an elegant villa in a rustic suburb of Tokyo,
and even before the novelist says a word about her we are sure she
is a kind of person entirely different from Kimie. The contrast is
obvious—perhaps too obvious by the standard of the modern Western novel.

As for Kafū's concept of style, it will be remembered that his
"Mutterings on a Gloomy Day" stresses melody as an important
ingredient of artistic language. Kafū appears to have used the term
"melody" in a very general sense; he once observed that he could
hear "a sorrowful melody" in some Japanese prints. In his essay
"The Tone and Color of Language," he first emphasizes that the
most important function of literary language is to convey the
writer's feelings exactly as they are. He goes on to observe that
when the feelings to be expressed are complex, as they often are,
words and phrases alone do not serve the purpose well. Under such
circumstances what can a writer do? Kafū's answer was that he
should use "tone" and "color." This is what he has to say about
tone:

I believe a prose writer can convey a delicate feeling—a feeling of evening twilight, a feeling of early morning, a felicitous feeling, a plaintive

feeling, or whatever—through a musical tone of the language. Personally, I take pains in creating a musical tone when I write. I weave words together in such a way that a certain tone naturally emerges therefrom, a tone that I hope will somehow impress the reader with a feeling that the individual words cannot express. That is the method I mean.

As for color:

Sometimes a passage describing a night fails to convey to the reader a sense of night. I mention night merely as an example. There are passages that, in depicting a daytime happening, give an impression of night, and passages that, though they talk about something that occurred early in the morning, sound as if it took place around noon. Such things happen because those passages are lacking in proper color. They fail to show the color of night or daytime or early morning, whichever is required. And it is not only the hours of the day that have colors; places do as well. A sea has its own color, a mountain has its own color, and a river has its own color. Some passages, depicting a sea, do not at all produce the feeling of a sea; others, depicting a lake, give the impression of an ocean. This is because, as I said before, the writer has failed to reveal the color sufficiently.

Kafū went on to make a distinction between tone and color. "To reiterate," he said, "a color is something that the subject to be depicted has in itself; a tone arises from a feeling or sentiment that is induced in the depictor when confronted by the subject."

Kafū's idea of tone comes fairly close to the meaning of that term as generally used in Anglo-American literary criticism, for in both instances tone has its origin in the writer's attitude toward his subject and is created by his deliberate choice of wording and phrasing. There is one important difference, however: Kafū stressed the musical qualities of tone considerably more than today's critics. Although he did not say so explicitly, he seems to have believed that certain vocal sounds, and certain arrangements of them, are closely associated with certain sentiments and emotions. The belief must have come naturally to someone like Kafū, with his ardent love of kabuki. In the kabuki, the actor is often accompanied by instrumental or vocal music, and there is a close connection between the musical phrases and the actor's emotion. Kafū once went so far as to say that some of Mokuami's kabuki plays are not based on his observation of actual life, but are a skillful dramatization of popular music in nineteenth-century Japan. The language of kabuki has to fit the music; a sorrowful monologue, for instance, would need to go well with certain melodies traditionally considered sorrowful. When Kafū said a writer should weave words and phrases in such a way as to create a specific emotional tone, he must have had in mind something like what Mokuami and other kabuki writers did.

Kafū's color, on the other hand, is something inherent in things themselves; it is not created by the writer who looks at them. Thus it resembles the term "atmosphere" as generally used in Anglo-American literary criticism. The main difference between color and atmosphere is that while the latter is usually applied to a scene or situation, the former is used in connection with an individual object as well. This is because of Kafū's emphatic insistence that everything in the universe is unique, and, therefore, that each object has to have its own unique color. In his view, a writer should suppress all his personal sentiments when he tries to catch that color. The same moon may look happy or sad to different onlookers. Its color, however, remains one and the same, as a good writer should be able to show by catching it in the clear mirror of his mind.

It follows, then, that the language of literature should be colorless, so that the subject described can be fully revealed in its own color. A description of a morning will fail if the writer does not let the morning speak for itself; a small lake described in a novel may give the impression of an ocean when the novelist's emotion has intervened in the description. In prose fiction, the writer's language should be simple, restrained, transparent. For this reason, Kafū admired the prose of Mori Ōgai (1862–1922) more than that of any other modern Japanese writer, comparing it to the best of Latin and classical Chinese writings.* He cited many passages from Ōgai to show this. Of two passages from Ōgai's "Achievements of Prince Yoshihisa," he says: "The concise, classical, quiet style fills

---

* Mori Ōgai, one of the most respected novelists in modern Japan, spent a considerable amount of his creative energy in writing historical and biographical studies. "Achievements of Prince Yoshihisa" was written in 1908.

the reader with infinitely deep emotion, especially when the author comes to narrate the most stormy scenes of life." These words could be used, with equal aptness, to describe the style that Kafū used in his diary, which spans a period of forty years. The diary is written throughout in an extremely terse style, and is especially effective in describing his life in 1945, when he wandered from place to place after his house had been destroyed in an air raid; indeed, this part of the diary bears a striking resemblance, stylistically at least, to "Achievements of Prince Yoshihisa." The same style, though not so conspicuous, can be found in his later fiction. Kafū himself once intimated that he was keeping a diary in order to improve his prose style; clearly, this is what he meant.

Kafū's concept of an ideal literary language, then, depends on a precarious balance between the two polar opposites, tone and color. On the one hand, the language has to be transparent enough to let the subject matter speak for itself; it has to be stripped of all superfluous, ornamental words, and of words that describe nothing more than the writer's personal emotion. On the other hand, it also has to show, in a delicate, subtle way, the attitude of the writer toward the subject; prose, as well as verse, should have certain rhythms and melodies that imperceptibly move the reader in a preconceived direction. In other words, the language of literature both must and must not express the writer's feelings. The conflict proceeds from Kafū's idea of the novelist: he is an objective observer, but must also have individuality and show it. At what point should tone be sacrificed for the sake of color, or vice versa? The answer in each case would seem to depend on the extent to which the writer wants to remain an objective observer.

The Poisonous Herb with Beautiful Flowers

Kafū's views on the uses of literature are best summed up in a postscript to his article on the kabuki. He wrote it when the kabuki was considered unrealistic, outdated, and vulgar by many Japanese men of letters, including his early mentor, Mori Ōgai, who preferred the more realistic Western-style theater. Kafū demurred, as follows:

The kabuki may be primarily a show to entertain the vulgar populace. Yet, if it can be kept in its old form, it will serve the same purpose as the decorative dolls, battledores, netsuke, and ukiyoe of the Edo Period, namely, to provide a momentary pleasure to those of us who continually suffer from the anguish of living in this modern age. The works of art created to cheer the populace in the authoritarian Edo Period appeal to those of us who cannot stand the political oppression in today's Japan; at least, they appeal to me personally in this way. Sometimes they appeal as biting satire, sometimes they incite fraternal sympathy, and sometimes they lead us into a beautiful world of spring sunshine that lies beyond this earth.

Kafū's emphasis on the escapist function of literature becomes even more explicit in a poem called "Flower of Grass":

> Life is a curse, and yet in the world of men
> There is a moment of consolation, a moment of pleasure.
> Don't we feel it when we read Musset's poetry?
> Isn't that the feeling when we listen to Mozart?

In Kafū's novels there appear a number of businessmen with escapist inclinations; the bank executive in *Sneers* is a typical example.

Of course, the idea that literature provides escape from the worries of life is universal, age-old, and, we might add, commonplace. But Kafū showed originality in stressing the negative aspects of escapism just as strongly as—sometimes even more strongly than—the positive ones. He did so with genuine sincerity. Literature is an escape from the binds of ordinary society, he would say; but he would seldom forget to add that those who can, or have to, live in that society should be careful not to become addicted to literature. In fact, few modern Japanese writers have taken Kafū's extreme stance that literature is not only useless but harmful to society. He once observed that all a novel purports to do is either to entertain women and children by describing fantastic incidents or to inflame the ardor of adolescents by allowing them to hear bedroom conversations; a gentleman, he went on to say, should not even lay hands on a novel. On another occasion he was irritated by some high school teachers who had asked him to donate his novels to their school libraries. It goes without saying, he answered, that a young boy still undecided on his future career should not read a novel, because a novel, in presenting the ways of the world as they really are, inevitably contains morally unacceptable elements. He said the same thing about poetry, and warned that students preparing themselves for careers should stay away from it. His most eloquent pronouncement along these lines is found in "Pleasure," where the novelist-hero compares poets to poisonous herbs, outlawed vagabonds, traitors, and gamblers. In this last instance there is a certain degree of calculated self-debasement, but it rings true despite the cynicism.

If the most that poetry has to offer the ordinary person is momentary relief from the pressures of everyday living, it follows that writing a literary work, just like reading it, should not be taken too seriously. Kafū confessed that he himself, as a young man of twenty or so, had begun writing fiction as a hobby, "just because I liked to write." He explained that he had made that hobby his lifelong profession because he was fortunate enough to have a wealthy father; he would not have been a novelist, he said, if he had had to look after his parents. For Kafū, then, writing a novel or reading one was for sheer pleasure; it had no practical use—or, more exactly, the fact that it had no practical use was itself the source of its pleasure. "To take a modest view of a novel, it is like a game—a diversion." In the passage just cited, he compares it to a high school student's taking photographs, playing a violin, or going hunting: he does so just because he likes to.

And yet, literature is something more than mere play. For, to repeat Kafū's words, it can "incite fraternal sympathy." By this he meant that as a spectator at the kabuki, for instance, he identified with some of the characters, and that he enjoyed the identification because he knew these characters felt the same joys and griefs that he felt in his own life. He made the same point in another essay. This time he was reading a biography of a physician named Ranken and came across a poem by Ranken lamenting the fact that his gardener did not understand how attractive weeds could be in the garden. Kafū was overjoyed and said, "When I read a book and find a man of long ago saying or doing something I would say or do myself, the joy of meeting a congenial friend uncontrollably wells up in me." The novelist in "Pleasure" says the same thing

even more explicitly: "I could not live without a collection of poems in my pocket. When I read a poem that sings with freedom and skill of joy or sorrow or any other feeling that I feel too, it seems to me as if I have met someone who has been my friend for a hundred years. I don't read books for research or for learning. I read them to console myself." In short, the pleasure of reading a novel, a poem, or a play is that of getting to know other people, alive or dead, who once felt the same way as the reader; basically, it relieves loneliness. For life is lonely, and reading a literary work is, along with sipping tea and drinking wine, the best companion one can hope for. A wife's love, Kafū thought, is far less dependable, and having a child produces more pain and grief than pleasure.

Again, there is nothing original about Kafū's idea that literature offers companionship. But his extreme pessimism about the possibility of a close relationship between individuals is the product of a unique personality. His works, he maintained, would be read only by a few people, but he would be satisfied if these few truly shared his views. He even went so far as to say that the publication of a novel was itself unnecessary, because the handful of genuine fiction lovers would not mind copying out any novel they wanted to read.

The third and final pleasure to be derived from reading a literary work, according to Kafū, was the pleasure of "biting satire." Again, he was talking about the kabuki, so by "satire" he probably meant something more like "social criticism": a kabuki play is seldom satirical in the narrow sense of the word. What he had in mind can be glimpsed, for instance, in a scene of *The River Sumida* where one of the principal characters, a young student, sees a kabuki play by Mokuami called *The Love of Izayoi and Seishin*. Kafū describes the student as being intensely envious of the free and passionate relationship between Izayoi and Seishin, who are robbers and social outcasts. Clearly, such people can love each other without restraint, while respectable members of society, like this student struggling to enter the university, cannot. In this sense, *The Love of Izayoi and Seishin* is just as much of a satire on contemporary

society as *The River Sumida,* since both extoll values that have no place in contemporary society.

In general, however, Kafū was an overly modest and diffident satirist. In one of his essays he even suggests that his stories about geisha and their clients may teach the reader how to behave in a house of assignation—as if that were their only value. The title of the essay, incidentally, is "Cranesbill," which suggests that its effect might be medicinal, like the herb of that name, traditionally a remedy for stomachaches and bowel upsets. But, again, he did not push the point; indeed, he seems to have felt that social criticism was better accomplished by other means. While still a young man, he observed that he did not condemn such artists as Tolstoy or Wagner, even though he sometimes found their works too didactic, but that he believed any message could be presented equally well or even better in nonartistic terms. Kafū did write works that, like *Sneers,* have a strong element of the satirical, but on the whole these are not up to the standard of his major works. He was too much of a poet, recluse, and epicurean to remain a satirist for long.

CHAPTER THREE

Tanizaki Jun'ichirō

✿

TANIZAKI JUN'ICHIRŌ (1886–1965) was never known as a literary theorist or critic. Always confident in his mission as a novelist, he had no urge to write a defense of literature or a social justification of the novel. Not a fast writer, he usually wanted to spend as much of his time as possible on writing fiction; he found little time for reading or evaluating the works of his contemporaries. And yet, by the end of his long literary career, he had produced a sizable number of writings that reveal his ideas on the nature of literature. There is, for instance, *The Composition Reader*, in which he said what he considered to be a good prose style and how one could go about attaining it. "In Praise of Shadows" and several other essays eloquently expound his ideal of beauty in life and art. Though he could seldom be induced to write reviews, his few essays in this genre, especially those on Sōseki's *Light and Darkness* and Kafū's *During the Rains*, leave no doubt that he could have become an exceptionally perceptive critic. His quarrel with Akutagawa on whether or not a novel should have a plot was one of the liveliest literary controversies of the time. In his fiction, too, aesthetic questions are often directly woven into the texture of the work, as in the well-known "Tattoo," *Some Prefer Nettles*, and "The Portrait of Shunkin," not to mention such lesser-known stories as "Creation" and "Gold and Silver."

Truths from the Mind's Deep Well

Tanizaki's concept of the relationship between nature and art was nowhere better expressed than in the following passage he wrote in 1918:

Some of today's writers—or I should say the great majority of them—are inclined to shun tales that present imaginings, labeling them all as "fabrications." Yet has there been any poet or man of letters, ancient or modern, who did not make free use of his imagination? Would a writer, even a naturalistic writer, be able to present truth if he were lacking in imaginative power? How could art exist if imagination were eliminated from the realm of art? In my opinion, only those who live by their imaginations are qualified to become artists. The artist's imagination may wander far from nature. But as long as it is a living, moving power in his brain, isn't it just as real as any other natural phenomenon? The artist justifies his existence only when he can transform his imagination into truth.

Obviously, the passage is directed at those contemporary Japanese exponents of naturalism who insisted that a literary work should copy real life as truthfully as possible. The nature of Tanizaki's reply to them is made clearer by another essay, "Random Thoughts on an Early Spring Day," which he wrote the following year. Here he presented examples to support his contention that all writers depended on imagination to some degree. He observed that an infinite amount of imaginative power had gone into *Anna Karenina* and *Crime and Punishment*. He also noted that even among the works of Zola, the naturalist par excellence, there was a masterpiece like *Paris* that could only have been written by a highly imaginative person. Flaubert, the father of naturalism, had produced *Salammbo*, which Tanizaki thought extraordinarily imaginative. He concluded: "Since Zola's time, people have often advocated that a writer should adopt a scientist's attitude. In my view, however, even a scientist cannot make a discovery without the power of imagination. As a matter of fact, aren't many scientific truths derived from abstract hypotheses?"

In Tanizaki's view, then, a novelist should be like a scientist who first conceives a hypothesis and then devises laboratory experiments to prove or disprove it. The hypothesis, a work of imagination, becomes a truth under certain conditions, conditions that the novelist can provide. Several times Tanizaki dealt with this theme in his works of fiction. One of the most obvious instances is "Tattoo." The beautiful heroine of this story does not know she is a vampire; it is the artist, in this case a tattooer, who awakens her to her true nature. In another early Tanizaki story, "The Cursed Play," the playwright-hero writes a play suggesting how he and his wife, despite all appearances, really hate each other, and how he would like to kill her. The wife at first refuses to admit that there is any truth in this, but later she finds herself being killed by her husband exactly as the play requires. This story, incidentally, begins with a quotation from Oscar Wilde: "Nature imitates art."

Imagination, according to Tanizaki, thus gives the artist extraordinary powers of perception; it enables him to see truths that the conscious mind has not recognized. Consider the following scene from Tanizaki's *The Secret Tale of the Lord of Musashi*, a macabre tale of a sixteenth-century Japanese warlord. One night the lord, about twelve years old at the time, happens to see a lovely young woman washing and making up severed heads of enemy soldiers in preparation for an official head inspection. He is inexplicably fascinated by this gruesome spectacle. Soon, he finds himself imagining how delightful it would be if his own severed head were fondled by her slender white fingers.

The young lord was startled at himself; he wondered how such a self-contradictory, strange fantasy could come to his mind, and how that fantasy could be so infinitely pleasurable to him. Before this time he had been the master of his mind; he had always been able to command it in any way he liked. But at the bottom of that mind there lay something alien, something like a deep well that no conscious effort of his could reach. Now, suddenly, the cover was removed from it. Clutching the edge of the well, he looked into the dark interior. The unfathomable depth frightened him. The shock was like that of a man who has never doubted his good health unexpectedly discovering that he suffers from a serious ailment.

Imagination has this capacity to reach for the depths because it is not controlled by the conscious mind; its truths are not moral but psychological. Imagination perceives what human nature is; it is not concerned with what human nature should be. A novel that, because it was written predominantly in the light of discursive reason, presents some ideal picture of human nature is deficient and unconvincing insofar as it ignores the human subconscious. Tanizaki sharply criticized Sōseki's *Mon* for this reason. The novel describes how a man, who has defied society in order to live with the woman he loves, finds himself leading a lonely life, without a child, without neighbors, without even much income, but still genuinely in love with her, though she has grown sickly and hysterical.

Tanizaki considered this plot untrue to human nature; he believed that any man, placed in such circumstances, would lose his love for his wife and fall into despair. With uncharacteristic cynicism, he concluded: "Sōseki's idea of love is of something far more serious and noble than I have found love to be." In Tanizaki's view, then, a work of art presents truths that, because they are hidden under the surface of ordinary life, can be grasped only by the creative imagination. They are at a higher level than observable truths because they pertain to the subconscious as well as to the conscious mind. Art imitates nature not merely in its visible appearance but in its hidden depths.

But what kind of subject matter do the hidden depths of nature present to the artist? Tanizaki gave no clear-cut answer in his essays. Had he been able to, one assumes that he would not have needed to write fiction. However, the following passage from one of his essays comes close to an answer.

One of the things I am currently interested in doing is to delineate the psychology of a Japanese woman of the feudal period, without giving it a modern interpretation and yet with such verisimilitude as to appeal to the modern reader's emotions and understanding. I want to draw a truly lifelike portrait of a woman who believed in the neo-Confucian moral codes and who was therefore bound by them—a woman of bygone days who was reserved in all things, who was taught to suppress her feelings on all occasions, and who seldom showed her face to any person of the opposite sex except her husband. Yet it would not be easy to portray the hypersensitive workings of such a woman's mind. Despite her wholly virtuous appearance, she could have been harboring thoughts of an illicit love that had not yet taken definite form. Jealousy, hatred, cruelty, and other dark emotions may have cast their dim shadows on her mind time and again without ever floating to the surface. It would be difficult, indeed, to create a vivid portrait of a woman of this type, a woman whose entire life was confined to her inner world.

For a successful novel of this type, Tanizaki pointed to Raymond Radiguet's *The Count's Ball*. Yet his own novels would serve equally well as examples. *A Blind Man's Tale*, "The Portrait of Shunkin," and *The Mother of Captain Shigemoto* have as heroines the kind of woman described in the passage above. She is reincarnated as a modern woman in *Some Prefer Nettles*, *The Makioka Sisters*, and *The Key*. In every case, the heroine has a profound psychological effect on the hero, or principal male characters around her, often to the point of changing their entire lives. Tanizaki was in fact profoundly interested in infidelity, jealousy, hatred, cruelty, and other dubious emotions that, he believed, were part of every woman's basic psychological makeup, even the most virtuous woman of neo-Confucian upbringing. He also wondered how such a woman, her psychological flaws masked by her beauty, would affect and change the life of any man who had anything to do with her. He was especially interested in sex, which he saw as both a constructive and a destructive force in the human subconscious. But instead of giving it a scientific interpretation, like Freud, he wanted to mythologize it. Such an attitude, he felt, was more in keeping with the novelist's function.

How, then, could the novelist give tangible form to the intangible truth that he had discovered? "I believe," wrote Tanizaki, "that things which have never happened in this world *can be made to happen* by means of art." This was possible because art created a world of its own. "In my opinion," he continued, "a novelist should aim ultimately at constructing an autonomous universe in his work." In that universe, the novelist could freely manipulate characters and events in such a way that truths originally revealed only to the creative imagination would manifest themselves in a form accessible to everybody. But in order to create his imaginary world, the novelist had better not choose a setting that too much resembled his own. Too much proximity to the facts was likely to cripple his imagination. For this reason, Tanizaki refrained from writing a novel about his first divorce, although it seemed like excellent material for fiction. "An incident like that," he explained, "impresses its factual nature on us so strongly that we would immediately feel literary inhibitions if we tried to change or replace, in the interest of the novel, the tiniest detail of what actually happened." In this respect, the material of a novel should be remote from the novelist's personal life in either time or space. "Recently I have acquired a bad habit," Tanizaki once said. "Whether in writing a novel myself or in reading one by someone else, I am not pleased unless it presents fictitious things. I do not feel like writing or reading a novel that draws on actual facts or, for that matter, any novel that is realistic." What he would read were either historical novels or imaginative tales; realistic novels were acceptable to him only when they had been written at least a century earlier. He could tolerate contemporary novels only if they were imported from the West, or some other society entirely different from Japan. As specific examples of the novels he liked, he cited Nakasato Kaizan's *Great Bodhisattva Pass*, George Moore's *Héloise and Abélard* and *Ulick and Soracha*, and Stendhal's *The Charterhouse of Parma* and *The Abbess of Castro*. This, of course, was why he wrote so many historical novels. In his preface to *A Tale of Disarrayed Chrysanthemums*, he wrote he had chosen mid-sixteenth-century Japan for the novel's setting because people in general knew least about that era. "The author set his eyes on this era," he explained, "not because he wanted to uncover unknown historical facts or characters, but because the age leaves free room for his imagination." He wrote some novels with contemporary settings, but they are settings that, for the most part, have remained isolated from the mainstream of Japanese life. Thus *The Makioka Sisters* is set in the Japan of 1936–41, but such climactic events in Japanese history as the Sino-Japanese War and the Second World War have hardly made a mark on the main characters' lives. The world of *Some Prefer Nettles*, *The Key*, or *The Diary of a Mad Old Man* is the private world of its hero and heroine; in the last two, the impression of privacy is enhanced by the diary form in which they are written. Virtually the only major Tanizaki novel with an obvious relationship to contemporary social phenomena is *An Idiot's Love*, although here again the main characters by and large enclose themselves in a world of their own.

On the other hand, Tanizaki tried to incorporate in each of his novels as many historical or scientific facts as possible, insofar as these did not detract from the intrinsic quality of the setting. He did this, of course, in order to give the setting authenticity. Thus *The Key* and *The Diary of a Mad Old Man* abound in current medical and pharmacological information. For *The Makioka Sis-*

ters, Tanizaki prepared a chronology of significant social events, so that the novel would contain nothing contradictory to actual facts. He took care, he tells us, not to be wrong about such facts as the rate of taxi fare, the availability of third-class sleeping berths on the national railway, or the cast of a kabuki play at a given theater on a given date. It goes without saying that his historical novels, too, were based on much historical research. A marvelous example is *The Mother of Captain Shigemoto,* in which the narrator, who is a scholar in the Japanese classics, freely alludes—with great accuracy—to a number of ancient Japanese books that still survive. But there are also references to one fictional book—Shigemoto's diary—that is treated in the novel as if it were an authentic Japanese classic. It certainly seems like one to the reader, because all the other books cited are authentic.

In sum, the outstanding feature of Tanizaki's literary aesthetic is his preoccupation with the subconscious. External nature, however beautiful it might be, did not interest him. His concern was with internal nature, with human nature and all that it hides—with the "deep well" that looms darkly in the heart of each man. To Tanizaki, then, imitation of nature came to mean imaginative representation of these mysterious psychological forces as they manifest themselves in life. The artist, with his imaginative power, perceives the forces and creates a self-contained world in which they are given free rein. In Tanizaki's view, this world was truer to reality than the real one, for it brought the hidden potential of men and women to fulfillment. The novelist might make use of historical or scientific facts, but they should play only a subordinate role; namely, to give a sense of reality to his imaginary world. In Tanizaki's opinion, the real world in which we live should be subservient to the imaginary world that the artist creates; nature should, indeed, imitate art.

The Artist's Brew

Tanizaki clearly made what he called "artistic imagination" the distinguishing mark of the artist's gift. "I believe," he wrote, "the basic difference between an artist's and a non-artist's temperament lies in the amount of artistic imagination possessed by each." The artist was a person gifted with an unusually rich imagination, so rich that he was compelled to give it public expression. He was, in Tanizaki's words, a man afflicted with "creative fever." Artistic imagination was the cause, creative fever the symptom. The artist at work was like a sick man struggling to master his delirium:

If I were asked how the creative urge takes shape, I would answer this way. It is like the trees and grass budding out with the coming of spring. Somewhere in the mind, artistic imagination begins to ferment. As soon as he becomes conscious of the ferment, the novelist feels an intense urge to write a creative piece. It is this urge that is known as "creative fever," I think. Of course, artistic imagination as such is nothing like an orderly, coherent vision that can be transformed into a tale at once. Rather, it is a cluster of wild fantasies, incoherent and disconnected, swirling up in disorder like masses of clouds. The faster the phantasmal clouds move, the more the creative urge is intensified. Yet no matter how high the fever, it alone is not enough to start the novelist off in his creative venture. Instead, he has to wait until the fantasies in his mind settle down here and there, gradually arranging themselves into a coherent whole. Until such a time comes, he must resist the intense pressure of the creative urge, without knowing either the theme or the eventual form of his forth-coming work. All he can do is to writhe in agony, chasing a succession of fantasies that appear and disappear in his mind.

In this process, as described by Tanizaki, the artist exercised little initiative or control; indeed, the process had its origin in the sub-conscious. The creative urge arises naturally, like a tree budding or a cloud rising; the artist cannot make it come, any more than he can control the seasons or the weather. Furthermore, the artist is powerless even after he knows a creative urge is there. He has to resist the urge to create until the fantasies come to rest by them-selves; he cannot make them do this by the force of his will. Thus, for most of the creative process, the artist is passive. Since his prime role is to uncover the mind's deep well, he has to let his conscious mind be taken over by the fantasies that escape from his sub-conscious. But he cannot summon them at will.* The most he can do is let them ferment in his mind like wine in a vat.

---

* An interesting case of a person attempting to summon fantasies by will power alone is described in the opening scene of "A Heretic's Sorrow," a novella that, by Tanizaki's own admission, was autobiographical.

There is, then, not much the artist can do except wait for the creative urge to visit him. He has to wait patiently, without knowing when it will return. "It may come back in no time, or not for many years," said Tanizaki. "In brief, all depends on the Muse's will; the novelist can do nothing for himself in this matter. Therefore, a novelist trying to support himself and his family by his creative work can be compared to a man precariously walking a tight rope." Only an unscrupulous writer, Tanizaki thought, would write when the creative urge was not present, shamelessly producing a mediocre work for the sake of money. But a conscientious novelist could never do such a thing; he would rather endure poverty and all the pain that goes with it, for he knew that such was the artist's lot.

One thing, however, the novelist could do: he could create for himself an environment that would encourage the Muse to visit him. He could, in other words, arrange his entire life in a way most conducive to his creative imagination. To this end, he should be thoroughly acquainted with his own imaginative bent. Tanizaki tried to do this throughout his life. In his youth, when he was interested in the fantastic and supernatural, he indulged himself in what he called dissipation. He then came to doubt whether decadence really suited him, whereupon he mended his ways and got married. When his tastes changed yet again and he became an admirer of classical Japanese culture, he made his permanent residence in the Kyoto-Osaka area, where many of the old ways had been preserved. Divorced twice by this time, he married into an old Osaka family.

Tanizaki went to great lengths in following his own precepts. For instance, he refused to have a child by his third wife, the woman from Osaka, on the ground that its birth might end his career as a novelist. He knew his wife had been the source of his creative imagination for many years; he once confessed he had written *A Blind Man's Tale*, *The Secret Tale of the Lord of Musashi*, "Ashikari," and "The Portrait of Shunkin" under her influence, even before he married her. She inspired him because she had so much of old Japan in her manner and appearance. Tanizaki feared that all this would disappear as soon as she became the mother of his child, even though she already had two children by her previous husband. When she actually became pregnant, he pleaded with her that, should the child be born, the artistic atmosphere of the household would be destroyed and that his creative urge would decline; indeed, he felt that he might no longer be able to write at all. After suffering agonies of indecision—she really wanted the baby—his wife had an abortion. "I believe," Tanizaki later recollected, "she loved me and my art more dearly than the child within her." He was profoundly grateful to her, and vowed to do his best to make her happy and to be as kind as possible to her two children.

One may well wonder why having a baby in the family should so irrevocably destroy its "artistic atmosphere." But Tanizaki, it appears, could not abide the thought of an Osaka woman—his wife—having a child by a Tokyo man; her purity would be lost. Furthermore, he felt that his need for a beautiful woman to stimulate his artistic imagination would not be met by a housewife with small children.* Like Kafū, he detested a domesticated woman. Nevertheless, he claimed that he differed from Kafū:

I am a feminist, while Kafū is not. On all matters where love is concerned, I am a fetishist, fanatic, radical, and purist, while he is not. Kafū tends to look down upon women and treat them as playthings, but I cannot bear doing so. I regard women as higher beings than myself. I look up to them. Any woman who does not deserve my respect is, to my mind, not a woman.

Clearly, Tanizaki's feminism was of a somewhat egotistical variety: he could not bring himself to have a child by the woman he adored because he could not bear the prospect of sharing her. He wanted her to be nothing except the personification of his aesthetic ideal; otherwise she was not a woman, or not in his eyes. Tanizaki was extraordinarily fortunate in having found a woman who was prepared to sacrifice herself to his art in this way. One wonders what

---

* Long before he came to know his third wife, Tanizaki had expressed his displeasure at the thought of his spouse having a baby. At that time he was married to a Tokyo woman; he did not have to worry about her losing her classic Japanese traits. She went ahead and gave birth to a baby girl.

would have become of him—or, at any rate, of his theory—if he had not.

In Tanizaki's opinion, then, the artist's imagination, stimulated from without, begets a succession of fantasies that are consistent with his subconscious desires. This is the first stage of the creative process. The second stage is when the novelist waits for the fantasies to settle: this waiting period has to occur before he can take up his pen. Again, the novelist can do nothing during this period; his fantasies have to simmer down by themselves.

Tanizaki said that the length of this waiting period obviously would depend on many factors. In his own case it seems to have been a period of several months. He said he was visited by fantasies most frequently during the summer months, but was too excited and intoxicated to give them artistic expression at once. His mind, he said, calmed down in December and January, and he therefore found it easiest to write in those months. Ideally, he would store his summer fantasies in his mind and transform them into a work of art when winter came. Needless to say, he also had numerous occasions when, for one reason or another, he did not follow that ideal plan. For instance, both "A Mermaid's Lament" and "The Magician" were conceived in October and written in December. He began writing "Ashikari" without any definite idea of how the plot would develop. After he had written the first quarter of the story, his thoughts gradually began to simmer down, and he was able to write without interruption for almost the rest of the way. But he did not know how to end the story, even when he came to the point where he knew he had to end it. He was in a quandary, when all of a sudden an idea flashed into his mind, and he was able to write the conclusion in fewer than ten lines. *Some Prefer Nettles* was also written extemporaneously, but in this instance Tanizaki had no difficulty ending the novel. As he grew older, his "waiting period" became longer. He waited for nearly two years after the initial inspiration to begin writing "Arrowroot Leaves in Yoshino." In the case of *The Makioka Sisters*, he had a long period of preparation, and set down a detailed plan before he wrote a word of it. He followed that plan almost to the end, with some minor revisions.

The third and final stage of the creative process is to give adequate expression to the fantasies as they present themselves to the artist after the waiting period. Tanizaki had in mind the importance of this stage when he said: "Art is expression; without expression, there cannot be art. A painter who does not paint, or a poet who does not write poetry, exists only as a metaphor. No such person exists in reality." The thought is commonplace enough. What is not commonplace is the use that Tanizaki made of it in developing a concept of the artist as creator rather than craftsman. Tanizaki refused to recognize artistic skill as separate from the subject to be expressed. In his view, artistic technique was "dead" or "counterfeit" unless it was permeated with the *esprit* and joy of creation. The form of expression, he thought, was spontaneously adopted by the artist; it was not something consciously devised by him. Each writer unknowingly created his own style, the style best suited to his natural endowments. The style was inseparably related to the writer, not merely to his personality but to his physique as well. "Whether the writer is conscious of it or not, his composition automatically assumes a style that corresponds to his constitution. A person emotional by nature writes in an impassioned style, while a calm person speaks in a low-keyed style. A man with a weak respiratory system writes a piece that is somehow short of breath, and a man with weak digestive organs produces a composition that reflects his pale, gloomy complexion." The logical conclusion is that style cannot be taught, since one's conscious mind can do as little to change one's style as one's physical constitution.

It must be said, then, that Tanizaki's concept of artistic creation is marked by his emphasis on passivity. The artist is little more than a container in which wine is fermented. The creative imagination that he needs lies beyond the reach of his conscious mind; he himself can do nothing but wait until his creative imagination breeds fantasies. Even then, he has to keep waiting until the fantasies sort themselves out. He does not have much choice in his mode of expressing the fantasies either, for this is determined for the most part by the fantasies themselves. Tanizaki's artist is a man endowed with the capacity to remain passive to the entreaties of his subconscious. He is a man who has the courage to give maximum freedom to the play of his subconscious.

The Lady of the Shadows

Tanizaki's concept of beauty is eloquently expounded in his celebrated essay "In Praise of Shadows." As the title indicates, the essay expresses his admiration for a shadowy and crepuscular style of beauty in both life and art. He prefers a Japanese-style washroom because it is darker than others inside; he is fond of lacquerware because it is most attractive in a dimly lighted room; he likes Japanese houses because of their large, drooping roofs; he is fascinated with the nō actors' gorgeous costumes that perfectly match the dusky stage. Why did he like shadows so much? His answer was that Orientals had always liked them, and that he was an Oriental. As for why Orientals liked them, he gave two reasons: Orientals were by nature passive, and had learned to live with darkness instead of trying to conquer it as Occidentals did; and Orientals, with their darker skins, had automatically cultivated a sense of beauty befitting their complexion. But the essay is much more than a comparative study of Eastern and Western ideals of beauty. It is written with enthusiasm, leaving no doubt that the author is far more fascinated than the average Oriental with this dusky ideal of beauty. In his youth, Tanizaki had in fact been an ardent admirer of the West and of Western female beauty. The main reason why he admired shadows so much was that they breed fantasies.

Support for this interpretation can be found throughout "In Praise of Shadows." The author intimates that he likes to "sink into meditation" in the dim light of a Japanese-style washroom. He also observes that Japanese soup, lying silently at the bottom of a lacquered bowl, makes one want to meditate rather than eat. He likes Japanese yōkan jelly because, looking on it, he feels as if it had "absorbed sunlight deep under its translucent jadelike surface and were emitting a dim light as in a dream." He loves to see gold lacquer work by candlelight because its surface glitters in the dark and creates "a strangely luminous dream-world" with its reflections. He likes to see a Japanese woman under the same circumstances, and imagines that in old Japan a high-ranking noble-woman must have spent many hours of the night sitting in a huge tatami-matted room lighted by a candle, its dim, rainbow-colored light filling the atmosphere like dense fog. He adds that

... people of today, long accustomed to the light of electric lamps, have forgotten there once was this type of darkness. Particularly in the house, the "visible darkness" makes one feel as if something imperceptible were wavering in it, and readily invokes fantasies in one's mind, so that it is more likely to induce a sense of mystery than the darkness outdoors. No doubt it was in such darkness that goblins and weird spirits hovered about; and weren't these women, who lived darkly behind so many doors and drapes and screens, also goblins after their fashion? I can imagine how tightly the darkness enfolded them, closing in on them through every opening in their clothes, downward along the neck, upward along the arms and legs. Or perhaps they emitted that darkness from within their bodies, through their blackened teeth or through their dark hair, as a ground spider spins its web.

"In Praise of Shadows" ends with the author's declaration that he would try to call back, through the art of fiction, the world of shadows that was so rapidly disappearing with the modernization of Japan. He did what he promised. Most of Tanizaki's later works create such a world, a twilight world inhabited by people who thrive on darkness. Many important happenings occur at night in *The Secret Tale of the Lord of Musashi*, "Ashikari," *The Mother of Captain Shigemoto*, and *The Key*. All of the events that happen in *A Blind Man's Tale*, "A Portrait of Shunkin," and *From the Notes of an Old Tale* are reported by blind men, living in darkness. The narrator of *The Diary of a Mad Old Man* is not blind, but he is nearing eighty years of age and his eyesight and other faculties are considerably weaker than an average person's. Among Tanizaki's later works virtually the only major novel not dominated by the world of shadows is *The Makioka Sisters*. But even here, daylight seldom enters. The four Makioka sisters were born and brought up behind the many doors and screens of a gloomy old house in Osaka. Of the four, Yukiko, the novel's hero-ine, has a particularly downcast appearance and an unusually introverted personality. She perfectly complements the traditional Japanese house, with its lack of interior lighting; indeed, at the end of the novel the author marries her to a viscount's son who, after many years of wandering in the West, has rediscovered the beauty of traditional Japan.

As is evident from the above-cited passage, shadows were also a prime factor in Tanizaki's concept of ideal female beauty. He adored women who looked their best by candlelight. He did not like women who passed for beautiful in today's Japan—the type of women who competed in Miss Universe contests—because "their facial features are too clear-cut and too self-sufficient to encourage dreamers." His ideal woman, he explained, had less distinctive features, creating an indefinable impression like a hazy spring moon. Many of the heroines in Tanizaki's later works can be viewed as personifications of this ideal. The heroine of "The Portrait of Shunkin," for example, has a face that, although exquisitely beautiful, is without individuality or any definite appeal. The principal female character in "Ashikari" has the features of a typical Japanese beauty, except that there is "something misty" about her face. Likewise, Yukiko in *The Makioka Sisters* has features less clear-cut than those of any of her three sisters, and is all the more attractive because of it. In each case, the heroine's face stimulates the onlooker's imagination by not being expressive of her inner feelings. It is a face capable of refusing the command of the conscious mind: it hardly shows an emotion, unless it is rooted deep in the subconscious. Yukiko, for instance, betrays no sign of happiness even when, at long last, a marriage is successfully arranged for her. Tanizaki liked a face of this type precisely because it so much resembled a mask.

In this respect, the theme of crepuscular beauty becomes a connecting link between Tanizaki's earlier and later heroines. His earlier ones are generally distinguished by their ruthless, possessive qualities, and his later ones by their calm beauty. But all of them have clouded, enigmatic features that mask the secret stirrings of the subconscious. And the subconscious knows neither good nor evil, but only the promptings of desire. Tanizaki's earlier heroines remain beautiful even as they follow their darkest impulses, paying little heed to the daytime world of public morality. Their beauty, as critics pointed out at the time (and as Tanizaki himself agreed), is daemonic. The heroines of "Tattoo," "A Spring Time Case," *Because of Love, An Idiot's Love,* and *The Whirlpool* all have this quality. The only major difference between them and the later heroines is that the former show what is hidden in their minds' secret depths. But the two types of heroine are sisters under the skin, just as the serenely beautiful heroine of *The Makioka Sisters,* all surface appearances to the contrary, in some ways resembles her more daemonic younger sister.

Among the types of daemonic beauty, Tanizaki seems to have been most attracted to the beauty of cruelty. This is probably because he thought of the human subconscious as basically destructive. Women, whose beauty came to full flower only at the expense of their male admirers, were naturally cruel; men, for their part, were never happier than when they were physically abused by the women they adored. One of Tanizaki's favorite film actresses was Simone Signoret, especially after he saw her play the role of a murderess in *Les Diaboliques;* he admired her for her "large, smutty-looking face and lusterless, tired skin, for the impression she gave of being a ruthless, fearless, cunning woman." Many of Tanizaki's earlier heroines have this ruthless quality, and are beautiful because of it. In his later works, the heroine of *The Diary of a Mad Old Man* comes closest to this type; in fact, she is directly compared with Simone Signoret.

Tanizaki's predilection for the beauty of cruelty also found expression in his fondness for members of the cat family. He once remarked that of all animals he would most like to have a leopard as a pet because it was "beautiful, lithe, elegant, as genteel as a court musician and as merciless as a devil." The same is true of his early heroines. Of course, he could not keep a leopard at home; he therefore kept cats instead. His love of cats is reflected in his short novel *The Cat, Shōzō, and Two Women,* which must rank as one of the world's finest cat stories.

Tanizaki also found mothers beautiful but daemonic. Maternal beauty in itself had no evil connotations for him. But when he related it to the child's latent sexual drive, he thought that it took on a distinctly equivocal aspect. Once, when Tanizaki was asked what woman struck him as being supremely beautiful, he answered that it was his late mother, as he remembered her, not in her last days, but as a young, beautiful woman. Such a young, beautiful mother is the heroine of his short story "Longing for Mother," in which the son, looking at the mother closely, cannot help feeling "a mysterious, daemonic eeriness" in her. "Her powdered face," he says, "created an impression of coldness rather than of beauty or loveliness." The hero of "Arrowroot Leaves in Yoshino," pining for his late mother, wishes that she were a fox, an animal with supernatural powers in Japanese folklore.* For Captain Shigemoto, too, his mother was a shadowy person who never showed herself outside the darkness of a dimly lighted room. When, after many years of searching, he as last meets her, he first takes her to be the spirit of an old cherry tree that is blossoming with "daemonic beauty" above her.

To conclude, Tanizaki's literary aesthetic centers on the beauty of half-light, of dusky visions that vibrate in the imagination. Living in the age of electricity, he nevertheless tried to create a world of shadows by means of literature. He preferred his world to be dimly lit because it permitted the weird creatures of the subconscious to come out into the open. In the kingdom of Tanizaki's fiction, women markedly outweigh men in importance, because he thought of them as creatures of darkness, belonging to the subconscious. Female beauty as worshiped by Tanizaki inevitably becomes equivocal: a woman who treats her lover sadistically or who seduces her son is always pictured as supremely beautiful. But this is logical, because for Tanizaki beauty and the grotesque are one and the same. The logic, of course, is that of the subconscious, the dark abode of Freudian goblins.

---

* In a puppet play known as *Arrowroot Leaves*, a female fox, taking on human form, marries a man and gives birth to a son, but has to return to the woods when her identity is revealed. The hero in Tanizaki's story, who has been familiar with the play since childhood, wishes that his mother had not been dead but had simply returned to the woods, in which case he might have had a chance to meet her again.

Plot like a Mountain Range, Style like a Flowing Stream

For all his emphasis on the subconscious, Tanizaki himself was a very self-conscious technician. Perhaps he thought a novel must have a form designed to engage the reader's conscious mind precisely because its contents made their appeal at a different level. In any case, his own novels are characterized by skillfully constructed plot and persuasive rhetoric, in sharp contrast to the uncanny, indefinable nature of their central themes and characters. In his literary essays he became unusually candid as soon as his topic led him to the technicalities of composition. On the question of structure, he even engaged in literary polemics—the so-called plotless novel controversy with Akutagawa. As for style, he wrote a textbook, *The Composition Reader*.

The much publicized controversy between Tanizaki and Akutagawa began when the former, in a magazine article, casually remarked that more and more he was coming to like novels with well-made, complicated plots. Akutagawa, on reading it, criticized Tanizaki for rating plot so highly; plot, he argued, had no value in itself. Tanizaki answered, in part:

Unfortunately, I cannot agree. The fact that plot is fascinating implies that the way the material is organized—namely, the structure—is fascinating; it implies the presence of architectural beauty. No one can say, then, that such a structure lacks aesthetic value. (The *material* and the *structure* are two different things.) Of course, the sole value of a novel does not reside in its plot. But, in my view, of all literary genres it is the novel that can make the most of structural beauty. A novelist who refuses to create a fascinating plot is throwing away one advantage that the novel has over other genres. The greatest weakness of Japanese novelists is that they have no power to construct, no talent for the geometry of building up a complicated plot.

In reply to this, Akutagawa conceded that the novel—and, in fact, all forms of literature, including the haiku—could have "architectural beauty." He disagreed with Tanizaki, however, on two points. First, he believed that "poetic spirit" was more valuable in the novel than "architectural beauty"; there could be fine novels without the latter, he insisted, but not without the former. Second,

Akutagawa thought Japan had produced a number of novelists who had the "power to construct," and he named some contemporary writers by way of example.

Tanizaki countered by saying that "poetic spirit" was too ambiguous a term. He also redefined his term "architectural beauty" so that it could not be interpreted as broadly as Akutagawa had done. True architectural beauty, he contended, needed space.

Mr. Akutagawa, who recognizes structural beauty even in a haiku, would probably find it in a teahouse, too. But in such instances there is no feeling of a great many things being piled one on top of another. There is scarcely any of what he called the *physical* strength that enables one to write a massive novel. In my opinion, the lack of such physical strength is the greatest weakness of Japanese literature. If I may speak frankly, I would say that as a short-story writer Mr. Akutagawa could never be a match for Mr. Shiga because he cannot create the feelings of physical strength in his work. Deep-breathing lungs, strong arms, muscular legs—a good literary work, even a short one, somehow produces an impression of having these things. Among long novels, too, a puny one gets short of breath in mid-course. A good novel, in contrast, creates beauty by introducing a great number of events one after another; it has a grandeur like that of a far-extending mountain range. That is what I mean by "power to construct."

Tanizaki, after defining "architectural beauty" in this way, went on to drop all but one of the contemporary Japanese novelists from Akutagawa's list of examples.* Akutagawa countered yet once more, but not very convincingly. In the end, he seems to have given tacit consent to Tanizaki's conclusion that the writer's physique is the final determinant of literary form.

Tanizaki's concept of structure, as it emerges from the controversy, is quite clear: a novel should have a tightly knit, skillfully woven plot. "Its components," he observed elsewhere, "should embrace each other so tightly that if one were to be removed the whole would collapse." Not many Japanese literary theorists have shared this approach. Japanese readers have always liked a loose, episodic kind of plot—if plot it can be called—far removed from what

---

* There was only one contemporary Japanese novelist who Tanizaki thought had any talent in plot construction: Izumi Kyōka (1873–1939), well known for such tales of mystery and imagination as *Kōya Mendicant* and "A Tale of Three Who Were Blind."

Tanizaki had in mind; they especially detested a plot that was constructed geometrically, like a classic French comedy. Tanizaki's notion of plot was also unusual in its preference for grandeur; plot, he thought, should be not only tightly knit but constructed on the grand scale. It should be like a long-distance runner with strong legs; it should demonstrate the writer's staying power.

Tanizaki's idea of plot thus turns out to be almost deterministic. Plot construction, ostensibly the fruit of the writer's conscious efforts, is determined willy-nilly by his physique. By his own criteria, Tanizaki's preference for a long, complicated story was instinctive, and his argument with Akutagawa had to end at this point because constitutional differences could never be reconciled. Once again, Tanizaki gave the subconscious an important role.

By and large, Tanizaki seems to have followed his own theoretical precepts about plot construction. His major works have plots that are considerably more complicated and more tightly woven than most Japanese novels. Few indeed of the latter have plots as complex as Tanizaki's *The Whirlpool.* Skillful storytelling contributes much to the charm of *A Blind Man's Tale,* "The Portrait of Shunkin," and *The Mother of Captain Shigemoto.* What Tanizaki termed the grandeur of a far-extending mountain range is seen in the plots of such works of his as *An Idiot's Love* and *The Makioka Sisters. A Tale of Disarrayed Chrysanthemums* reads like a popular adventure story; in fact, Tanizaki amused himself by calling it "a popular novel," apparently in reference to Akutagawa's charge that any work of fiction that tries to attract readers by an ingenious plot is a "popular" novel, not a "genuine" one. Some of his early tales—"The Thief," "Devils Talk in Broad Daylight," and "In the Street," among others—are plotted as carefully as detective stories; indeed, they are usually assigned to that genre. The same type of suspense is built up in "Arrowroot Leaves in Yoshino," which relates the search for a missing person, while *The Key* approaches the detective story when the wife begins to plot her husband's death. No doubt one reason why so many of Tanizaki's works have been made into films is because they have interesting stories to tell. Tanizaki himself, more than any other modern Japanese novelist, seems to have considered himself a storyteller; in fact, he entitled one of his last books *I Am a Modern Storyteller*, and he liked to call his fictional works "tales."*

As a storyteller, Tanizaki was always extremely sensitive to the use of language. Already in his twenties he was concerned enough about the confused state of the Japanese language to contribute to a political magazine an article proposing the standardization of Japanese orthography. He never lost this concern. Almost half a century later we find him writing a short article headlined "What Disturbs Me"; its subject was the incorrect and imprecise use of many words by contemporary Japanese writers and journalists. His desire to do something to improve the quality of Japanese writing led him to produce *The Composition Reader*, a comprehensive guidebook to good prose. While intended for a broad range of readers, the book reveals a good deal about his own literary practice.

What was distinctive about Tanizaki's approach to the language of literature was his denial that any such thing existed. He even said: "I believe there is no difference between practical and artistic language." By practical language, however, he meant language that efficiently carries out its practical purpose, which is to make the reader understand the writer. The most practical language is therefore the most artistic. "If you think there is some art of speaking or writing reserved exclusively for the novel," he said, "read any one of our contemporary novels. You will immediately discover that it contains no sentence that cannot be used for a practical purpose, and that any sentence serving a practical purpose well is also useful in literary composition." More than anything else, Tanizaki believed, the language of literature had to be persuasive; to be beautiful or euphonious was of secondary importance.

In this regard, Tanizaki must be said to have had a healthy respect for the reader. Many of his colleagues were concerned above all with being honest to themselves; they made no special attempt

---

* For example, "The Tale of a Woman Who Turned into a Monkey," *A Tale of Disarrayed Chrysanthemums*, *A Blind Man's Tale*, *The Secret Tale of the Lord of Musashi*, and *The Tale of My Youth*.

to accommodate their audience. Those with aesthetic temperaments close to Tanizaki's were more inclined to write poetry than novels, because poetry seemed so much more expressive. Tanizaki, though in his youth he had admired Poe and Baudelaire, seldom composed verse, and when he did he almost exclusively wrote in the traditional tanka form, without a hint of fashionable surrealistic hermeticism.* No doubt he had many reasons for so doing, but one of the main ones must have been that he was eager to be understood by a large number of people. He wanted his story to look convincing to the unsophisticated reader, and in order to make it convincing he wanted to be an expert stylist. And he was.

According to Tanizaki, good style was a matter of two rules, both of them quite relevant to his general conception of literature. The first was not to be too concerned with the rules of grammar. The reason for this, as he explained, was that the Japanese language in its very nature was not very grammatical. The writer could turn this to advantage by cultivating a certain ambiguity, which Tanizaki found elegant; indeed, he compared the effect of a passage written with no ambiguity to that of rudely exposed thighs and knees. A passage that omitted as many words as possible, even to the point at which a strict grammarian would object to it, was at once graceful in impression and provocative in meaning.

The second piece of advice Tanizaki had for beginning writers was that they should cultivate their literary taste. In order to become a good writer, one had to be able to distinguish good writing from bad. But this was like distinguishing between good and bad wines; one had only one's own taste to rely on. Here Tanizaki was retreating to subjectivism, and he knew it. He still insisted, however, that there would emerge a semblance of objectivity if the reader had developed a refined taste. Once more, Tanizaki com-

---

* The Japanese were introduced to Western symbolist poetry in 1905 with the publication of *The Sound of the Tide*, a collection of poems by Baudelaire, Verlaine, Mallarmé, and others in Japanese translation. For the next several decades, symbolist and surrealist modes of expression dominated the poetic scene. Readers outside the poets' circles, however, were considerably less enthusiastic about the new trend. Discouraged by the abstruse language, many of them turned away from the Western-style poems written by Japanese poets in this period.

pared this to wine tasting: the experts' opinions, he observed, almost always agree. "Human faculties," he concluded, "are made in such a way that, after an adequate amount of orientation, they respond in the same way to the same stimulant." Just as connoisseurs of wine refined their taste by trying a great many wines, so novice writers should improve theirs by reading as widely as possible, and by practicing the art of composition. Education had little to do with it; inborn taste, polished by experience, was all. Here again Tanizaki's distrust of intellect was apparent.

The Composition Reader also classified prose styles in terms of two main categories. The first included the "flowing style," the "laconic style," the "calm style," the "airy style" (a light, casual, unconventional style; Tanizaki advised that a writer practice Zen to learn it), and the "craggy style" (a deliberately rugged, uneven style; Tanizaki compared it to the surface of a crag); it referred, as these terms imply, both to the mode of sentence construction and to the way in which one sentence followed from another. The second referred to vocabulary and idiom; it comprised the "lecture style" (normal written style; professors often used it in their lectures so that students could copy them verbatim), the "military style" (more polite than the lecture style; so called because typically a serviceman used it in addressing his superior), the "salutatory style" (even more polite than the military style; used on highly ceremonial occasions), and the "conversational style" (used in normal conversations). Though in both instances the classification involved no value judgment, Tanizaki made sufficiently clear which styles he favored. In the first category, Tanizaki seems to have had a natural predilection for the "flowing style," a style that, with its long sentences and carefully but inconspicuously engineered continuity, was like a smoothly flowing stream. He recalled the days when smooth readability of this type was the prime requisite of good Japanese composition, and lamented the contemporary trend that prized clarity above all else. Someday, he hoped, the flowing style would come back into vogue again. He was fond of it because he thought it suited the genius of the Japanese language better than any other. This is what we would expect from someone for whom the greatest masterpiece in Japanese literature was *The Tale of Genji,* a novel written in the flowing style throughout. In the second category, he seems to have been most attracted to the "conversational style." He liked it because, as he pointed out, this style had four main strengths: (1) expression was freer; (2) sentences could end in a greater variety of sounds; (3) the reader could feel the tone of the writer's speech and almost see his feelings and facial expressions; (4) the reader could tell whether the speaker was a man or a woman. Tanizaki seems to have especially liked this last fact. He observed that as a rule a male reader read a book in a male voice even when he was not reading aloud, but that if the book was written in the conversational style he would read it in either a male or a female voice, whichever the sense required. For this reason, Tanizaki recommended that writers use the conversational style more frequently.

Tanizaki's predilection for the flowing and conversational styles is clearly seen in his own writings. Though he was a very versatile writer, who could command a variety of styles with consummate skill, these two styles underlie most of them. The flowing style is the one in which he wrote many of his novels and short stories in his mature years; the most notable example of it is *The Makioka Sisters.* It is also conspicuous in *The Cat, Shōzō, and Two Women,* "Ashikari" (in which many quotation marks are deliberately omitted in order not to interrupt the flow of words), and "The Portrait of Shunkin" (in which most of the punctuation is omitted, for the same reason). Some parts of *The Diary of a Mad Old Man* are written in the "craggy style," and *Chronicles of Our Peaceful Kitchen* inclines somewhat toward the "airy style"; yet in both instances the overriding tone of voice is unmistakably that of the flowing style. The same style is latent in his earlier works, too—in "The Clown," for instance.

As for Tanizaki's use of the conversational style in his fiction, examples are too numerous to cite. The most striking one is *The Whirlpool,* which is told entirely in the peculiarly feminine vernacular of a woman brought up in the Osaka area. In one of his last works, called "A Chat," he assumes instead the voice of a

Tokyo woman. *A Blind Man's Tale* is narrated in a kind of modernized version of sixteenth-century colloquial Japanese. In several other works the main story is told by one character to another, as in "The Tale of a Woman Who Turned into a Monkey," "An Incident at Yanagi Bathhouse," and "Ashikari." *I Am a Modern Storyteller*, written in the "salutatory style," gives the impression of a traditional Japanese storyteller sitting on a high platform and telling a lively tale to the audience. Works like "The Mermaid's Lament," "The Magician," *The Idiot's Love*, and *The Composition Reader*, which use the "military style," give the impression of a speaker talking to the reader in a polite, even tone. *The Mother of Captain Shigemoto*, written in the "lecture style," is almost a long rambling talk by a scholar in Japanese classics. *The Key* is narrated by a male and a female voice, speaking in alternate chapters, though in both instances the surface language is that of the "military style."

It has often been claimed that Tanizaki's style went through drastic changes during his long literary career. But his basic style does not seem to have changed much, when judged in the light of his classification of styles, since it always inclined toward the flowing and the conversational. Many of his readers would be willing to concede that there is a good deal of stylistic difference between "Tattoo" and *The Makioka Sisters*. Yet how many of them would be ready to say of the former that it approaches the "laconic style," the opposite of the "flowing style" in which the latter is written? And this is so in spite of the fact that "Tattoo," as we know it today, is a condensed version of a longer work that he discarded. Likewise, Tanizaki's fondness for the conversational style was lifelong. If one thinks this style is not often used in his early works of fiction, one has only to be reminded that the young Tanizaki wrote a good many plays. Among his early stories, too, there are those that, like "Creation" and "From a Certain Protocol," consist solely of dialogue. It does not appear, then, that Tanizaki ever attempted to change his basic stylistic preferences, or that the attempt would have made any sense to him, since he saw style as a natural product of physique.

Venus Redemptrix

For Tanizaki, the use of literature lay, to a considerable extent, in the pleasure it gave. He was caught by the charms of reading fiction early in his boyhood, and that more or less determined the subsequent course of his life. When he was eleven, he recalled, he read a children's story called *The New "Tale of Eight Dogs,"* and was completely absorbed by the strange world it created, a world of exciting adventures undertaken by eight toy dogs. He says that from this time on he knew "the happiness of letting the mind wander in the world of fantasy" and began indulging in that happiness himself. He went on to read more and more adventure stories for boys, as well as historical tales like the *Taiheiki* and foreign novels like Mark Twain's *The Prince and the Pauper*. He soon learned the pleasure of writing tales himself, and so creating his own world of fantasy.

Tanizaki's career as a novelist can be viewed as an extension of this boyhood hobby. As a grown-up writer, he continued to write stories for the happiness of roaming in a land of make-believe. Almost half a century later and nearing the end of his career, he still talked in the same vein about the pleasures of his craft.

I am often tempted to write an essay called "The Happiness of Being a Novelist," or something like that. No one but the novelist can enjoy the happiness of being able to work in complete isolation from other men, enclosing himself in a world of his own. Even at home I retain my own secluded world—a world unknown to my wife and her relatives—into which I can flee whenever I am inclined to.* Once within my castle, I am like a child playing with its favorite dolls: I bring out a number of phantasmal dolls and enjoy myself to my heart's content, with no one to interfere with my play. This privilege, I believe, is vouchsafed to the novelist alone. At such times, I never dream of taking even one step outside this private world.

For Tanizaki, then, the enjoyment of literature was ultimately the pleasure of dreaming. There is, of course, nothing new about

---

* The wife mentioned here is Tanizaki's third. After marrying her, he associated himself closely with her relatives. Her children by her first marriage, as well as her younger sister (who was the model for the heroine of *The Makioka Sisters*), lived in his household for a considerable length of time.

this idea. But it is profoundly characteristic of the man himself. His works, more than those of any other modern Japanese writer, give the impression of having being written with genuine enjoyment. This is true even of *The Makioka Sisters*, which is closer to the reality of contemporary life than most of his other works. In fact, Tanizaki wrote that he was happy throughout the long period in which he was writing it. This is all the more striking when one remembers that this was during the Second World War, when times were particularly hard for Japanese writers. And, in fact, he did meet many difficulties. Long before its completion (it was being published in installments), the novel was censored by the authorities for not promoting the cause of the war. Several times he moved his residence, trying to escape air raids. His health was deteriorating, especially while he was working on the last part. And yet he could say he was happy during all this time, and one does get that feeling when one reads the novel.

The pleasure of roaming in an imaginary world must also have been a large part of the reason why Tanizaki spent a great amount of time and energy in translating *The Tale of Genji* into modern Japanese. In fact, he translated that massive classic three times, a feat equaled by no one else before or since. That it was a worthwhile feat is undeniable; each time, the translation was superb. Yet, when one counts how many years he spent doing it, one sometimes wonders what new novels or tales he might have written if he had never undertaken such a project. Yet Tanizaki seems to have had not the slightest regret, because the process of translating that masterpiece of classical Japanese literature gave him as much delight as composing his own works.

However, it is also characteristic of Tanizaki that he seriously wanted to share the pleasures of literature with as many people as possible. While some writers of his time (Kafū, for example) thought that a literary work needed to be enjoyed only by its author and a small number of connoisseurs, Tanizaki wanted his novels to delight a mass of people. As has been mentioned, he did not mind writing deliberately popular works; he spurned Akutagawa's view that a conscientious novelist should write nothing but "genuine" literature that might or might not have a popular appeal. Tanizaki had nothing against "genuine" literature. But if he had to choose between two novels whose artistic values were otherwise equal, he preferred the one with more popular appeal. "Take the case of Shakespeare or Goethe or Tolstoy," he once said. "All great masterpieces are popular literature." He also referred to Stendhal's *The Charterhouse of Parma* in the same vein. Obviously, what he meant by "popular literature" was somewhat different from the ordinary sense of the term, but his intention is clear enough: he preferred a literary work to have an entertaining story to tell, and so to entice the reader into a world of imagination. An unsophisticated reader might read it for no reason other than diversion. But that was perfectly all right with Tanizaki; literature to him was play, whether with dolls or with the characters in a novel.

Tanizaki said basically the same thing about drama. He expressed his misgivings about the type of drama fashionable among the intellectuals of his day, the type that "makes the audience think" with its social and moral messages. "Of all forms of art," he said, "the theater has the greatest number of hedonistic, sensual, fleshy, and lustful elements. More than anything else it has to appeal to the spectator's emotion in order to make its effect felt. A drama without any hedonistic elements, a school-like theater to which one goes for learning—no such thing exists." Here Tanizaki was expressing his preference for the kabuki and allied dramatic forms to plays of the Ibsen variety. A kabuki playwright writes a play for his actors. A spectator goes to the kabuki theater to see his favorite actors; he pays little attention to the moral message of the play. And yet the kabuki has a peculiar significance, as Tanizaki explained:

If the actor has real versatility and charm, a spectator with refined taste and sensitivity can, as he watches the sensual and bodily beauty being created on the stage, feel something eternal emerging from it: he can feel spiritual beauty. In the actor's face, eyes, or posture, the spectator can get a momentary glimpse of that eternal beauty found in a masterpiece of painting or architecture. Beauty of form, elevated to this height, is worth as much as beauty of content. And since the large majority of people who go to the theater are neither scholars nor philosophers, they respond more readily to a play that has a supremely beautiful form than to one that has an important message.

Tanizaki's logic here is the same as when he said that the masses read a novel for its amusing story, not for its philosophical or moral implications. Again, he was not against moral or philosophical implications as such, but he thought that a play centered on them could be read at home. Why should there be living actors on the stage at all if their physical charms were not displayed to advantage? The spectator, he thought, might as well enjoy the actor's bodily beauty as long as the actor was there.

Despite all this emphasis on the idea that literature is play—and play for a very large number of people—Tanizaki seems to have secretly harbored a belief in literature's didactic function. This can be seen, for instance, in the passage quoted above, where he said that beauty of form is ultimately the same as beauty of content, that physical beauty is essentially no different from spiritual beauty. Tanizaki seems to be implying here that art at its highest level is as capable as religion of bringing spiritual enlightenment to its devotees—more capable, in fact, since visible beauty is more readily appreciated than spiritual beauty. Buddhism appeals to more people when the Buddha takes on a beautiful female form.

Again, this is hardly a novel idea. But when we consider Tanizaki's daemonic ideal of beauty, it takes on some very strange applications. Can an admirer of one of Tanizaki's she-devils be led thereby to the realm of religious enlightenment? Tanizaki's answer was emphatically in the affirmative. In his opinion, art was valuable precisely because it had that function. In most Oriental religions, the worshiper had as a rule to be a good man to be saved, but art could redeem even a bad man, a worshiper of evil beauty. "I believe," he said, "that art is the only way by which an evil man can attain a realm of perfect liberation without becoming an entirely different person. While religion spurns evil men . . . art permits them to enter its realm, as long as they believe in it. This is so because evil is only of this world; in the other world there is neither good nor evil; all there is is beauty."

The argument gains in force if "this world" is equated with the conscious mind, and "the other world" with the subconscious. Religion teaches man to be good in this world; it wants him to discipline himself by his conscious effort. A good man in religious terms is a person whose conscious mind has complete control over his behavior, so complete that he follows the religious codes automatically. But some people (everybody, potentially) are more faithful to the subconscious; they follow its commands because they come from a deeper level and speak to deeper needs. Religion would label such people wayward and refuse to save them unless they reformed. Art, in contrast, would both accept and save them, because it understands these needs.

A characteristic instance of art functioning as redeemer is cited by Tanizaki in a short polemic piece called "The Censor." The literary work being censored here is a play called *First Love*, and the playwright (modeled after Tanizaki himself), summoned before the censor, vigorously defends himself by insisting that the play is not at all immoral, that in fact it serves a didactic purpose.* The hero of the play is a young student who falls in love with a maidservant in his father's household. She, however, loves another man, and these two scheme to murder the student and grab the family estate. The student, well aware of the woman's evil design, willingly meets his death. "The flame that was burning in this boy's heart cannot be explained away by the logic of this world," the playwright remarks. "Nevertheless, the play does not give the spectators the impression that he met an unfortunate destiny. Or, even if some spectators should feel he was unfortunate, they will not believe his death was meaningless. They will be convinced that something remains after his death." The young student, Tanizaki is saying, is "saved" in the sense that he has been awakened to something higher than death, something that makes him readily meet his death. In this sense, though the object of his passion was unworthy, the play is didactic, even highly moral, since death is overcome as truly by passion as by religion.

Some of Tanizaki's novels are "religious" in the same sense, but more plainly so. Plainest of all is his last novel, *The Diary of a Mad Old Man*, in which the aged hero worships his young and beautiful

* This must have been based on Tanizaki's own experience. The censors banned his *An Age to Know Love*, a play that has the same plot as *First Love*.

daughter-in-law like a female Buddha. Keenly aware of approaching death, the old man buys a lot for his grave and prepares a plan for his tombstone, on which are to appear the young woman's footprints carved in the manner of the Buddha's.* Once the plan is set, the old man is no longer afraid of death, since he can dream of his departed soul lying at peace under her feet. A similar identification of a beautiful woman with a female Buddha is suggested in *The Whirlpool*: here, too, her admirers are not at all afraid of dying when they dream of being with her after their death. A more pathetic case is that of Captain Shigemoto's father, in the novel named after his wife. This old man is robbed of his beautiful wife, whom he worshiped. In deep grief and agony, he tries every means of salvation available to him—he reads the poetry of Po Chü-i, he drinks wine, he devotes himself to the practice of esoteric Buddhism—but to no avail. It is only his wife that can save him. His futile search for peace is awe-inspiring, and it is with relief that one finally reads of his son, Captain Shigemoto, being reunited with his mother, and so saving the old man's soul. However strange, even perverse, these emotions, they ennoble the characters who are driven by them. If the reader, too, is momentarily ennobled, perhaps he has gained from literature the best that Tanizaki thought it had to offer.

---

* When Sakya died, his disciples copied his footprints and had them carved on stone. Those sacred stone footprints are treasured at several temples in China and Japan and are worshiped by local Buddhists.

CHAPTER FOUR

Shiga Naoya

✿

MORE THAN MOST other contemporary Japanese novelists of importance, Shiga Naoya (1883–1971) seems to have been fond of writing about his own works. When the first collection of his prose was published in 1928, he wrote a postscript explaining the motive and intent of each work included in it. He did the same for the nine-volume *Collected Works of Shiga Naoya* (1937–38), and for the five-volume *Library of Shiga Naoya's Writings* (1954–55), so that today's readers have the author's notes on virtually all his fiction. The works themselves also throw a good deal of light on his attitude toward literature, because many of them have a writer, often identifiable as Shiga, for their principal character. This is true of his only full-length novel, *Voyage Through the Dark Night*, as well as of his three novelettes, *Ōtsu Junkichi, Reconciliation*, and *A Certain Man: His Sister's Death*. Then there are such literary essays of his as "Notes in My Leatherbound Box," "Rhythm," "Notebook of a Green Youth," and "On the Appreciation of Art," which directly touch on the art of writing or problems in aesthetics. When all these are put together, Shiga's views on the nature of literature emerge with unmistakable clarity.

Instinctive Wisdom and Recovery from Misfortune

In writing about his own works, Shiga was preoccupied above all with the question of their factuality. In almost every instance, he wanted to tell his readers to what extent the work was fictional. As it turned out, a large number of his stories were based on his own experience; many of them, indeed, purported to be faithful records of actual events. For instance, of his story called "Influenza" he said, "I wrote down the facts as they were," and of "At Kinosaki," "This too is a story that tells what actually happened." As for his methods of composition, he said of a story entitled "Morning, Noon, Evening": "In a relaxed frame of mind I wrote down the day's happenings as they actually occurred." When a certain critic made some derogatory remarks about his novelette *Reconciliation*, Shiga defended himself by saying that it was true to fact. He had written it, he said, not to present a moral thesis but to vent a "more immediate sentiment" of his—namely, "the joy of having arrived at a reconciliation [with my father] after a long period of estrangement." He concluded: "I simply kept on writing down the facts as they were, without any artifice, and I ended up producing a work of art. That is the strength of this work." Underlying all these comments is Shiga's idea that literature is in the last analysis a record of events that actually took place in the author's life. A literary work, he thought, should be autobiographical in the strict sense of the word; that is, it should be a conscious effort at self-revelation.

To Shiga, then, the difference between fiction and nonfiction was minimal. Indeed, to carry his views to their logical conclusion, there would not seem much need for writing fiction at all, since the facts of daily life could be most satisfactorily presented in the form of a diary, an autobiography, or an essay. And to a certain extent Shiga himself found this to be the case. Of the seventeen-volume *Collected Works of Shiga Naoya* (the 1955–56 edition, in which each volume has roughly the same number of pages), nine volumes are devoted to his works of nonfiction—essays, diaries, and personal letters. Among his stories, too, there are a considerable number that border on nonfiction. In the case of "Harvest Bugs," Shiga himself did not know which category it belonged to, and he remarked that this was characteristic of his work in general. In the case of another prose piece, he had first entitled it "Kusatsu Spa, an Essay" and sent it off to a publisher. But when it came back for proofreading he changed it into a short story by simply erasing "an Essay" from the title. It is difficult to think of any other major writer in modern Japan who could have done such a thing.

The fact remains, however, that Shiga was primarily a novelist, not an essayist or a diarist. His main creative energy went into writing works of fiction—a novel, three novelettes, and a sizable number of short stories, which include such obviously imaginative tales as "Han's Crime," "Claudius' Diary," and "Akanishi Kakita." Why did he think fiction was the best mode in which to record the facts of his own daily existence? His answer can be found in his notes on *Voyage Through the Dark Night*. "Kensaku, the hero, is by and large myself," he wrote. "I would say his actions approximate the things I would do, or would wish to do, or actually did, under the given circumstances." The prime function of a diary, like most other genres of personal nonfiction, was to record only what one actually did. A work of fiction, on the other hand, could present what one "would do, or would wish to do" in various imaginary situations. It described man not only as he had been or was, but as he might be or might want himself to be.

Likewise, in Shiga's view, a novel presents facts not only as they are but also as the novelist imagines they are or as he would wish them to be. He might, indeed, write down things contrary to actual fact, if they seemed imaginatively more convincing to him. Once, on devising a scene for a short story, Shiga placed the moon in a geographically impossible position, but knowingly let the description stand because that was the way he had long visualized the scene in his mind. At another time he described a certain temple in Nara from memory and later discovered the description was wrong in many details. But again he left it intact, for the same reason. In a more striking instance, Shiga consciously created an imaginary incident and placed it among other events that were obviously autobiographical. Later, he was amused to hear his sister say that she remembered the incident well. "My sister had no reason to tell a lie about that [incident]," he observed. "It had floated most naturally into my imagination, and because of that naturalness it was recalled to my sister's memory as a fact." Shiga also tells of instances in which his imagination seemed to sense an event before it actually happened, despite the fact that he had no foreknowledge of the circumstances. On one occasion, he was writing a short story and was trying to visualize a scene in which a barber kills his customer with a razor. By coincidence, one of his next-door neighbors committed suicide with a razor just about the same time. On another occasion, he wrote a short story about a boy who was hit by a streetcar and narrowly escaped death. That same evening Shiga himself was hit by a streetcar and was seriously injured. All these instances seemed to him to substantiate his idea that some imaginary facts are just as valuable as, or even more valuable than, actual facts.

What kinds of facts, whether actual or imaginary, are most suitable for a work of fiction? Ordinary facts would not do; they would merely provide material for a chat, or for a popular novel at best. "A story that can be told in a chat," Shiga once said, "should be told in a chat. Only a story with something in it that could not be told in a chat could be made into a work of literature." Shiga did not elaborate on what that "something" was. But other writings of his show clearly enough what he meant. For instance, there is the revealing anecdote about the way he welcomed a close friend who had just returned from a year-long trip to Europe and North America. His wife showered the friend with "Welcome home!" and other such greetings. But Shiga did not utter a word of welcome; he did not even make the customary bow. It had always been this way between him and that friend of his, Shiga explained; he did not know why it should be so, but he felt "it was most natural." In the same essay, Shiga cites another instance, this time involving two naval officers who had been close friends since childhood. One of the officers had been shipwrecked and had barely managed to survive; the other officer, welcoming him at a naval station, said just one word, "Hi!"—and smiled. Shiga, after telling this anecdote, muses that such a scene would never occur in a work of popular fiction. Popular fiction described an event according to common sense, visualizing it as an average person would; when two intimate friends met after a long interval, they would greet each other effusively. Fiction above the popular level was different: it presented an event in the way the author thought most "natural." A serious writer of fiction presented men and women who behaved themselves more "naturally" than the average person; he presented facts that were more "natural" than facts usually were. A "naturally" conceived fact was one that, even though it had never existed in reality, would strike a person as being true and real, as had been the case with Shiga's sister.

Exactly what did Shiga mean by the word "natural"? The obvious answer, as we have seen, was that he used it to mean the opposite of "commonsense" or "conventionally accepted." When he said literature presented "natural" facts, he implied that it revealed facts ordinarily hidden beneath the surface of conventional appearances. At a deeper level, however, the term assumed a more positive value for him. To be "natural" meant to be true to nature. A person who behaved "naturally" was not a mere eccentric who pays little attention to conventional norms; he was a person who, having awakened to his innermost nature, was trying to return to it. When Shiga said a work of fiction presented things that he would do or would wish to do, he meant the things that were most natural to him in this sense. With such a creed, a writer of fiction becomes a seeker after his own and others' true nature.

Shiga must have arrived at this conclusion fairly early in his career as a novelist. An entry in his diary dated May 27, 1911, reads as follows:

The mission of art is to achieve a deeper understanding of nature's beauty. The mission, to put it another way, is to observe nature with an artistic mind, a mind bent on discovering beauty. Therefore, the kind of nature that the average person sees does not make art when it is reproduced. One must have a deep, deep understanding of nature. But men have become more and more forgetful of nature and are creating art out of art alone. Thereupon, men arise who cry, "Return to nature!" Art, when it is forgetful of nature, degrades itself. Degraded art is, I feel, like the expressionless face of a lovely princess born of a noble family.

Thirty-eight years later, he was still emphasizing the importance of "nature" as the source of literature and art. "I am still of the opinion," he said, "that the one thing man can certainly depend on is this 'nature.' There have been various literary and art movements, but I cannot think of any alternative other than to follow the trail of nature." The question of where this trail led is more of a philosophical than a literary one. We should pursue it, nevertheless, since it affected Shiga's concept of literature by influencing his definition of artistic imitation.

Shiga's answer seems to center on the word "wisdom." As against some of his literary colleagues, who tended to see human nature as founded on sexual drives, he believed that man possessed a kind of instinctive wisdom so deep-seated that it sometimes overrode even his sexual impulses. It was almost an animal instinct, an instinct that maintained man's physical and mental health. In "Film Preview in the Morning," another of his autobiographical pieces, Shiga called it "the law of nature." The narrator of the story, obviously Shiga himself, is walking along the street with a male dog of his called Yone, when a neighborhood dog, a female, happens to come by. Yone becomes excited and goes up to her, but calmly leaves on discovering that her mating season has passed. The narrator is impressed to see that dogs act according to "the law of nature." He recalls a film, *The Charterhouse of Parma*, that he saw a week ago. The film's characters had become embroiled in a tragic crime of passion. "In the world of dogs a male would never kill a female for love, no matter how much they were at odds," Shiga wrote. "But in the human world, men have been known to kill women for precisely this. Man, by his wisdom, should be able to avoid such senseless tragedies." Man has impulses; Shiga would not deny that. Yet man has wisdom also, instinctive wisdom given him by nature for his own health and survival. Shiga advised that every man be attentive to it, understand it, and follow it; this was the way to return to nature. A work of art should present a man doing just that, under the specific circumstances in which he happened to have been placed. In short, a novel should describe a "wise" man.

Shiga's idea of a "wise" man is further clarified by two of the short stories written by the novelist-hero of *Reconciliation*. One of them is about a man who, though basically a decent enough fellow, is a chronic philanderer. Once, when his wife is away from home for an extended period, a maid in his household becomes pregnant. He has had nothing to do with the maid, but he has no way of proving it. When the maid's condition can escape his wife's

notice no longer, he simply says to her, "I've had nothing to do with the maid, you know." The wife takes his word for it, fully believing in his integrity. At this point the narrator cuts in and says: "Both the husband and the wife were wise. Tragedy missed its last chance to feast on them." Another story in the same series is about a young man and a young woman, both postal workers, who fall in love and have an affair, though the norms of contemporary society prohibit any such thing. The local postmaster dismisses them both, terming their love affair shameless and scandalous. The young man's parents, however, have no hesitation in allowing the two lovers to marry; indeed, they are more than delighted to give them their blessing. The narrator likes this story because it showed the opposite of what usually happens: no tragedy takes place, because the parents are sensible people. There is no doubt that the narrator-hero of *Reconciliation* is Shiga himself.*
He, too, believed that people have this wisdom buried in their innermost selves, and that many tragedies occur unnecessarily because it goes unrecognized. But wise people, like the married couple in the first story and the parents in the second, make the best use of it that circumstances allow.

Many of Shiga's own stories depict such people. Explaining the theme of his lone full-length novel, he said: "Everybody, wise or foolish, has misfortunes that are due to fate; it is impossible to avoid them. Yet one should wish to tide oneself over them as wisely as possible. That is the theme of *Voyage Through the Dark Night*." The novel's hero, Kensaku, suffers two misfortunes that he was powerless to prevent: his incestuous birth and his wife's rape (though Shiga preferred to call the latter incident adultery). Shiga's three novelettes, which he once compared to three branches of a tree, combine to tell the story of how a man, in trying to be faithful to his inner feelings, arrives at a tragic clash with his father because of their basic difference in personality, and how he eventually reaches a reconciliation with the latter in a way acceptable

---

* The closeness of this narrator-hero to Shiga is indicated by the fact that these stories, attributed to him in *Reconciliation*, are obviously the same as Shiga's "A Good-Natured Couple" and "Parents and a Child."

to them both. The same type of hero appears in many of Shiga's short stories; his progress is always from disaster to recovery. The theme is obvious in "Mother's Death and the New Mother," "Seibei's Gourds," "An Incident," "Han's Crime," "At Kinosaki," "Influenza," "Tree Frogs," "Morning, Noon, Evening," "The Dog," and many more. In some stories, like "The Razor," "Claudius' Diary," and "Kuniko," the disaster part is heavily emphasized. In others, like "A Snowy Day," "The Fires," and "Yajima Ryūdō," a more peaceful mood prevails, since the protagonist has completely recovered from a disaster as the story begins. Also falling into the last category are many short prose pieces that deal with animals, birds, and insects—"Dragonflies," "Harvest Bugs," "Kuma," "Insects and Birds," "Cats," "White-Eyes, Bulbuls, and a Bat," "Animal Sketches," "On Sparrows," etc. It is hardly surprising that Shiga, who recognized true wisdom in dogs, was so much at ease with so many other members of the animal kingdom.

Shiga's adverse criticism of certain literary works can also be explained in terms of this highly individual view of human nature. He did not like *Othello, Hamlet,* or *Romeo and Juliet* because they were, in his opinion, tragedies caused by human folly. He felt that, in each case, the tragedy could have been averted if the protagonists had been "wiser" in the sense already discussed. He also disliked naturalist writers, because the characters they described had nothing beautiful about them. In an obvious reference to them he said: "It is hazardous to health to be frequently exposed to the ugliness and folly in human life." For the same reason, Shiga was careful enough not to read those pages of the daily newspaper that reported on murders, burglaries, rapes, and frauds. He did not like Stendhal's *The Charterhouse of Parma* because, he thought, its hero differed little from the kind of delinquent one read about in newspapers. "At all events," he said, "we should take a little more severe attitude toward a person who conducts his life without wisdom or anything of that sort, and who, driven by his instinctive impulses, brings tragedy upon others and becomes the cause of all sorts of misfortunes."

Shiga's idea of artistic imitation thus assumes a didactic character. Literature should be factual, he believed, but that did not mean a writer should present all facts indiscriminately. Some facts were more "factual," more "natural," and therefore more convincing than others. Autobiographical facts were an important source of material for fiction, but only insofar as they resulted from the natural, instinctive behavior of the person in question. Events that took place as a result of social and moral convention were less valuable; even though they might actually have happened, they were less convincing than "natural" events that existed only in imagination. These "natural" events and facts were characterized, according to Shiga, by the "wisdom" that lay behind them. This "wisdom" was of a specific kind, a kind that had its roots deep down in man's biological nature and served to maintain his physical and mental health. Fundamentally, man was a wise being. It followed that a novel, if it was to be as factual as possible, should prove him to be so. In this way, the reader would be awakened to the fundamental wisdom lying dormant within himself.

Ultimately, Shiga's theory of literature is limited in the same way as his view of human nature. Even if it be granted that man has some basic animal wisdom such as Shiga recognized, it may be argued that he was being too optimistic. When he said that "Hi!" was enough to greet a really close friend, was he not attributing too much to human powers of communication? When he advised men to emulate dogs, which know when and when not to mate, was he not assuming too easily that man's sexual urge is basically controllable? He never seems to have visualized himself in an extreme situation; certainly, few of his heroes have been in them. To be born of an incestuous mother, to have one's wife raped, to live with a stubborn, domineering father—these are lesser disasters than, say, to be born crippled, to be born of an insane mother, or to have one's marriage forcibly broken up. Shiga's characters are never faced with such agonizing choices as either eating human flesh or starving to death. His theory seems reasonable enough as long as it maintains that literature must be true to fundamental human nature. But to make wisdom, or anything resembling it, the very essence of human nature seems a little far-fetched. Inevitably, much of his fiction seems far-fetched as well, as far as its philosophical implications are concerned.

The Writer Who Does Not Write

If a novel's primary purpose is to depict the life of a man who, having met with a catastrophic misfortune, recovers from it by his innate "wisdom," it seems that the novelist would do well to become such a man himself. To be sure, he can draw on hearsay (as Shiga himself did in "The Righteous") or a newspaper story (as he did in "Sasaki's Case"). He will be on safer ground, however, if he writes directly out of his own experience—safer, because he knows his own fundamental nature better than anyone else knows it. How he will instinctively feel or act in a given situation is unpredictable, at times even to himself; better, then, to have the experience before writing about it. It follows that there are two prerequisites for being a novelist: first, one must be somewhat disaster-prone, whether by circumstances or by character; second, one must have the physical and mental vigor to rebound from a disaster. There is sufficient evidence to show that Shiga thought this was so.

Shiga's concept of the artist as a disaster-prone person is best expressed in his short story "Kuniko." The heroine, named Kuniko, is married to a playwright who is suffering from writer's block because his family life is too peaceful. She of course likes things to be that way; she cannot understand how he could sit at his desk and work if his home were not peaceful. Her husband, however, thinks of himself as having been rotting "like a peach" during those peaceful years. Finally he starts having an affair with a flighty young actress. When the affair is picked up by the newspapers as a juicy piece of scandal, news of it reaches his wife. The happy atmosphere of the household is completely shattered. At the same time, however, the playwright regains interest in his craft and begins work on a large-scale play. Kuniko, on the other hand, is utterly crushed by this turn of events. Having lost all hope of saving her marriage, she commits suicide.

While it would be rash to identify Kuniko's husband completely with Shiga, there is no doubt that Shiga was similarly exercised by the basic predicament of the artist's personal life. In fact, he said as much in an earlier essay. "When the day is windy, cloudy, and chilly," he wrote, "the weather alone is enough to fill people's minds with gloom. This is natural. On such a day, however, a novelist is seized by a desire—a desire more intense than an ordinary person's—to express that gloom in a work of fiction. And when he succeeds in expressing it well, he feels happy." Kuniko, then, is a victim of this unfortunate antinomy lying between the artist's happiness and the ordinary man's. The average person is happy when the weather is pleasant; the artist is happy when the weather is rough, because it is then that he can be creative.

Why does an unhappy personal life stimulate the writer to write, while a happy life does not? Shiga's answer, as might be expected, is that an unhappy man has a stronger motive for expressing himself, suffering as he does from frustrations that he cannot contain. A person may be unhappy because he believes he is right but few people sympathize with him; he therefore appeals to their sympathy in words. Shiga cites several instances of unhappy people who vented their frustrations through literary composition. In one instance, a college student is moved to write a novel when he violently disagrees with the minister of his church, who regards adultery as on a level with murder. In another, a young writer, when told about the checkered life of a certain geisha, thinks little of it. But when he hears his brother, who has also heard the gossip about her, retell it with emphasis on the geisha's depraved nature, he becomes thoroughly irritated, and begins to think of transforming the gossip into a work of literature. Shiga also gives an instance from his own life: he once saw *Hamlet* staged at a Tokyo theater, and was repelled by the scheming, heartless, selfish behavior of its hero—so much so, in fact, that he was moved to write a short story, "Claudius' Diary." All these cases support Shiga's view that creative writing functions as an emotional purge. The motive for writing a novel is to find an outlet for one's hatred, anger, and frustration, including the frustration of being treated unjustly. A peaceful life, devoid of these emotions, offers no such motive.

Characteristically, however, Shiga thought of creative writing as something that, while it might help to relieve tension, did not necessarily restore mental equilibrium. Venting one's frustrations in the form of a novel did not remove the cause of the frustrations. Literature was, after all, an inferior substitute for life, not life itself. The cause of one's unhappiness has to be dealt with and overcome in the sphere of one's actual life; this was as true of novelists as of ordinary people. But there was a clear distinction between a poet and a novelist in this respect. "A poet is emotional and tends to destroy his personal life," he observed, "like Baudelaire, Verlaine, Rimbaud, etc. But this would never do in the case of a novelist. . . . Poets and novelists are both men of letters, but there is a good deal of temperamental difference between them." Hence Shiga disliked a novelist who was like a poet—that is, a novelist who did not rebound from a misfortune. For instance, he did not like Tanaka Hidemitsu (1912–49), because the latter showed "no spirit of prose literature" and was completely overcome by his own misfortunes.* He also did not like Tanaka's idol, Dazai Osamu, because he thought Dazai was a weak man who adopted a conceited pose to hide his weakness. "However hard I tried, I just could not bring myself to sympathize with Dazai's love suicide," he wrote. "If he had to die, why didn't he die alone?"† He liked a novelist who was strong enough to die alone or, better, a novelist who refused to die in the face of disaster. A novelist, he thought, should have enough vitality to rebound from any misfortune he might have to face. Most of the artist-heroes in Shiga's stories have such vitality and do rebound from their misfortunes. The most striking example is the young novelist-hero of *Reconciliation*, who has a violent clash with his father and is disinherited as a result. The novelist, however, does not yield to defeatism; he is determined to fight on, and even imagines a scene in which he engages in a mortal

---

* Tanaka Hidemitsu is best known for the short stories that he based on his dissipated life. He was an ardent admirer of Dazai, before whose grave he eventually committed suicide.

† Dazai and a woman friend committed suicide by jumping into a river on June 13, 1948. Moved by the event, Shiga wrote an essay called "Dazai's Death," from which this quotation is taken.

duel with his father. The same can be said of Kensaku, the novelist-hero of *Voyage Through the Dark Night*, who prompts his half-brother to say of his character: ". . . you are strong. You have a strong self that enables you to do whatever you want to do. . . . You always have a focal point inside yourself, and all your indicators are always ready to point to it." It is this strong ego, this "focal point," that enables Kensaku to survive two major disasters. The protagonist of "Han's Crime," who can also be called an artist, actually kills his wife because he can think of no other way to ensure his own survival. Because of his will to survive as a playwright, the playwright-hero of "Kuniko" also causes his wife's death, though not so directly. The Shiga-like narrator of "At Kinosaki" first longs for the peace of death, but regains his desire for life when he recalls the strong natural instinct for survival that he showed when caught in a traffic accident. The strong, vigorous character that Shiga demanded of a novelist is further illustrated by his diary entry for January 9, 1926, which is a kind of New Year's resolution:

This year, I want to lead a vigorous life, in every sense of the word. I want to live in a positive frame of mind. No tearful complaints. No grumbling, slandering, or nagging. No flattering, no overconscientious acceptance of tiresome duties. I will love my wife and children. I will love them, without doting upon them. I must avoid, as much as possible, doing the sort of thing that I know will make me unhappy later on. I will make my living as a writer this year. I want to be free, natural, honest, vigorous, and carefree.

If this seems to present an image of an ideal man rather than an ideal novelist, that is consistent with Shiga's idea of a novelist. For Shiga, the ultimate goal in life was to become a man of moral strength. This was a logical conclusion for a writer who considered literature as at best an inferior substitute for life. Problems in life had to be solved in the realm of life; the solutions offered by art were, in the final analysis, no more than substitutes for real solutions, dreams that might or might not be fulfilled. The artist, Shiga thought, should not be a mere dreamer; he had to have vigor and strength to make his dreams come true in real life. He had to lead a "vigorous life" in a "positive frame of mind."

Shiga actually seems to have attained the goal he set for himself. The protagonists of his later works (say, after 1928), easily identifiable as Shiga, are by and large "free, natural, honest, vigorous, and carefree" persons. In fact, they are so vigorous and carefree that they hardly ever allow anything untoward to happen. When it does, it rarely amounts to more than a ripple on calm waters. In "Kuma," for example, the "disaster" that befalls the hero is that his family dog goes astray for a few days. In "Morning, Noon, Evening," it is that the hero's eldest daughter, who is recovering from a cold, goes to visit her grandmother on a chilly day without first asking his permission. In "Film Preview in the Morning," the worst inconvenience suffered by the narrator is that the film he saw, *The Charterhouse of Parma*, was not to his liking and that the theater was poorly heated. In other stories—"Harvest Bugs," "Sunday," "Typhoon," "Rabbit," "Cats," "My Youngest Child," and "Kusatsu Spa," to name a few—hardly anything happens to disturb the equilibrium of the hero's mind. It seems that, as time progressed, Shiga succeeded in establishing his own and his family's well-being on such a firm basis that no serious misfortune could ever befall them again. Inevitably, given his view of literature, he lost the urge to write; he had no frustrations to vent, no disasters to rebound from. He wrote less and less frequently, his yearly production dwindling to fewer than five short prose pieces—normally two, one, or none—after 1928. Very likely he could not have cared less. "I have felt," he once said, "the important thing for me to do is to spend this unrepeatable life of mine in the best way possible. The fact that I have written works of fiction is of only secondary importance."

In Shiga's view, then, the ideal novelist is an inactive novelist, a writer who feels no urge to write. For if he remains active, he is forced to lead an ambivalent existence, keeping a delicate balance between his disaster-prone character and his strength to recover from disasters. If he is too disaster-prone, he will make a good poet (like Verlaine) but a bad novelist (like Dazai). If his character is too wholesome, he will hardly meet with any real misfortunes, and will therefore have little motive for writing a novel. In his younger days Shiga managed to keep this balance, and produced some fine pieces of literature as a result. But as he got older he lost it, and remained largely inactive as a writer. For most other writers this development would have constituted a painful setback. For Shiga, it was progress.

Natural Beauty, Vigor, and Spiritual Elation

Ideally, what kind of impression should a novel give its readers? Naturally Shiga's answer is derived from his concept of the ideal novel. This, as we have seen, presents the life of a man meeting misfortunes and rebounding from them. Such a life has to be presented in a certain way in order to make a convincing impression on the reader. Although it would be impossible to list all the qualities that go into such an impression, at least three can be singled out as important—natural beauty, vigor, and spiritual elation.

An impression of natural beauty comes from observing a man who conducts himself honestly, in accordance with his inmost feelings. Such a man would not repress his true feelings in the interest of social convention. He would say "Hi!", and nothing more, to an old friend who had just survived a tragic mishap, if he really felt that this was the only proper thing to do. He would follow the dictates of his innermost self even if that would lead to an explosive clash with his father or even to the death of his wife. A man fighting for his survival was beautiful, because he was, if nothing else, pure in his motives. A fight for material gain or for lust was ugly, but a fight for bare existence, physical or mental, had its own dignity.

It goes without saying that natural beauty is also to be found in the behavior of an animal, bird, or insect following its instinct for survival. Shiga's short prose pieces on such little creatures—and there are a great many of them—all speak of this. In "Amateurs and Professionals," for instance, he describes how a mongoose expertly wins its fight with a cobra; he compares the beauty of the scene to the art of fencing. In "Cats" he tells how a neighbor's female cat regained possession of her kitten by artfully deceiving a number of human beings. In "Yajima Ryūdō" he describes a shrike that has succeeded in remaining wild despite the fact that it was reared in captivity. Shiga's sketches of children have the same quality; a characteristic example is "My Youngest Child," which describes his little daughter's carefree behavior.

Shiga may have had a special feeling for natural beauty, but nature in the conventional sense—flowers, trees, mountains, rivers, etc.—seems to have meant little to him. The vegetable and mineral worlds hardly feature in his occasional writings. There indeed is one short piece called "The Morning Glory," but in its second sentence the author makes clear that he valued this plant not for its flowers but for its medicinal leaves. Shiga was not impressed by the beauty of mountains and rivers because they had no life and did not struggle for survival. Similarly, he was not much attracted by Japanese flowers because they seemed too passive in asserting their right to live. Shiga's works of fiction are generally lacking in descriptions of beautiful natural scenes.

The only notable exception is the most celebrated scene in the entire Shiga canon, the climactic episode of *Voyage Through the Dark Night* in which the hero spends a night on Mount Daisen. At dawn, he looks down on the world below. The beauty and tranquillity of the scene enable him to overcome his fear of death; finally, as he becomes absorbed by it, he feels ready to die at any time. This is a rare moment in Shiga's works, which seldom show man's vitality overwhelmed by the forces of nature. Here, inanimate nature is almost personified; in fact, Mount Daisen is a holy mountain in both Buddhism and Shintoism. This, of course, makes it more suitable as an opponent. To Shiga's hero, inanimate nature is beautiful in this instance precisely because it is not passive; instead, it works on him and transforms him, so that he becomes the passive one. This explains what many critics regard as the novel's most serious flaw: the abrupt change of viewpoint in the last few pages. Hitherto, nearly everything has centered on Kensaku. But now, without warning or explanation, his wife takes over. Shiga later explained that he had done this deliberately, and claimed that the average reader would hardly be bothered by it. A more convincing explanation is that since Kensaku has now become ill, and so lost much of his vitality, he is disqualified, in Shiga's eyes, as the novel's narrator-hero. The person who takes his place has to be his wife, who is beginning to recover from her misfortune. Thematically, however, the novel ends at the point where Kensaku regains his mental equilibrium and feels readiness for death. Shiga chose to write further, and had therefore to find a new protagonist.

Natural beauty—the beauty of powerful creatures living violent lives—gives an impression of vigor and strength. Things that are strong are beautiful, and when they become protagonists the stories create a powerfully beautiful impact. Shiga, in sharp contrast to Tanizaki and Kafū, made nearly all his protagonists men. They are all healthy, with firm confidence in their body and its functions. They shed tears unashamedly when they lament; when they are angry, it is without restraint. They consider weeping or getting angry to be healthy bodily functions, and so nothing to be ashamed of. When they feel a sexual urge and have no other means of satisfying it, they have no hesitation in visiting a brothel. When they get married, they become self-assertive husbands. They are usually young; when they are not, they still retain youthful, even childish qualities. Shiga's preference for a masculine type of beauty is also evident in his prose pieces dealing with animals and birds. Unlike Tanizaki, he likes dogs better than cats. Unlike Kawabata, he likes wild birds better than tame ones.

Shiga once described this untamed energy of the wild in terms of what he called "spiritual rhythm." He thought a dynamic, passionate person lived a strongly rhythmical life, and when such a person became the protagonist of a story the rhythm transmitted itself to the readers, stirring them up and moving them. Even when the story did not feature such a person, it could still create a strong rhythm of life if the storyteller had that rhythm and injected it into his narrative. Second-rate novelists, he continued, write with skill, not spiritual rhythm; the results might be expertly written, but were lacking in strong emotional appeal. A good novel, with its powerful rhythm, never failed to move its readers. Shiga cited *Tales from the Provinces* and *The Last Fragments of Saikaku's*

Cloth, by Ihara Saikaku (1642–93), as well as Charles-Louis Philippe's *Chronicles of the Wild Duck*, as having such a vigorous rhythm. Though he did not spell it out, he apparently recognized the same type of rhythm in the oil paintings of Umehara Ryūsaburō (b. 1888), which made his heart "jump with joy." He also liked the calligraphy of Tomioka Tessai (1836–1924) because "it has power and gives the impression of penetrating the paper."* Of various Japanese gardens he liked the one at Ryōanji best because it was most "intense, strong, and spacious," thereby making his heart leap. In all these cases, the artist has a vigorously rhythmical mind—so much so that it makes the onlooker's mind vibrate with it. To Shiga, this kind of mental vibration became a criterion even in the visual arts. For instance, when he published an expensive art book called *My Treasures of Oriental Art*, he selected works for illustration according to "the degree to which the given art object moved my heart with its vibrations."

Conversely, Shiga decried works of art that showed a weak rhythm of life. "Trying to create a novel out of rotten material," he said, "is like trying to cook a good meal out of rotten fish." If the novelist's life is rotten, his novels become rotten, too. Shiga's adverse criticism of Dazai seems to have been directed more at his life than at his works. Shiga was also critical of Japanese proletarian writers because they drew inspiration more from their ideology than from their experience; he thought even Lenin would have advised that they emulate Saikaku. He disliked Mori Ōgai's works because he felt they were too cerebral, and failed to show any evidence of innate vitality on the author's part. Shiga also felt that any attempt to accommodate the reader inevitably weakens an author's rhythm of life, at least insofar as it is embodied in his work. Shiga was firmly against "literature for the millions." He did not like his stories to be made into films or translated into foreign languages. He preferred to be read by a select few, with their number to increase gradually as the centuries passed. He valued a work

---

* Umehara Ryūsaburō, a leading Japanese painter who once studied under Rouault, was a good friend of Shiga's. Tomioka Tessai, an influential *nanga* painter of his time, was very much admired by Shiga. As a young man, Shiga had sought to visit his studio to see him work. But the chance never came.

of art that made no concessions to its audience, a work that had something unapproachable about it. He liked Cézanne, Renoir, and Rouault because he felt their works had that quality. He was less fond of Matisse, because Matisse's paintings seemed to him too easily understandable. He said so even though he confessed he was not sure whether Matisse was a crowd-pleaser by temperament or whether his paintings just happened to have become popular without any intention on his part. In brief, Shiga demanded a considerable effort of appreciation from readers and spectators. He believed that an artist whose creative energy was at all powerful did not stoop to make his audience's understanding easy; on the contrary, it was his audience that should make a positive effort to understand his works.

The "elation" of which Shiga talked so much was the reverberation, so to speak, of the reader's spirit in response to the author's mental vigor, which was embodied in the book. Thus of Saikaku he said:

Of Japanese novelists I admire Saikaku the most. The spirit underlying his writings has a certain powerful rhythm, and when its vibration reaches me I feel an incomparable delight. The subject matter is the events of ordinary people's lives. They do not make particularly moving stories, and yet the impressions they create in me are marvelously powerful and vigorous, filling me with spiritual elation.

Shiga felt the same sort of elation when he read Gide's *The School for Wives* and *Robert*. He observed that on reading them he had experienced "a happy feeling of myself being all stirred up . . . a joyous feeling of total elation." A good work of literature succeeded in conveying the author's vital rhythm to his readers and so in raising them to a higher level of experience, where they felt elated. Elation of this sort consisted in a happy feeling of recognizing one's own true potential. Every person had moments of disillusionment, self-disgust, and despair. But on reading a good work of literature he gained, or regained, faith and confidence in humanity, as he observed the author facing stark reality with honesty, courage, and perseverance. Such a reader would feel that the human race was after all not as despicable as he had once thought, that he himself had the potential to live a vigorous, meaningful life. He would feel that he could not go on living as he had been. Shiga's "elation," then, was not a passive emotion; it was a dynamic passion that stimulated people to take positive action in the moral realm. It moved them to return to their inmost nature and live according to its directives.

Raw Life as Structure and Texture

Shiga said little about plot. This is understandable, in view of his emphasis on spontaneity in creative writing. Constructing a plot is basically an intellectual undertaking, far removed from the sphere of impulse. It is also an area in which the novelist's desire to accommodate his readers is often only too obvious. An intriguing plot, Shiga thought, might be necessary for a popular novel, but it did nothing but harm to a genuine work of literature, whose prime purpose was to convey the author's vigorous rhythm of life. A fascinating plot made the reader read the novel for the plot alone, neglecting its thematic content.

Shiga especially disliked a story that built up suspense by hiding facts from the reader. He cited Sōseki and Akutagawa (two novelists to whom he paid due respect otherwise) as being guilty of this charge. Referring to Akutagawa's "The Martyr," he wondered why the author waited until the story's end to reveal that the protagonist was a woman. The climax was as effective as the revelation was shocking, but this distracted the reader from the central theme, which was the nature of martyrdom. Though the readers might be more entertained, they would be less moved by the intrinsic importance of the theme. Shiga would rather have made the climax less shocking in order to sustain the readers' interest in the theme from beginning to end. "I prefer placing the readers in the same spot as the author and letting them watch the action from there," he said. Obviously, the closer the readers are to the author, the more easily they can become attuned to his life rhythm.

Another reason, Shiga thought, why a story that depends too much on plot is second-rate is that no one would want to read it again after finding out how it ends. Shiga criticized a Dazai story for this very reason. He was reading "The Criminal," and midway through the story he found he could predict how it would end. He thought the author should have stated the story's conclusion at the outset and then concentrated on describing how it was arrived at. If this had been done, he thought, the story might have withstood a second reading.

Shiga's devaluation of plot in storytelling makes sense in that context and with those examples, but as a yardstick it has to be applied with caution. Of course, a story that has nothing to offer except an entertaining plot is an inferior work of literature by any yardstick. Yet plot can be used to enforce theme; indeed, it would seem incumbent on every good novelist to do just that. For instance, he may hold back some facts from the reader, in the hope that revealing them later on will reinforce his theme. The element of surprise at the story's end can also be used to reinforce the theme rather than detract from it. If the subject is a stimulating one, the reader may well give the work a second reading whether it has a surprise ending or not. In short, plot is not itself the chief criterion of a novel's worth, and it was rather academic of Shiga to single it out.

However, Shiga's remarks on plot would seem to be well taken as long as he is talking about the *ich-Roman*, or "I-novel." In this type of novel, the hero obviously has to evoke as much sympathy as possible. If the author holds back too many facts, readers will find it hard to identify with him. He is better off taking the first opportunity to tell them all the essential facts about himself. Shiga's criticism of Sōseki, Akutagawa, and Dazai was not fair, because he applied the standards of the I-novel to works not in that category. It should be noted, however, that he did not direct his attack at Tanizaki, who was writing stories with more complex plots than most of his contemporaries. Perhaps Shiga respected the vital rhythm of Tanizaki's works, even though it was of a type quite different from his own.

Shiga's view, then, was that a novelist did not have to pay much attention to plot, since if he had a vigorous rhythm of life the story would develop one of itself. Plot, in other words, marched to the rhythm of the author's own life. If that rhythm of life was weak, the plot would refuse to develop; the author, then, would have to make up the story by using his brains. The story should spontaneously "flow" out of the author; it should not be imposed on the material. In short, it had to be natural, as the author's life had to be natural.

What would such a "natural" plot be like? We can see from Shiga's own works. A typical Shiga story has a hero very much like himself. Its actions are narrated from the standpoint of the hero, often in the first person. The setting, which is contemporary, may be Tokyo, Nara, Kinosaki, Mount Daisen—in any case, places familiar to the author. The incidents in the story are related in chronological order, except for ones that were unknown to the hero when they happened. These incidents usually throw the hero's health off balance, physically or mentally. The main body of the story tells how the hero came to lose his equilibrium, or how he came to regain it without being false to his true nature, or both. The story is usually short; when it is long, it is by repetition— that is, the cycle in which the hero regains equilibrium is repeated.* All these attributes of a Shiga story illustrate his general concept of life. In his view, life is a series of episodes in which man faces a minor (rarely a major) catastrophe, strives to overcome it, and eventually does so (he has to, if he is to stay sane and healthy). The structure of a Shiga story is "natural" in the sense that it is based on this fundamental pattern or rhythm of life.

Predictably, being "natural" was also Shiga's leading stylistic principle. He made this clear on one of the rare occasions when he talked about the art of writing:

One should not write sentences that do not follow the rules of grammar. Such sentences unnecessarily tax the reader, irritating him unbearably. Grammar (apart from the use of particles) has to do with something more basic than a set of agreed rules. Constructing a sentence that does not accord with grammar means more than a mere disregard of agreed rules; it means a disregard for the way in which the brain is structured. This is wrong. I know very little about grammar, but when I write I try to be faithful to the structure of the brain.

* Shiga's only full-length novel, *Voyage Through the Dark Night*, was in part published as a series of short stories. While still in the early stages of writing it, he had thought of undertaking such a series with the same hero, rather than being burdened with the task of writing a long novel.

Shiga is thinking of two types of grammar, artificial and natural. Artificial grammar is school grammar, a set of rules devised by scholars. This is the kind of grammar that Shiga says he knows very little about; evidently, he could not have cared less. But he did care a great deal about natural grammar. He thought of language as a gift given to man by nature, and of speaking and writing as something natural and spontaneous. An ideal writer, he believed, would just let words flow out of his brain naturally, and let them form sentences of their own accord.

It is easy enough to imagine Shiga's ideal novelist and his style. The style would be, above all, powerful, reflecting the vigorous rhythm of his life. The sentences would be powerfully short and concise. There would be few conjunctions, so that the sentences would look even shorter than they actually are. The words and phrases would be sonorous in sound and clear in meaning; vagueness would be avoided at all costs. Visual images would predominate over auditory ones. Chinese characters would be used plentifully, because they create a more powerful, masculine impression than Japanese letters.* In brief, Shiga's idea of a "natural" style has all the attributes of Tanizaki's "laconic style." And this was Shiga's own style, too, as Tanizaki rightly pointed out.

One might wonder why Shiga, while aiming to reproduce the natural rhythm of life, arrived at this laconic style, the exact opposite of the "flowing style" that attracted Tanizaki for precisely the same reason. The answer lies in their different concepts of the human psyche. For Tanizaki, the ultimate source of psychic energy was the sexual instinct, the will to reproduce one's own kind. Since woman, with her ability to give birth, was closer to this source than man, her rhythm of life was correspondingly more vigorous. Shiga, on the other hand, found the source of life not in woman's reproductive power but in man's will to survive. Hence he favored the male, who had more physical strength, as more typical of a human being who was faithful to his inner impulses. Shiga's

* Shiga resented the ordinance of the postwar Japanese government that limited the use of Chinese characters in Japanese. Once he even declared he would refuse to contribute to any newspaper or magazine that insisted on editing his writing to conform with the ordinance.

laconic style is as masculine as Tanizaki's flowing style is feminine; it is difficult if not impossible to say which is better, since each mirrors a different human reality. Which reality one considers to be the "ultimate" reality would appear to be a matter of taste.

Be that as it may, Shiga's style has been widely admired as the best in modern Japanese prose. Whereas Tanizaki's style is inimitable, samples of Shiga's prose appear in every school textbook. A number of professional writers have succeeded in writing very much like him. In fact, it has been pointed out that all top students in Japanese composition classes write like Shiga. This fact probably has little to do with the intrinsic value of Shiga's style. But at least it is ample proof that his style is a "natural" one, since it lies within a range attainable by a great many Japanese, including students in elementary school.

Conscious and Unconscious Use of Creative Writing

I have already said a good deal about Shiga's views on the uses of literature because, as we have seen, these views were essentially didactic. A literary work, he thought, should improve its readers' self-knowledge and self-confidence, and bring them a sense of elation as it does so. Characteristic of Shiga was the fact that, with all this emphasis on what the novel could do for its readers, he still urged the novelist to write for himself, not for them. In Shiga's view, the novelist wrote for primarily personal motives, namely, to vent his own emotions and so recover his own mental equilibrium. If his readers also found themselves purged of their frustrations, that was only incidental; the novelist did not consciously intend the novel to have this effect. "When a literary work is completed, the author releases it from his hands," Shiga wrote. "From that point on, it develops an independent relationship with its readers and performs various functions for them. It may help an unexpected person at an unexpected place. I have had a few pleasant occasions to witness my work functioning in this way." If the work was deliberately made to teach something, it lost vigor, spontaneity, and natural beauty. Shiga confessed himself bored with the final part of *Anna Karenina* because it was here that, in his opinion, Tolstoy became consciously didactic. For the same reason, he disliked so-called proletarian literature. In a letter to a noted Marxist writer, he said: "Your story is in servitude to a master, and I do not like that. What you have done is inevitable, I suppose, for a writer devoted to the proletarian movement. All the same, it makes a literary work impure, which in my opinion reduces the work's effectiveness." Of course, Shiga could not grant the name of genuine literature to any novel that tried to please its readers. He once declared that a novelist was neither a geisha nor a clown. I have already remarked on his preference for works of art that had something unapproachable about them. The dichotomy between pure art and the mundane world is the theme of "Seibei's Gourds." A novelist, Shiga thought, should stand aloof from the general populace.

Shiga did not deny, however, that a novelist felt great satisfaction when he knew his novel had had an edifying effect upon the general public. That satisfaction, Shiga felt, arose when the novelist was able to believe that he had left something good and permanent in the all-too-fleeting world of humanity. Death was inevitable; indeed, all mankind would perish at the end of the earth. Thinking about this could produce an intolerable sense of isolation. One sure way to overcome this isolation was to attain immortality by performing some great work that mankind would cherish forever. "There is no death for a man who has wrought a truly lasting work," muses Kensaku, obviously speaking for Shiga. "I have come to feel that this is true not only of a great artist but also of a great scientist. I don't know too much about the Curies, but I would think that their sense of security about their contribution to mankind must have given them a peace and satisfaction that would remain undiminished no matter what else they may have had to face." The artist's satisfaction was of the same type as that of any man who had made a great contribution to humanity. The novelist, though standing aloof from the rest of mankind, should try to produce a work that would eventually be seen as a major contribution. In similar fashion, the scientist might do research purely for his own pleasure but produce results of great benefit to society.

Both the artist and the scientist worked consciously for themselves, unconsciously for others.

There is, however, a serious flaw in this line of thinking—a flaw that constitutes the main limitation of Shiga's views on art. To be sure, the artist or scientist may gain results while following his own bent. But it does not necessarily follow that these results will prove beneficial to all men alike. A delightful intellectual adventure may end in the horror of atomic weapons. The gloomy tale that the novelist feels better for having written may drive some of his readers to desperation or suicide. Shiga would have denied that his works could have any such effect; his heroes, he would have said, always end up victorious. But he never really admitted the moral ambivalence of literature in general. There is no Satan or Iago in his works of fiction; indeed, he would not even read about murders and rapes in the newspapers. Yet these should be part of literature, too, as they are part of life. Shiga's theory of art applied only to works that he considered morally edifying; it did not apply, for instance, to a novel like *The Charterhouse of Parma*, which Shiga thought could inspire only disgust. Even Shiga's own work did not always edify; it is even said to have helped drive Akutagawa and Dazai to their suicides. Did this knowledge give him the "peace and satisfaction" that he reserved for the artist?

The charge, however, is not entirely fair. For, with all his emphasis on the usefulness of literature, Shiga was also well aware of its uselessness, its lack of power. After all, in his view literature was subservient to life; indeed, it was an inferior substitute for life. A person driven to suicide could not have been leading the right kind of life to begin with; creative writing might have helped to relieve his tension, but not to solve his problems. For Shiga, literature could be immensely useful insofar as it could fill a particular need in one's life. It was useless for a person who did not have that kind of need, especially one who needed more than literature could give. Shiga, with his pragmatic view of art, could not ignore its limitations. He coolly abandoned it in later life, when he no longer had any need for it.

CHAPTER FIVE

Akutagawa Ryūnosuke

AKUTAGAWA RYŪNOSUKE (1892–1927) was a writer who could easily have become a scholar or literary critic. An extremely self-conscious man, he never failed to criticize the artist within himself, usually with unforgiving scrutiny. Naturally the basic problems of art and artist are abundantly reflected in his works. "The Hell Screen," a masterpiece of his early period, centers on a painter caught between the conflicting demands of life and art. *Kappa*, a major work of his later years, has a poet, an aphorist, and two composers among its main characters. A sizable number of his other major pieces, such as "Absorbed in Letters," "Withered Fields," "Genkaku Sanbō," "Cogwheel," and "A Fool's Life," also have artists for their principal characters and deal with problems relating to art. As an essayist, too, Akutagawa wrote a good deal about literature, from the casual and polemic "Literary, Too Literary" to the more theoretical "Ten Rules for Writing a Novel," "Literature: an Introduction," and "On the Appreciation of Literature." There can be no doubt that, like his mentor Sōseki before him, he devoted many hours to pondering the nature of literature.

Taming a Monster

One of Akutagawa's clearest definitions of literature appears in his essay "Literature: an Introduction," where he calls literature "an art that uses words or letters for its medium." He continues: "To elaborate, it is an art that transmits life by means of three elements: (1) the meaning of words; (2) the sound of words; (3) the shape of ideograms." This definition reveals two factors that are basic to Akutagawa's concept of literature. The first is his emphasis on the medium of literature, namely, language. The second is his assumption that literature aims to "transmit life."

Of course, literature does use language for its medium. But Akutagawa seems a bit overemphatic on that point. In a definition of literature as brief as this, one would usually forgo mention of sound and meaning; certainly, one would not want to refer to the visual effect of ideograms. To Akutagawa, however, those formal elements of language were so important that he could not help bringing them in. This fact is substantiated in the essay itself: two of its three sections are devoted to words, letters, sounds, ideograms, structures, etc. Although the shape of ideograms was hardly a universal issue, Akutagawa could not bear to leave it out. For him, literature was above all an art of words.

The reason for his emphasis on words is explained in the same essay. It is that words, when arranged in an orderly fashion, create form, without which contents cannot exist. "Contents that lack a form are like a desk or chair without its form," he wrote. A work of literature could exist only when it took on a form, just as a desk was a desk by virtue of its form. Life, before it had been given form by the artist, was nothing but crude material, just as a desk was coarse lumber without the carpenter. Words were the very means by which wild nature was molded into form and given a place in human life.

As might be expected, Akutagawa favored unambiguous words and lucid syntax. Explaining his principles of composition, he once said:

More than anything else, I want to write clearly. I want to express in precise terms what lies in my mind. I try to do just that. And yet, when I take up my pen, I can seldom write as smoothly as I want to. I always end up writing cluttered sentences. All my effort (if I can call it that) goes into clarification. The quality I seek in other men's writings is the same as the one I seek in my own. I cannot admire a piece of composition lacking in clarity. I am sure I could never bring myself to like it. In matters of composition, I am an Apollonian.

What aspects of life should the literary artist try to clarify with the words that are his shaping tools? Akutagawa's answer is implied in the word he used for "life" in the definition of literature already quoted. The Japanese word is *seimei*, usually translated as "life" but primarily referring to "the source of life." Akutagawa chose this word in preference over *seikatsu*, which can also be translated as "life," but which more precisely means "activities in life." Seimei is energy, vitality, the inner biological force that keeps a living thing alive and vigorous. Seikatsu is the outer manifestation of seimei—eating, drinking, talking, walking, running, fighting, and every other kind of human behavior. Literature, Akutagawa seems to be saying, should transmit the source of life; it should not aim merely to copy outward manifestations of that source.

As can be imagined, Akutagawa was against those who insisted that a novel should copy the tangible realities of life as they are. In one of the first critical essays he published, he attacked a school of tanka, quite influential at the time, that was known as the Seikatsu School. "I know I am being rude in saying this," he wrote, "but I cannot understand what makes those distinguished poets write exclusively in the style of that school. If they wish to express nothing more than those plain—if the word is offensive, I would be willing to say 'realistic' or 'plebeian'—those plain feelings, they need not go to all the trouble of confining themselves to the 31-syllable form. Instead, they might as well choose such forms as free verse or the novel, which are more conducive to narration." Akutagawa was saying, in effect, that the Seikatsu School poets presented seikatsu but not seimei. He made the same point about fiction, a literary form that by his own admission was more conducive to description of everyday life. A target of his attack was Flaubert, then one of the reigning deities among Japanese novelists. After citing Flaubert's words that an artist should be like God, manifesting Himself in all His creations but remaining invisible to man, Akutagawa caustically remarked: "For that very reason his *Madame Bovary* lacks emotional appeal, even though it creates a microcosm." The author of *Madame Bovary*, he thought, might well have succeeded in his creative task, but why had he concealed himself so thoroughly, as if he wanted nothing to do with his readers? There was such a thing as being too godlike. As a commentary on Flaubert, this is hardly just. But Akutagawa was aiming his barbs at the Japanese naturalists of his day, who had made Flaubert an idol, and here he was much nearer the mark. The Japanese naturalists, as he correctly pointed out, wrote boring novels because, with all their attention to surface facts, they had neglected the one essential ingredient: the source of life itself.

But where was this all-important "source of life" to be found? Akutagawa's answer is best expressed in his works of fiction. However, there are answers of a sort to be found throughout his other writings. Among them is the following, which appears in a letter he wrote to a friend when he was still an undergraduate student:

These twain, sprung from the same homeland, are named Good and Evil. They were given these names by folk who knew nothing of their homeland. Let us now rename them, to mark their common origin. Shall their name be Logos? A high-sounding name, you say. But Logos pervades the universe. Logos is in all men. The Greater Logos moves the constellations; the Lesser Logos moves the human heart. Those who reck not of Logos shall surely perish! Such behavior, for want of a better name, we call evil. Logos is neither emotion nor intellect nor will. If we have to define it, we might say it is Supreme Intellect. Good and Evil are only utilitarian concepts that vaguely define men's conduct in terms of their relation to Logos. Sometimes I feel as if the stars are mixed in my blood and circulating in my veins. The founders of astrology must have felt as I do, only more strongly. Unless we know the Logos, there is no health in us. Whatever we write must partake of its influence, else it will be worthless. It is only by and through the Logos that a work of art becomes meaningful.

Clearly, whatever Akutagawa meant by "Logos," it was neither good nor evil; rather, it was the prototype of them both. It was not an external power like fate; rather, it was part of one's very existence, as familiar—and as close—as one's own heartbeat. From this point of view, his "Supreme Intellect" was a misnomer.

Akutagawa stressed that art must partake of this Logos, this power that lies deep in the existence of man. Most of his major stories can be interpreted as attempts in this direction. "Rashōmon" is a study of how man's survival instinct supersedes moral values. "In a Grove" takes the reader into a subterranean world of sex and death where the so-called facts and truths of the daylight world disappear in the murk. The priest's monstrous nose in "The Nose" is symbolic of an incurable deformity in human nature—a deformity with which every man has to live. The hero of "The Hell Screen" has a more tragic fate: *his* deformity is the artist's irresistible passion to copy the dark hell that is human life. Akutagawa's Logos finds even more direct expression in "Doubts," the story of a man who kills his wife when he is unable to release her from under a fallen beam in their burning house. He chooses to beat her to death with a few swift and savage blows rather than leave her to meet a slower, more painful end in the fire. After the incident, however, doubts begin to fill his mind that, somewhere deep within him, he had always wanted to kill her, because she had not been a sexually ideal wife for him. His doubts grow more serious and more importunate with time, until he has a nervous breakdown. "I may be a lunatic," he finally reflects, "but, then, wasn't my lunacy caused by a monster that lurks at the bottom of every human mind? Those who call me a madman and spurn me today may become lunatics like me tomorrow. They harbor the same monster."

The young Akutagawa, after dutifully pursuing his Logos, found such a monster waiting for him in the end. Seimei, the "source of life" that made men want to go on living, turned out to be a monstrous force capable of driving a man to bludgeon his wife to death. An ordinary person does not do such things simply because he has never been faced with an extreme situation. This dreadful wisdom casts an even darker shadow on Akutagawa's stories as time goes by. The heroine of "A Clod of Earth," known to her entire village as a model of diligence, is a merciless, egotistical monster at home; her industry and her egotism spring from the same internal source. "Genkaku Sanbō" is a story filled with monsters: the old painter who often wishes for his concubine's death; his invalid wife who is silently jealous not only of the concubine but of her own daughter; his grandson who in his childish innocence hurts everyone who gets close enough to him; and his sickroom nurse who takes a sadistic pleasure in watching others suffer. *Kappa* is not a social satire, as has often been claimed; it is the story of a man who has become awakened to the monstrous "source of life" (symbolized by kappas),* and who eventually goes insane as a result. Doubts,

---

* Kappa is an aquatic monster that appears in Japanese folklore. It looks like a large frog, with a saucerlike receptacle growing on its head. "Weird" is the adjective Akutagawa uses most often to describe this creature in *Kappa*.

anxiety, and fear about the weird forces that underlie human existence make up the atmosphere of "Cogwheel." "It is unspeakably painful to live with these feelings," says the hero at the end of the story. "Isn't there anyone who would kindly strangle me to death while I am asleep?"

Akutagawa's last thoughts about "the source of life" are unmistakably expressed in his famous suicide note entitled "Note to an Old Friend." "What is known as the source of life is in reality nothing more than animal energy," he wrote near its end. "I, too, am one of the human animals." Finally, he confesses that when he was young he wanted to think of himself as God, but that at last he realized he was wrong. No doubt he was recalling his student days —the days when he believed in the Supreme Intellect as the source of human life. Now he found that what he had taken to be divinity was no more than animality.

For Akutagawa, then, to depict nature was to depict the monstrous animality that was the source of human life. The agreeable part of nature—the part that was pleasing to the eye and mind— was all on the surface, even though it might be all that an ordinary person saw in his daily life. Akutagawa would have no part of such superficiality. He wanted extreme circumstances under which man would be forced to face his own monstrous nature. His tales are full of such circumstances for that very reason. He himself wrote in explanation:

... suppose I have a theme and would like to make it into a novel. In order to give it an artistically powerful expression, I need some extraordinary incident. But the more extraordinary I imagine it to be, the less plausible today's Japan becomes as a setting for it. If I give it a contemporary setting, I will most likely strain my readers' credulity. This will probably ruin my chances of getting the theme across. I already suggested one solution to this problem when I said it was difficult to place an extraordinary incident in a contemporary setting. The solution is nothing other than this: to make the incident happen in some remote past (the use of the future for this purpose would be possible but rare), or in a country other than Japan, or both.

The microcosm created by Akutagawa in his fiction was simply a means to an end, namely, illustration of his theme; it was not an end in itself. Here he differed from Tanizaki, with whom he otherwise had much in common. Tanizaki created a world of fantasy according to the dictates of his imagination; Akutagawa first conceived his theme, then made up a fantasy world to suit the theme.

The reason why Akutagawa took this attitude is clear enough: he had a stronger faith in the power of words as such. A novelist, he thought, could penetrate to and express the source of life through his mastery of words. Unfortunately for Akutagawa, mastery of words proved no substitute for mastery of life. His definition of literature thus fell prey to conflicting principles. Literature, he said, was an art that used words to transmit life. But what if life should resist transmission by words? Language is Apollonian, life Dionysian. Akutagawa wanted art not merely to imitate nature, but to conquer it. He wanted too much.

The Novelist Must Be a Poet

It follows from Akutagawa's concept of literature that a novelist needs two qualifications above all else: command of words, and deep feeling. He is a verbal artist, but he is also sensitive enough to penetrate the surface of life and reach the source of human vitality beneath.

That a novelist must be a competent prose writer is a truism. Probably for that reason, Akutagawa did not stress this point in his essays. In "Ten Rules for Writing a Novel," he put style in seventh place. Nevertheless, he held up an ideal of literary craftsmanship.

Literature is an art that depends on language for its expression. It goes without saying, then, that a novelist must work hard to improve his writing. If he finds himself indifferent to the beauty of language, he must realize he lacks one of a novelist's chief qualifications. Saikaku gained the nickname "Saikaku the Dutchman" not because he broke the contemporary rules of fiction, but because he had learned the beauty of words by writing *haikai*.*

The passage is noteworthy for its rather peculiar reference to Saikaku. This seventeenth-century novelist has often been praised

---

* Saikaku was a writer of *haikai*, a popular form of linked verse, before he began writing prose fiction. As a haikai writer he shocked his contemporaries by the use of quaint, unconventional words, so much so that he was nicknamed "Dutchman." His use of unconventional words in his fiction was just as striking.

for his sturdy prose style (Shiga, as we have seen, admired him in this respect), but rarely for his quaint vocabulary. Akutagawa here seems to be advocating a highly individual style, including an unusual vocabulary, together with a certain disregard of ruling literary conventions.

Akutagawa's high regard for individuality in writing probably accounts for some unique advice of his: "High school students wanting to become writers should waste as little time as possible on such subjects as Japanese literature or Japanese composition." He did not want aspiring novelists to produce model schoolroom compositions or imitate the styles of famous writers. Instead, he recommended that they concentrate on two subjects usually loathed by young would-be writers in Japan: mathematics and physical education. The choice is interesting because it seems to reflect Akutagawa's concern with language as an organizer of chaos rather than as a means of communication. Just as mathematics creates an arbitrary universe completely controllable by discursive reason, so physical education provides the means of controlling physical circumstance. In both cases, the theme of control is paramount. In Akutagawa's view, a novelist works on human experience in the same manner as a mathematician works on his universe of mathematical concepts or an athlete on his physical constitution. In short, he saw the creative process as strenuous and deliberate.

The artist's creative activities are conscious, however much of a genius he may be. Take, for instance, the case of Ni Yün-lin, who drew a pine tree with all its branches outstretched in one direction.* I do not know if he knew why the stretching of the branches produced a certain effect in the painting. But I am certain he was fully aware that the extended branches would produce that effect when he drew them. If he had done it without knowing what the result would be, he would have been no more than a robot. So-called unconscious creative activities remind me of the imaginary seashell vainly sought by the nobleman in the old story.† Rodin despised *l'inspiration* for that reason.

* Ni Yün-lin (1301–74), also known as Ni Tsan, was a leading painter in the late Yüan period and was especially skilled in landscape painting. He also wrote many volumes of poetry.

† In a ninth-century Japanese tale called *A Tale of a Bamboo-Cutter*, the beautiful heroine gives a test to each of her wooers. She asks one suitor to bring her a seashell that does not exist in reality.

According to Akutagawa, the creative process was to represent the human life-force, in the sense discussed. The second of the artist's two chief qualifications was that he has plenty of that force in himself; otherwise he would never be able to grasp it, far less give expression to it. Akutagawa once wrote that someone who composed a work of literature must be a barbarian deep down, no matter how cultivated he might be on the surface. By "barbarian" he meant a man with superabundant animal vitality. He used an English word, "brutality," to describe the dominant quality of the medieval Japanese tales collected in *Ages Ago*.* Akutagawa gave that quality to Yoshihide, the painter-hero of "The Hell Screen," who originally appeared in *Ages Ago*. The painter is described by Akutagawa as creating a "weird, truly bestial impression" with his ugly appearance, particularly his bright red lips. This appearance has earned him the nickname of Yoshihide the Monkey. A pet monkey that appears in the same story is also named Yoshihide, and the close relationship between the painter and the animal is unmistakable. The same sort of animality is seen in Bakin, the novelist-hero of "Absorbed in Letters," another major Akutagawa story about an artist. Bakin is sixty years of age in the story, yet he is described as showing "an awesome flash of vigorous animal force" on his cheeks and around his mouth. It should be noted, however, that Akutagawa gives noticeably more animal vitality to Yoshihide the painter than to Bakin the novelist. Yoshihide has headstrong energy and barbarous pride that make him sneer at the tyrannical ruler of the country. Bakin, on the other hand, is put out when a frivolous gossiper in a public bathhouse adversely criticizes his work. The difference can be attributed to several factors, not the least important of which is that one is a painter and the other a novelist. A painter, Akutagawa believed, could express himself more freely than a novelist. Indeed, Bakin is described as being envious of a

---

* *Ages Ago* is a collection of more than 1,200 tales compiled in the early twelfth century. Unlike most of the literary works that preceded it, the collection was intended to appeal to a large segment of the contemporary Japanese populace. Accordingly, it did not shy away from presenting vulgar or even bawdy aspects of life in a direct, unsophisticated manner.

painter because the latter did not have to worry about government censorship.

There is evidence that painting, to Akutagawa, was a better medium than prose for embodying the human life-force. The novel, he thought, was a rather impure art form. The very first item in his "Ten Rules for Writing a Novel" is an affirmation to that effect: "One should realize that the novel is the least artistic of all literary genres. The only one that deserves the name of art is poetry. The novel is included in literature only for the sake of the poetry in it. In other respects, the novel differs not at all from history or biography." Of course the question here is what Akutagawa meant by "poetry." This is made somewhat clearer in the second of the rules: "The novelist is a historian or biographer, in addition to being a poet. Hence he is compelled to relate himself to the human life (of a given age and of a given country). This fact is proved by the works of Japanese novelists, from Lady Murasaki to Ihara Saikaku." Akutagawa seems to be implying that a poet is the only kind of literary artist who does not depend on contemporary society for his subject matter. A novelist can and should be a poet, but he is also obligated to be a historian or biographer, and that makes him an impure poet. In this respect, a painter has more artistic freedom than a novelist, because he can be more subjective, and therefore more faithful to the source of vitality within him.

Akutagawa's term "poetic spirit," which became a subject of controversy in his famous quarrel with Tanizaki, can be interpreted in the same light. Akutagawa did not explain the term clearly— not to Tanizaki's satisfaction, anyway—but he must have meant the poetic residue of the novel, after the elements of history and biography had as it were evaporated from it. The poetry corresponded to his conception of what life ultimately was, as opposed to what it had been on such and such an occasion. The theme of human bestiality is present here, but perhaps not fully realized. At any rate, this is what is suggested by Akutagawa's remark to Tanizaki that "by poetic spirit I mean lyricism in its broadest sense." Elsewhere he suggested that the most lyrical examples of Japanese poetry were to be found in the tanka of *The Collection of Ten*

Thousand Leaves, primitive poems of the eighth century and earlier that expressed "simple feelings in a moving way." In another
essay he recalled how touched he was one day when he heard a
deer's cry in the mountains. "It seemed to me," he continued, "that
all lyric poetry must have had its origin in such a cry—the cry of a
male deer calling for his mate." Akutagawa's unconscious syllogism
is here complete: the poetic spirit, in its purest form, is contained
in lyrics; lyrics originate in a male animal calling for a female;
therefore, poetic spirit has its source in animal instinct. "Poetic
spirit" ultimately goes back to animal instinct.

If this interpretation is accepted, it follows that a novelist should
nurture the beast in him, for it is the very source of his artistic
creation. He should try to improve his physical condition by ex-
ercising, as Akutagawa advised high school students who aspired to
become writers. The weaker the artist's health, the weaker his creative urge. The artist with failing health would inevitably meet
a tragic end, like Tok, the poet in *Kappa* who kills himself while
longing to reach the Valley of Life where clear water flows and
medicinal herbs flower. Akutagawa himself committed suicide
when he felt he had lost the "animal force" in himself. "I, too, am
one of the human animals," he wrote in his suicide note. "But I
seem to be losing the animal force. Witness the fact that I have
lost my appetite for food and for women."

Loss of animal force is a characteristic ailment of modern man,
surrounded as he is by the products of human intellect. A novelist, Akutagawa thought, should resist these pressures and never
lose sight of human bestiality. The ninth of Akutagawa's ten rules
for writing a novel touches on this point:

A person aspiring to be a novelist should always be cautious not to respond to philosophical, scientific, or economic theories. No ideology or
theory is capable of controlling man's entire life, as long as he remains
a beast in human form. A person who responds (knowingly, at least) to
such theories will meet needless inconveniences in following his life's
course—the animal life.

This is a sad verdict on the role of ideas. But Akutagawa in later
life seems to have reached a point at which he was forced to

acknowledge the powerlessness of modern learning in the face of man's biological nature. In *Kappa*, for instance, Mag the stoic philosopher cannot quite overcome his sexual drives; Gael the millionaire businessman is at the mercy of his wife; the doctors in kappaland have not found an effective way of controlling undesirable hereditary traits. In short, the products of human intellect are no match for basic human animality, and a wise artist should put no trust in them.

It is ironic that Akutagawa, who stressed the intellectual power of language and the artist's command over it, eventually had to face up to the powerlessness of intellect. Akutagawa began by regarding the novelist as a specialist in language on the one hand and a seeker after experience on the other. As it turned out, the two functions were incompatible. After all, to the extent that the novelist was still a historian or biographer—which he could not help being part of the time—he continued to depend on the generalizing power of intellect. This was the heart of his dilemma. If he became too much of a historian or a biographer, the poet within him would be overwhelmed and his work would lose its "poetic spirit." On the other hand, if the poet within him grew too powerful, he would not be able to relate to the outside world; he would end up as a social misfit, a misanthrope, or a madman. According to Akutagawa, then, there could not be a happy novelist.

Akutagawa offered three solutions to this dilemma, none of which was very attractive. One was not to become a novelist, or at least to stop being one. "If a person wants to live a relatively happy life," he said, "the best course he can take is not to become a novelist." The second was suicide, the course taken by Yoshihide the painter, Tok the poet, and, finally, Akutagawa himself. The third was prolonged perseverance. Bakin, the other notable artist-hero in Akutagawa's fiction, is an example of this: he keeps repeating to himself: "Learn! Don't get upset! And endure harder!" Each of these solutions is so drastic that it is clear Akutagawa regarded the novelist's situation as desperate. This tragic view may well be a reaction to his earlier optimism (if not arrogance), when he thought the chaos of human reality could be given order by means of language, a human invention. He thought a novelist could overcome the world with mere words. The world proved to be too powerful, and Akutagawa was too perceptive not to realize when he was beaten. He could not console himself with belief in the redemptive power of ethics, religion, or Marxism; he had too clear a view of human bestiality. On the other hand, he was also too proud, or too afraid, to embrace the powers of chaos. He was too much of an intellectual to accept the prospect of insanity, of being a burden to others simply in order to stay alive. His ideal of the novelist, then, had to be a tragic one—as tragic as his own life.

Gauguin Versus Renoir

Akutagawa's dualistic concept of art is also reflected in his ideal of beauty. On the one hand, he was very much attracted to the primitive, dynamic type of beauty that is created by an artist with more natural vitality than formal training. On the other hand, he could not help feeling an affinity with the elegant, urbane type of beauty produced by the professional artist who is completely at home in modern society. This, then, was yet another of his dilemmas.

Akutagawa made his views on art abundantly clear in two successive sections of his long essay "Literary, Too Literary." These two sections are entitled "The Call of the Wild" and "The Call of the West." In the first, he recalls how repelled he was when he first saw Gauguin's painting of a Tahitian woman who was, as he felt, "visually emitting the smell of a barbarian's skin." He then goes on to say that, despite his initial reaction, he gradually became fascinated with this orange-colored woman. "Indeed," he wrote, "the power of the image was such that I felt almost possessed by the Tahitian woman." Why he was so enchanted by her is clear enough. He saw in her a "source of life," the vigorous life of primitive people. "Gauguin—at least as I see him—meant to show us a human beast in that orange-colored woman," he reflected. "Furthermore, he showed it to us with more power than the painters of realistic schools." Naturally he recognized the same type of beauty in the works of other Postimpressionist painters. He saw it, for instance, in Van Gogh's paintings of the Arles period. He especially adored Matisse, of whom he said: "What I am seeking is his type of art, the kind of art that is brimming with vitality, like grass in the sunshine vigorously growing toward the sky."

Akutagawa also recognized a "Tahiti School" in literature. His subtitle, "The Call of the Wild," is obviously a reference to Jack London's novel, though there is no clear evidence to show how much he liked it. The strongest expressions of his enthusiasm in this regard are directed at *Ages Ago*, Bashō, and Shiga Naoya.

Akutagawa has generally been considered the "discoverer" of *Ages Ago* for modern Japanese readers. That massive collection of old tales had attracted little attention through the centuries, until Akutagawa published an essay called "On *Ages Ago*," praising it in the highest terms. The chief value he found in *Ages Ago* was what he termed "the call of the wild," which he explained as follows. "I finally discovered the sterling worth of *Ages Ago*. The artistic value of *Ages Ago* lies not only in its vigor. It lies in its beauty— the beauty of *brutality*, if I may borrow a word from the English. It is the type of beauty farthest removed from anything elegant or delicate." He then cited a tale from *Ages Ago* that he thought exuded this brutal beauty. The tale was about a man who was suddenly gripped by sexual passion while traveling alone in the countryside. Unable to calm it in any way, he at last pulled out a large turnip from a field by the road and satisfied himself with it. Some time later the turnip was picked up and eaten by a young maiden who had no knowledge of how it had been used by the traveler. In due time she became pregnant and gave birth to a baby boy. The story makes clear what Akutagawa meant by "brutal beauty": it was an artless, lowbrow, crude type of beauty, tempered by bawdy humor. Certainly, as Akutagawa noted, it was far removed from elegant or exquisite beauty. Also noteworthy was the way in which the story revolved around the traveler's virility: primitive vigor—the vigor of the life-force—is an essential ingredient in "brutal beauty."

Akutagawa has also been credited with throwing new light on Bashō. Before he published "Miscellaneous Notes on Bashō," the seventeenth-century haiku poet had been visualized as a lean, travel-worn sage who had no interest in mundane affairs. Akutagawa presented a new image of Bashō by describing him as a sturdy, energetic man with a great many fleshly interests, including heterosexual and even homosexual ones. Here, for instance, is his condensed version of Bashō's biography: "He committed adultery and thereupon eloped from his native province Iga; arrived at Edo, where he frequented brothels and other such places there; and gradually evolved into one of the age's great poets." As an example of Bashō's superabundant energy, Akutagawa quoted a haiku of his:

> In the summer woods
> I kneel before the divine footwear:
> my journey's start.*

Akutagawa did not spell this out, but it is obvious that the poem, with its images of summer trees, giant footwear, and a traveler just setting out, gave him an impression of vigorous life far removed from exquisite, graceful, or delicate beauty.

The same type of beauty can be found in the works of Shiga Naoya, who, as we saw in the last chapter, tried to capture the beauty of a healthy animal vigorously pursuing its natural way of life. Largely for that reason, Akutagawa admired Shiga's works more than those of any other contemporary Japanese writer. "Mr. Shiga's works," he once wrote, "show they are by a writer who, above all, is living a wholesome life in this world." He went on to point out that they show "poetic spirit" and that Shiga was a poet as well as a novelist. Referring to a scene of *Voyage Through the Dark Night* where the hero enjoys a night with a prostitute, Akutagawa commented: "Only a poet could have sung 'It's a rich year! It's a rich year!' at the sight of a woman's voluptuous breasts. I feel a little sorry for my contemporaries, who have given relatively little attention to the sort of 'beauty' that Mr. Shiga has created."

---

* The haiku was written by Bashō in the summer of 1689, when he visited a rural temple at the beginning of his long journey to the far north. Enshrined in the temple was a mountain priest noted as a tireless traveler through the wilderness. Unlike other holy statues, that of the priest normally wore wooden shoes.

Again the beauty Akutagawa spoke of is not elegant or urbane. Though not as "brutal" as that of *Ages Ago*, it has the natural appeal of animal good health and vitality—the call of the wild.

Yet, with all his admiration for a dynamic, masculine beauty, Akutagawa did not produce a literary oeuvre in which that quality predominates. He did write stories about primitive, violent men— "The Robbers," for example, and "Lord Susanoo"—but they are not among his more successful efforts. He also wrote a number of tales based on *Ages Ago*, "Rashōmon" and "The Nose" among them, but they are noticeably lacking in the beauty of "brutality." As has been pointed out, his friend Tanizaki noticed this fact and told him that he could not write stories like Shiga's because he lacked the physical strength. Akutagawa himself admitted that none of the contemporary imitators of Shiga, including himself, had succeeded in emulating Shiga's "poetic spirit." The hero of "Cogwheel," who is obviously Akutagawa himself, confesses that *Voyage Through the Dark Night* has turned out to be a frightening book for him. Akutagawa listened to the call of the wild, but his own work does not have it.

Why was this so? Tanizaki's explanation is surely inadequate. Akutagawa may have been fascinated with the call of the wild, but he was also drawn to an opposing force, a force that he termed "the call of the West." It is this latter force that seems to predominate in his works of fiction, though he says less about it in his essays. The reason may well be that Akutagawa himself was somewhat at a loss to explain this other "call" in analytical terms. In fact, he called it "mysterious."

Underlying the West, as we call it, is ever-mysterious Greece. As an old saying goes, one cannot know the temperature of water until one drinks it. The same applies to Greece. If someone were to ask me for a concise explanation of Greece, I would advise him to look at the few examples of Greek pottery on display in Japan. Or I might recommend that he study photographs of Greek sculpture. The beauty of those works is the beauty of Greek gods.

"The call of the West," then, seems to be the call of ancient Greek civilization, of the Hellenism that lies at the roots of Western culture. If that is the case, Akutagawa's attraction to the West is quite consistent with his admiration for Supreme Intellect, the force that conquers chaos. As we have seen, he called himself an Apollonian. The Western style of beauty is, above all, the beauty of intellect organizing chaos into order. Applied to a literary work, it is the beauty of a tale with a logically ordered structure that gives form to the chaos of raw life and the human psyche.

Akutagawa's stories, especially his early ones, show this type of beauty. "Rashōmon," "The Nose," and "Yam Gruel" all have a well-ordered structure patterned on the hero's thinking. They have a beginning, a middle, and an end. Progression from beginning to end is attained through analysis of the hero's psychology; the general effect is of light thrown on the dark corners of the mind until everything is revealed. The weird, uncanny part of the human mind is brought under control; fear of the dark is dispelled. The servant in "Rashōmon," who is at a loss when the story begins, clearly knows what to do at its close. At the same time, the reader learns how to behave in a chaotic, war-ridden society. The priest in "The Nose," unable at first to tolerate his grotesque nose, finally makes peace with himself as he comes to know his mind better. The petty official in "Yam Gruel," who makes himself ridiculous by his fondness for yam gruel at the tale's beginning, succeeds in overcoming his weakness, whereupon the tale ends. The reader of these stories is left with the feeling that life, chaotic and uncontrollable though it may seem, can be brought under control by intelligence and self-knowledge.

Intellect, in reordering the conventionally ordered world, sometimes begets humor and irony. In some of his tales, Akutagawa laughs at people who are important only because they are wedded to the existing social order. In "The Handkerchief," he gives a highly satirical picture of what really goes on in the mind of an internationally known philosopher and moralist. In "The General," he shows a greatly respected general to be petty, inconsiderate, and vainglorious. In "Lice," he has fun with the spectacle of some ostensibly courageous samurai being completely stripped of their dignity when attacked by lice. Akutagawa once remarked: "According to Pascal, man is a thinking reed. Does a reed think?

I really can't say. But I do know that a reed, unlike a man, does not laugh. I cannot imagine a man being serious—or, indeed, having any humanity—unless I can also imagine him laughing." By "humanity" he must mean intellect; only a creature with intellect can laugh. Akutagawa's stories, especially his early ones, are often humorous because of their intellectuality.

Human intellect, while begetting humor and irony on the one hand, evolves elegance and delicacy on the other when it functions as an aesthetic principle. A man-made world is self-insulated; having no room for such "animal" activities as procreation, it tends to cut itself off from the roots of life. Art in such a world is, above all, artificial. It therefore has no greater goal than its own refinement. The artist, however confident of his dexterity, has to make his work meticulously artificial in order to prove it. Such elegant beauty is a mark of civilization in the sense that it shows a distance from barbarism. Akutagawa liked elegant, sophisticated beauty; he had to, as long as he approved the progress of civilization. While attracted to Gauguin and Van Gogh, he confessed he was also fascinated by the works of Renoir and Redon. "Like all art lovers of my generation," he recollected, "I was first an admirer of those moving, powerful works of Van Gogh. But slowly I began to develop a taste for Renoir's works, the ultimate in elegant beauty." He drew a similar parallel between Gauguin and Redon. "I feel the call of the wild in Gauguin's orange-colored woman," he wrote. "But I also feel 'the call of the West' in Redon's 'Young Buddha.' " He attributed his fondness for an elegant, sophisticated style of beauty to the fact that he was a city dweller. His claim that a civilized person like himself could never really understand Gauguin or Van Gogh seems at times to proceed from a genuine inferiority complex. At other times, however, he seems to have been overcome by a sense of superiority before such "barbarous" works.

Of all Akutagawa's works, the one that shows elegant, urbane beauty in its most touching form is "The Lady Roku-no-miya." This court lady, precisely because of her courtly refinement and elegance, is lacking in the will to live and eventually has to meet a passive death. An elegant, courtly atmosphere also prevails in

"Heichū, the Amorous Genius," and its hero, who is a courtly, sophisticated Don Juan, meets a similar fate. Indeed, the Akutagawan protagonists who are urban dwellers with delicate sensitivities and impaired vitality outnumber the more primitive and vital ones. The stories in which the latter appear do not always produce a graceful effect, but none creates a crude or vulgar impression, either. If one is to make a comparison, they are closer to Renoir than to Van Gogh.

If elegance and sophistication are marks of advanced culture, so are pluralism and complexity. The more intellectual a person is, the more skeptical he tends to become. Akutagawa liked to create deliberate ambiguity in his stories, because he did not believe in simple truths. In an aphorism entitled "Interpretation," he wrote:

Any interpretation of a work of art presupposes a degree of cooperation between artist and interpreter. In a sense, the interpreter is an artist who, using another artist's work for his theme, creates his own work of art. Hence, every famous work of art that has withstood the test of time is characterized by its capacity to induce a multiplicity of interpretations. But, as Anatole France has pointed out, the fact that a literary work has the capacity to induce multiple interpretations does not make it ambiguous in the sense that the reader can easily give it any interpretation he likes. Rather, it means that a good work is like Mount Lu; it is many-sided, and therefore encourages viewing from many angles.*

A work of art, Akutagawa is saying, is the better for being many-sided and multilayered, because life is many-sided and multilayered. A simple-hearted rustic may see all human life in black-and-white terms, but a modern intellectual would not and should not do so. Truth in human life is always complex, always elusive. A good work of literature recognizes that fact and creates a complex effect.

The multilayeredness of Akutagawa's stories is well known. The

* In *The Garden of Epicurus* Anatole France remarked that words in a book were magic fingers that played on the harp strings of the reader's brain, and that the sounds thus evoked depended on the quality of the strings within each individual reader. Mount Lu is a famous mountain located near the Yangtze River. Because of its scenic beauty and its close associations with Buddhism, it provided fitting material for poetry and the arts through the centuries.

most famous is "In a Grove," in which the same event is narrated in such widely different ways by its three participants that the reader is left wondering what really happened. The reader knows exactly what is going to happen in "Kesa and Moritō," but he also knows that Kesa (or her ghost), Moritō, Wataru, and others will have widely differing interpretations of it when it happens. In "Doubts," the hero is unable to decide on his true motive for killing his wife and finally goes insane. The hero of "Cogwheel" cannot look reality in the face because phantasmal cogwheels in his eyes obstruct his sight; as a result, he has difficulty distinguishing between what he sees and what he imagines. The painter in "Dreams," likewise, cannot discern reality from dreams, and the reader also does not know what really happened to the model who just disappeared. *Kappa*, a story narrated by a mental patient, has inspired a good many controversies about its meaning. In "The Painting of an Autumn Mountain," multiplicity of interpretation is itself the main theme: the famed Chinese painting of the title gives such different impressions at different times that the onlookers are not sure if they have seen the same painting.

It can be said that this skeptical disposition of Akutagawa, while it gave his fiction complexity of meaning, prevented him from pursuing "the call of the wild" with wholehearted devotion. He was torn between "the call of the wild" and "the call of the West," as he himself conceded. The tales he wrote show, as a result, neither the vigorous strength of the former nor the graceful beauty of the latter—or, at least, not as much as he would have liked them to show. Many of them are both logical in conception and orderly in construction. Nevertheless, something raw and weird remains lurking beneath the surface. Other tales of his try to present human animality in its primitive form, and yet they lack a strong lyrical appeal because the theme has been intellectualized. It was Akutagawa's unhappy fate as an artist to pursue two conflicting sets of aesthetic ideals without being able to reconcile them. In the final analysis, however, the best of his works—"The Hell Screen," "In a Grove," *Kappa*, "Cogwheel"—derive their basic appeal from that conflict. These stories move the reader by showing a penetrating intellect desperately trying to cope with the murky, chaotic realities of the human subconscious and ending in failure. Despite their author's nostalgic longing for ancient Greek civilization, their beauty is not that of classicism. Rather, it leans toward the grotesque.

Form for a Versatile Writer

Akutagawa revealed his ideas on the structure of the novel in the course of his famous controversy with Tanizaki, even though he did it in a somewhat haphazard way and invited misunderstandings as a result. As against Tanizaki, who argued that a novel would be better for having an ingenious, well-constructed plot, Akutagawa maintained that plot itself has no artistic value, and that a novel without a complicated plot can be a fine work of art if it has plenty of "poetic spirit." As the controversy became famous, he came to be considered the champion of the "plotless" novel, in spite of his repeated insistence that he did not necessarily regard it as the best form of fiction.

Akutagawa's use of the term "plot" was also widely misunderstood. Certainly he did not mean a novel without structure. "I am not insisting that every writer should write a novel lacking a plotlike plot," he stressed. "In fact, most of my own works have a plot. Without *dessin*, there cannot be a work of painting. It is through plot that every work of fiction comes into being." Here Akutagawa was using the word "plot" to mean "structure," and he approved of plot in this sense without reservation. When he talked about the "plotless" novel, he had a different type of plot in mind: it was a more "plotlike" plot, a plot with a sequence of events the reader would find interesting (Akutagawa once used the term "shocking" in this context and was consequently misunderstood still further). Roughly, it meant a story in the popular sense. In advocating a "plotless" novel, Akutagawa was advocating a novel without a "good story."

What he meant by the plotless novel becomes clearer when one reads his argument in favor of the plotless play: "Now I am sick and tired of watching a playlike play—that is to say, a play with plenty of dramatic interest. I want to see a play as free as air, a play that hardly has a plot." This is an unusually forthright statement for a diffident man like Akutagawa; perhaps he found it easier to make because he was talking about a genre to which he was an outsider. What he was objecting to was the "well-made," Ibsenesque plot, with its series of clashes between protagonist and antagonist. He liked a more lyrical plot—a plot with "poetic spirit," as he would have said. He expressed his sympathetic approval of a certain Japanese producer whose favorite Western playwright had changed from Ibsen to Maeterlinck to Andreev.

The form of prose fiction Akutagawa advocated, then, was a poetic, and not dramatic, novel. It might or might not have a protagonist. In all likelihood, it would not have an antagonist. It might or might not present a series of events; when it did, the events would not be sensational ones, and they would be arranged loosely rather than with tight dramatic logic. There would be no single story line that would hold the different parts of the novel together. In general, it would create the impression that the novelist wrote it in a casual mood, digressing whenever he felt like it. Ostensibly, the structure was so loose that a careless reader might think the novel had not ended when it actually had.

Have there been such works of fiction? Akutagawa cited Jules Renard's "Ways of the Philippes" and Shiga Naoya's "The Fires" as leading examples. "Ways of the Philippes," included in *The Winegrower in His Vineyard*, is a short story made up of some dozen brief episodes with a rustic vinedresser's family for their common characters. The episodes are varied in their time, setting, and subject matter. The first is a casual conversation exchanged between Philippe and his wife concerning their centuries-old house, with the narrator cutting in from time to time. The second episode takes place a few months later: it describes the Philippes waiting in vain for their soldier son to come home for the New Year. In the third episode, the Philippes are seen butchering a pig. In the fourth they have just been married. The bridegroom eats fourteen plates of food at the wedding dinner, while the bride sits there silently with no appetite at all. Other episodes are of similar nature, all dealing with the daily events of life normally following their course in a peaceful French village. The same uneventfulness is also seen in Shiga's "The Fires," though it ranges over a much shorter span of time and space. The story describes the happenings of just one day in the life of a man building a cottage with his wife and friends near a lake in the woods. They play cards in the morning since it is rainy, but they begin working on the cottage when the sky clears in the afternoon. After supper they go boating on the lake. When it gets dark they make a bonfire on the shore; as they sit around the fire one of them tells a strange experience he had the previous year. That is all.

"Ways of the Philippes" and "The Fires" seem to fit well with Akutagawa's idea of a plotless novel. Certainly, the reader would not read them for their story's sake. In both instances, the plot is loose or nonexistent; various episodes from the life of an ordinary Frenchman or a Japanese are just put together, seemingly at random. Pervading the episodes are the personalities of the dramatis personae, who are all simple, honest, sincere people (in the case of Philippe, this simplicity of character is developed to the point of naiveté). Together they create a warm, congenial atmosphere in a rustic setting. The reader visualizes good-natured, simple-hearted people leading wholesome lives entirely removed from the strains and stresses of "keeping up with the times." The sincerity of their basic attitude creates a lyrical mood. That mood, and not a well-developed story line, is the unifying principle in these works.

Akutagawa did make a few efforts to write in the vein of Renard and Shiga, notably in a series of short autobiographical pieces that have Yasukichi, a teacher of English at a naval academy, for their common hero. The results are largely unsuccessful because the characters are far from attractive, and the narrator's observations are too unimaginative to animate the trite events he describes. Markedly more successful in this genre are several works of his last years, notably "On the Seashore" and "The Mirage," both of which describe the leisurely life of a recent college graduate who is vacationing at a beach resort for a few days. Most of the scenes in these two stories show the young man walking and talking on the sandy shore with friends from his college days; that is all. Yet the stories impress because the few incidents they depict, while trivial in themselves, are presented through the eyes of a hypersensitive young man, a young man abnormally sensitive to decay, death, ghosts, and the dark side of life in general. The young man is totally different in personality from Philippe or the narrator in "The Fires," yet he grips the reader's attention by his uncanny capacity to sense weird things hidden from the ordinary eye. His presence creates an eerie mood that holds the different episodes together. Admittedly, "On the Seashore" and "The Mirage" have somewhat more structure than "Ways of the Philippes" or "The Fires." But of all Akutagawa's works they are the ones that best embody his idea of the plotless novel.

Nevertheless, the fact remains that those pieces constitute only a small proportion of Akutagawa's canon. He himself admitted that most of his works had a story to tell. Even when arguing most vehemently in favor of the plotless novel, he still declared that he had no intention of confining himself to writing essaylike stories. It would be misleading, then, to conclude that Akutagawa's concept of plot centered on the plotless novel. If he seemed to have become its champion at the time of the famous controversy, it was partly because Tanizaki drove him into that position, and partly because he associated the idea of an intriguing plot with the "popular" novel, which he detested. His stand in favor of the plotless novel was never so strong that he had to label other kinds as inferior. He championed the essaylike novel mainly because Tanizaki appeared to overpraise the novel that had an interesting story to tell.

In the final analysis, what Akutagawa really wanted to say in his controversy with Tanizaki seems to be that novels can have different types of structure, and that it is wrong to say one type is better than another. As a novelist, he did not like to be restricted in form; he wanted to be completely free to use any kind of structure he saw fit. Life, he thought, had many layers of meaning. Since literary works should present many types of life, it followed that novels should have many types of form and structure.

Akutagawa did write stories in a wide variety of forms. To mention only the principal types, he wrote essaylike stories like "On the Seashore" and "The Mirage"; dramatic pieces like "In a Grove" and "Kesa and Moritō"; märchen like "The Spider's Thread" and "Tu Tzu-ch'un"; traditional tales like "The Robbers" and "The Hell Screen"; lyrical stories like "The Mandarin Oranges" and "Flatcar"; fantasies like "Strange Island" and *Kappa*. Akutagawa also tried his hand at many literary forms besides prose fiction. He was one of the period's major haiku poets. He also wrote poems in the tanka form, and revived an obsolete verse-form called *sedōka* that had a 5-7-7-5-7-7 syllable pattern. He had some free verse to his credit, too. In the area of nonfiction, he made lasting contributions with his aphorisms and journals. His aphorisms, serialized in a magazine under the title *Maxims of a Midget*, attracted a great deal of attention at the time. His journals were also quite popular; some readers who do not like his fiction consider his *Records of a Journey to China* to be his finest work.

It can even be said that one of the main charms of Akutagawa's writings lies in the great variety of literary forms that he employed. He was a versatile writer, and he enjoyed displaying his versatility. In fact, he once said he had become a novelist because it gave him the opportunity to do so. "I write prose fiction," he explained, "because it is more all-embracing than any other form of literature, allowing me to toss in anything and everything." Accordingly, his idea of plot had to be a comprehensive one.

The same applies to his idea of prose style. He did not say it specifically, but it is obvious that he wanted to see a great variety of styles in prose fiction. His own works are, indeed, sufficiently varied in this respect. "Ogata Ryōsai's Affidavit" and "The Old Murder" are written in a certain style that used to be employed in the official language of the past. "The Martyr" and "St. Christopher's Life" have a very peculiar style, apparently modeled after the language of sixteenth-century Japanese Christians. In "The Hell Screen" and *Heresy*, though they are written in modern Japanese, he tried to convey the flavor of the language spoken by an ancient Japanese courtier. "A Clod of Earth" and "Genkaku Sanbō" are written in a simple, matter-of-fact style, stripped of all the decorative elements usually associated with literary language. "The Dog Shiro" and "The Three Treasures" show stylistic features reminiscent of a tale for children. "On the Seashore" and "The Mirage" are, as can be imagined, written in a lucid, precise style that approaches Shiga's.

Akutagawa never attempted to classify Japanese prose styles in a methodical manner, but he did set up two examples at opposite stylistic poles: Shiga and Sōseki. He thought that Shiga and his followers "wrote in the manner of speaking," while Sōseki was a writer who "spoke in the manner of writing." By the former he meant simply a colloquial style, that is, a style that reproduces the vocabulary and rhythm of daily speech. But the meaning of the phrase "spoke in the manner of writing" is more ambiguous. He did not mean a bookish style, for that would have been to "write in the manner of writing." A short essay of his entitled "Composition That Makes One Visualize" throws light on this point:

I like the kind of composition that makes the reader visualize the scene. I detest the kind that does not do so. In my view, there is a fundamental difference in sensibility between a person who writes "The sky is blue," and one who writes "The sky is blue like steel." While the former feels the color as merely "blue," the latter feels it as "blue like steel." He added the phrase "like steel" not because he was a better technician in composition; he did so because he had a more accurate grasp of what he saw. Sōseki had such a grasp and, as can be seen from his writings, it was of a highly individual and yet superb kind. Here is the opening sentence of "Snake," from his *Spring Miscellanies*: "As I opened the wooden door and stepped outside, I saw a horse's tracks, large and brimming with rainwater." With just one sentence, the impression of a country road full of rain puddles is vividly created. I like this type of writing.

In an ordinary conversation one does not say "The sky is blue like steel," or "As I opened the wooden door and stepped outside, I saw a horse's tracks, large and brimming with rainwater." These sentences are too calculated in their effect to be spoken extemporaneously, at least by an ordinary person. Yet what they lose in spontaneity, they gain in accuracy and individuality. Since they make more use of similes, metaphors, and symbols, they also gain in vividness. Their meaning is at once more complex and more accurate, as any figurative language is. In short, the style that "speaks in the manner of writing" is the style of poetry (one recalls that Sōseki was himself a writer of haiku).

It goes without saying that Akutagawa, who stressed the importance of "poetic spirit" in the novel, favored the style that "speaks in the manner of writing." Indeed, his typical style is the polar opposite of the style that "writes in the manner of speaking." It is anything but spontaneous; indeed, Akutagawa was a perfectionist. He once reflected:

I know I overtax my nerves unnecessarily in composing a piece. I cannot help it. There are certain words that I simply cannot bring myself to use on certain occasions. The tone of certain phrases disturbs me too much. For instance, I find it difficult to use a place name like Yanagihara ("willow-field")* because, to my mind, it makes the entire passage green; I cannot use the word unless the passage includes a word of another color to tone down that green.

Akutagawa was here talking about the writing of prose fiction, but what he said can be applied, with equal aptness, to the writing of haiku. Haiku poets take great care to create a harmony of colors, sounds, tactile sensations, etc., and they often go about doing so in a very self-conscious manner. Akutagawa's style is deliberate in the same way as the language of haiku is deliberate.

Akutagawa was often criticized for his artificiality by contemporary critics, many of whom were admirers of Shiga's more natural style. Always sensitive to criticism, the young Akutagawa tried hard to write more spontaneously, but without satisfactory results. One day he brought this problem to the attention of his mentor, Sōseki, and asked how he could possibly learn to write like Shiga. Sōseki answered: "He [Shiga] can write in the way he does because he writes spontaneously, without trying to create a piece of prose," and added that he, too, could not write like Shiga. Later on, however, Akutagawa seems to have been more confident of his own style. He remarked, for example, "My friends tell me: 'Your writings are too deliberate. Don't be so deliberate.' But I don't recall ever having been more deliberate than necessary. More than any-

---

* Yanagihara is the name of a district in Tokyo. It is written with two characters meaning "willow" and "field," respectively.

thing else, I want to write clearly." He went on: "No matter what other people may say, I shall go on trying to produce composition as clear-cut as calcite, one that permits the minimum amount of vagueness." Consciously or unconsciously, he did what he said. Even when he wrote such Shiga-like pieces as "On the Seashore" and "The Mirage," his style remained somewhat less spontaneous than Shiga's. Given his view of language, this was probably inevitable. He considered words—and the arrangement of words known as style—as so many tools with which to organize the chaos of life. As long as he held such an Apollonian view of literature, he had to be an Apollonian in matters of style, too.

Negation of a Negative Spirit

Akutagawa was adamant in repudiating the idea that literature was merely play or entertainment. For him, a literary work written to amuse the reader was "popular" literature, a product of commercialism that had nothing to do with "genuine" novelists. He wrote:

Today I stopped by the roadside to watch a fight between a rickshaw man and a motorist. I found myself watching it with a certain interest, and wondered what kind of interest it was. No matter how hard I tried to convince myself otherwise, I could not but feel that it was the same sort of interest I would have in watching a fight on the kabuki stage. . . . I have no intention of denying the value of literary works that produce this sort of interest. But I believe there can be interest of a kind higher than this.

The main question is what Akutagawa meant by a "higher" kind of interest. Instead of explaining, he simply observed that the first few pages of "Kylin," an early Tanizaki tale, produced that kind of interest. "Kylin" is the story of how Confucius, in his old age, toured China to propagate his teachings. Its first few pages describe his encounter with a venerable Taoist sage and then his travel to the state of Wei. There are no fights, nor any other kind of sensational incident. All that happens is a brief discussion on human happiness between Confucius, a disciple of his, and the Taoist sage. This is followed by a description of life in the state of Wei, where people are starving while the ruler and his beautiful wife indulge in luxury. The interest generated by these few pages is philosophical and moral to the highest degree, leaving no doubt about Akutagawa's meaning.

Indeed, Akutagawa repeatedly emphasized the didactic use of literature. "In a way, all novels are textbooks in the art of living," he once said. "Therefore, they can be said to be educational, in a very broad sense of the word." On another occasion, he called the poet "a microphone created by God." His reason was that "in this world of men no one proclaims the truth. It is the poet who amplifies people's whispers in an instant." Akutagawa was most persuasive on this point in his autobiographical story entitled "The Youth of Daidōji Shinsuke":

Shinsuke learned everything through books. At least, he could not think of anything he did not owe to books in some degree. As a matter of fact, he never tried to improve his knowledge of life by watching people in the street. Rather, he tried to read about men's lives in order to watch people in the street. A roundabout way to learn about life, you may say. But for him real-life people were merely passersby. In order to know them—to know their loves, hatreds, and vanities—he had no means other than to read books.

Shinsuke may have had a rather more withdrawn personality than the average person. A more extroverted person may learn more directly from actual life. Yet Shinsuke was also a man with a greater thirst for knowledge than the average person. He was not satisfied with a superficial knowledge of men; he had to know love, hatred, vanity, and all the other emotions hidden in their hearts. Good books present the facts of life at a level deeper than everyday events. A person like Shinsuke, who seeks hidden truths about men, goes to books rather than to actual life.

Literature, however, is far more than a mere supplier of knowledge. The point is made unobtrusively by Akutagawa a little later in the same story. Here, beauty rather than truth is the issue:

"From books to reality" was an unchanging truth for Shinsuke. In his past life, he had not been without some women he found himself in love with. Yet none of them showed him what feminine beauty was. At least, none showed him anything more than what he had read about feminine beauty. Thanks to Gautier and Balzac and Tolstoy, he noticed the beauty of a woman's ear glowing translucent in the sunlight, or of her eyelash casting a shadow on her cheek. He could still remember her beauty because of that. If he had not read these books, he might have seen nothing in a woman but a female animal.

In this instance, books taught Shinsuke how to look at life. Life might be ugly, but it could be beautiful if looked at in a certain way. The woman might not be beautiful, but her partner could see in her an image of his favorite heroine in Gautier, Balzac, or Tolstoy. Literature might reveal hidden truths that were better left hidden. But it might also reveal beauty such as an ordinary person would never see in his lifetime. A literary work could depict people as more beautiful or noble than the reader had ever thought they were. In this way, it could give him support and encouragement in fighting the battle of life itself.

From his earliest youth, Akutagawa seems to have considered art a guiding light. As a young man of twenty-four who had not yet established himself as a writer, he wrote to a friend of his: "At some moments I find myself in the presence of a current that flows through life and art. The next moment, I lose sight of it again. And the instant I lose sight of it, I am overcome by the immense darkness and solitude that loom around me." This is the same current that Bakin, the novelist-hero of "Absorbed in Letters," eventually discovers "flowing like the Milky Way in the sky"—a sight that drives away all the unhappy thoughts from his troubled mind. Yoshihide, the artist-hero of "The Hell Screen," is so swept up by that current he forgets that the model being burnt to death before his eyes is his beloved daughter. The Akutagawa-like narrator of "Cogwheel," depressed, nervous, and on the brink of insanity, reads *Voyage Through the Dark Night* and gains peace of mind for a while.

Another revealing testimonial to the power of art is given by Akutagawa in an essay that records his experiences in the ruins of Tokyo immediately after the great earthquake of 1923. He was walking among the debris of fire-ravaged buildings with a heavy heart, when suddenly he heard the voice of a youngster in a nearby moat. He was singing "My Old Kentucky Home." "I felt strangely moved," Akutagawa later recalled. "I felt something within me that wanted to join in with the youngster. No doubt he was simply enjoying himself singing a song. Yet the song, in a trice, overcame the spirit of negation that had gripped my mind for some time."

Akutagawa went on to reflect on the uses of art. He concluded: "What I saw was something that even the flaming fire could not destroy." That "something" was the power of art, a strange power that could overcome the darkest of negative spirits. Even a simple song by Stephen Foster could do that; great masterpieces of literature should be able to do the same or more.

At this point art approaches close to religion—that is, if the purpose of religion is to overcome the spirit of negation. Akutagawa—at least the young Akutagawa—thought so. For instance, he wrote in a letter to a friend in 1914: "There is no need to force oneself to seek faith in God. One is compelled to debate whether or not there is a God because one thinks of faith only in terms of faith in God. I have my faith—a faith in art. I cannot believe that the exaltation I gain through this faith of mine is inferior to the exaltation gained through other faiths."

Could art really be a religion, in the sense Akutagawa thought it could? The available precedents were not very hopeful. There was the case of Bashō, who tried to unite art and religion, but failed because religion required him to be passive before the Supreme Being while art wanted him to be an active creator. Akutagawa, who was the first to point out that dichotomy in Bashō, came down firmly on the side of art. "Goethe once said he was possessed by a daemon while he was writing poetry," he wrote. "Wasn't Bashō too much under the influence of a poetic daemon to become a religious recluse? Wasn't the poet within Bashō more powerful than the religious recluse within him?" Akutagawa's answer was, of course, in the affirmative. For him, Bashō exemplified the sad fate of a poet who wrote poetry in the belief that it brought him closer to religion, but who finally came to the realization that he was wrong. How, then, did Akutagawa try to resolve a dilemma that had defeated Bashō?

Akutagawa's proposed solution was the opposite of Bashō's. While Bashō tried to bring poetry close to religion by writing a passive kind of poetry, Akutagawa attempted to humanize religion and thereby bring it closer to art. Increasingly interested in Christianity in his later years, he wrote essays describing the Holy

Scriptures as literature. Jesus, he thought, was more human than divine. "Christianity," he once wrote, "is a poetic religion rich in ironies, a religion that Jesus himself could not practice. He laughingly threw away his life, even, for the sake of his genius. No wonder Wilde discovered in him the first of the romantics." "Christ became an early-day journalist," he wrote in another instance. "He also became an early-day Bohemian. His genius marched on in leaps and bounds, overriding the social codes of his time. On occasions, he grew hysterical with disciples who did not understand him." He added:

Jesus would ask his disciples, "What am I?" It is not difficult to answer that question. He was both a journalist and a subject for journalism; or, to put it another way, he was the author of short stories called "The Parables" as well as the hero of fictional biographies called the *New Testament*. A number of other Christs, it appears, had similar characteristics.

By "other Christs" Akutagawa meant Goethe, Tolstoy, Ibsen, and all other "journalists" who were possessed by a "daemon," and who kept on writing about themselves as they searched for something nobler than human bestiality. For Akutagawa, the Holy Ghost that fathered Jesus was merely another name for that "daemon," which also moved Jesus to teach, preach, and be crucified. In that sense, Jesus was a writer like the others. "In the final analysis, Christianity is a work of art, a didactic literature created by Jesus," Akutagawa concluded. "The works of Tolstoy's last years come closest to this ancient work of didactic literature [the Bible], though they lack the romantic color he (Jesus) added." Here, Akutagawa was implying not only that the Bible is literature if Tolstoy's *Resurrection* is literature, but also that *Resurrection* is a religious classic if the Bible is a religious classic.

Thus Akutagawa attained a unification of literature and religion by making the former include the latter. Religion, in his way of thinking, was a type of literature, a romantic type. This was, of course, far more than a literary judgment, and should not be judged on literary grounds. The only question one can legitimately ask in a biographical context is whether Akutagawa did actually derive from literature the religious consolation he apparently demanded from it.

Ostensibly, the answer must be in the negative. Admittedly, the young Akutagawa seems to have found in art the kind of exaltation that a religion might give. Thus the writer Bakin attains "mysterious joy" and "ecstatic, moving exaltation" by means of art, and the painter Yoshihide shows the "splendor of ecstatic joy" on his face as he works at creating a masterpiece. Yoshihide eventually commits suicide, but this is depicted as a triumph because he leaves behind him a masterpiece that is immortal. And yet, Akutagawa seems to grow less and less confident in the saving power of art as he grew older. The suicide of Tok the poet is described in *Kappa* as being far less glorious than Yoshihide's: there are obvious indications that poetry failed to function as a redeemer for Tok. The neurotic narrator of "Cogwheel" does get solace from reading *Voyage Through the Dark Night,* but it is a temporary solace. And, of course, Akutagawa himself committed suicide. Does this not indicate that his religion of art had failed him? Could he not have lived on if he had become a Christian, for example?

From Akutagawa's point of view, his suicide indicates neither that art had failed him nor that religion could have saved him. To him, it appeared that even Jesus had died a suicidal death. And as Jesus had died because he would not compromise his ideals, so did Akutagawa. He had a lofty ideal of man in his youth, and he kept on refusing to abandon it, even when he grew older and came to discover bestiality at the source of human life. He chose to keep believing that man was considerably nobler than a beast. Unfortunately, his health rapidly deteriorated in his later years, threatening to reduce or even incapacitate his intellectual power. He could have lived on, had he been ready to accept a less intellectual life for himself. He could have stopped being a writer, if he found himself unable to write. He could have lived on in retirement, as a good-for-nothing, or even as a mental patient. But he was too proud; he could not and would not compromise his idea of human nobility. Likewise, he could have lived on as a

Christian. But, in his view, becoming a Christian would have meant surrendering his humanity to God; it would have meant recognizing an existence higher than man. His religion, which was art, dictated that man be his own master in death as in life. His suicide, in this context, was therefore a vindication of art; it was comparable to the suicide of Yoshihide in "The Hell Screen." Yoshihide the man died, but his hell screen, a proof that man is not a mere beast, remained. And so it is with Akutagawa: he killed himself, but his works remain as the record of his struggles to prove human nobility.

CHAPTER SIX

Dazai Osamu

✿

I T MAY AT FIRST seem strange that Dazai Osamu (1909–48), noted for his garrulity, said little about literature or about his own works in his essays and letters. One should recall, however, that he was basically a very shy person who could not bear talking much about himself in an open manner. Writing about his own works seemed to him like bragging about his looks. "A writer should be ashamed of himself," he once said, "to give even one word of explanation or apology regarding his own work." Such being the case, Dazai's idea of the novel has to be sought mainly in his works of fiction. Fortunately, he was an autobiographical novelist, and a writer or an artist often appears in his fiction as a thinly disguised spokesman for the author. Dazai's attitude toward literature is therefore everywhere visible. In this respect he was very much like Shiga, a writer he intensely disliked in his later years.

Drowning of a Shipwrecked Man

Of all Dazai's works, the one that most directly reveals his ideas on the art of writing is a relatively unknown novel called *A Women's Duel*. It is based on a short story of the same name, "Ein Frauenzweikampf" by Herbert Eulenberg (1876–1949). Dazai read this German work in Japanese translation, and was so dissatisfied with it that he was moved to rewrite it in his own way.* By examining why he was dissatisfied and how he went about rewriting it, we can learn much about Dazai's attitude toward literary real-

* This information is given by the narrator of the story. Since his name is Dazai, the assumption is that Dazai himself is speaking.

ism, as well as toward the relationship between art and objective external reality.

"Ein Frauenzweikampf" is a story only a few pages long. Its main character is a Russian woman named Constance, who has just discovered her husband's infidelity. She wants to dissolve the love triangle by a duel between herself and her husband's young mistress, a medical student. They duel in a field at the edge of town, and Constance, who has never handled a revolver before, somehow manages to shoot her opponent to death. Immediately, she gives herself up to the authorities and enters a jail, where, before anyone notices, she starves herself to death. In a letter left behind she testifies that she is killing herself as a martyr of love; she lost all purpose in living, she says, when she discovered that her victory at the duel saved her honor, but not her love.

Why was Dazai dissatisfied with the story? Because, he said, the author was too realistic in describing the incidents. After quoting the first couple of pages from the original story, Dazai addressed his readers:

How about that? If you are a seasoned reader of fiction, I must have quoted enough for you to notice something strange about the writing. In a word, there is a certain *coldness* about it; there is *indifference*—so much so that it is almost insulting. If you ask what is being insulted, I would answer it is the facts themselves. Too accurate a description of an actual fact has a disquieting effect on the reader. Newspapers, in reporting a murder or some even more repugnant crime, sometimes carry a sketch of the scene of the crime, outlining, among other things, the body of the slain woman sprawled like a doll in her bedroom. You surely know the kind of thing I mean. I can't stand that sketch. I feel like yelling "Take it away!" This story has the same sort of nakedness. Don't you begin to feel that way as you read it?

Elsewhere, Dazai compares Eulenberg to a camera; in his judgment, Eulenberg's story is just a police photograph of the scene of a crime. From all this he concludes that "when a story describes a scene with outrageous frankness, the reader, though impressed, will come to hold serious misgivings."

Dazai had a theory to explain why the author wrote the story in a way so realistic as to make the reader sick. According to him, Eulenberg had been physically exhausted at the time of writing.

When a tired man writes a story, he tends to write in a hostile tone—even, at times, a reproachful one. On such occasions, he is capable of revealing the bitterest, cruelest aspects of reality with the utmost nonchalance. Perhaps man is cold and heartless in his innermost nature. With his body exhausted and will power diminished, he is capable of attacking someone off guard and unceremoniously cutting him down. Sad, isn't it?

Dazai imagined that Eulenberg had been a tired man when he wrote "Ein Frauenzweikampf." In fact, he must have been so tired that he allowed himself to "take an unkind attitude toward human life, toward the humble way in which man lives day by day." Such was Dazai's verdict on realism.

If a novelist should not portray reality as it is, how should he portray it? Dazai's answer is revealed in the way in which he rewrote Eulenberg's story. The greatest difference between Eulenberg's original and Dazai's adaptation is that the latter tells us far more about what is going on in the minds of the story's three main characters. The German writer says almost nothing about the medical student's feelings when she received Constance's challenge to a duel. Dazai, on the other hand, delves deep into her mind and makes clear the psychic process through which she reaches the decision to accept the challenge. As he tells us, she has already become disillusioned with her lover, whom she finds ugly, weak-willed, and snobbish. Constance's challenge to a duel deeply chagrins her, because she has just awakened to her role as a marriage wrecker; she has even begun to feel sympathy toward the married woman, who, she thinks, has also been victimized by the same hypocrite. Her sympathy, however, quickly evaporates from her mind on the day of the duel, when she meets Constance for the first time and recognizes dogged determination in her. At once she resolves to accept the challenge.

The difference between the original story and its adaptation is even more noticeable in the treatment of Constance's husband, for, whereas he makes no appearance in the former, he plays a major role in the latter. As might be expected, in Dazai's version he is Eulenberg himself. According to Dazai, the husband was an indecisive intellectual who had two vices characteristic of the artist: amorousness and curiosity. He remained indecisive even when he knew that his wife and his mistress were to fight a duel on account of him; not knowing what to do, he timidly watched the duel from behind a tree. When he saw his mistress shot to death, he hurried back home and sank back in his sofa. At the police interrogation he answered that he knew nothing about the duel, that he wished both women were alive. He was deeply moved, however, when he learned of his wife's suicide and her motive for it as revealed in her letter. He was touched by the "violent seriousness" with which human life could be lived—so touched that he even thought of killing himself to join his wife. Real life, however, was not so romantic, and he did not commit suicide. Instead, he became a writer of popular fiction and lived a long, comfortable life. He never married again.

The portraits of the medical student and her lover, thus drastically modified by Dazai, change the entire story and affect the image of its heroine, Constance, too. In the Eulenberg story she is depicted with a detachment that prompted Dazai to imagine that the author had harbored personal hostility toward her. In contrast, Dazai's adaptation presents her as an intense, pure-hearted woman who thinks life is not worth living if it is bereft of love. The proud, almost arrogant woman who feared neither God nor man in the original story turns into a young idealist who lives for love and dies for love. Although Dazai does not delve into her psychology, he contrasts her both with the medical student and with the artist-husband. Out of the contrast she emerges as a person of heartfelt sincerity.

The reason why Dazai was tempted to change the story and its three main characters is now clear: he wanted to make every one of the characters a person worthy of the reader's sympathy. Constance, her husband, and his mistress, being human, are all potentially "cold and heartless"—as Eulenberg seemed to imply in his original story. Dazai did not deny this, but he also felt that they were redeemed from complete egotism by a degree of insight into their own emotions. The medical student found herself sympathizing with her rival in love, the wife who shot the student felt obliged to commit suicide, and the husband who learned of the suicide gave up his ambition to be a respectable writer. The situation was an ugly one, but the characters in the story were painfully aware of this. To depict them as if they were not aware of it, or as if no one ever had a decent thought or feeling, was to distort reality, not copy it.

As people live their daily lives, all sorts of beautiful and ugly thoughts cross their minds from one moment to the next. Nevertheless, some people conclude that ugly thoughts alone are true, forgetting that people are capable of beautiful thoughts, too. This is wrong. The images that keep passing through the mind may exist as "fact," but it is a mistake to regard them as "truth."

The same idea is suggested elsewhere in Dazai's writings. *A Women's Duel* was not the only story by another author that he reworked. In every case, he made his characters more sympathetic figures than they had been in the original. By and large, these characters were well aware of their own depravity. In *The New Hamlet*, Claudius, Gertrude, and Polonius are far more sympathetic characters than in Shakespeare's play, because they are more aware of their own weaknesses. Similar traits can be found in the stories collected as *Nursery Tales*. The Bad Old Man in "The Old Man with a Wen" is pitiably obsessed with a large wen on his cheek. The Bad Badger in "The Rabbit's Revenge" is a clumsy, ugly-looking animal who is hopelessly in love with the Good Rabbit and is cruelly victimized by her. The Bad Old Woman in "The Tongue-Cut Sparrow" is a former maid who for many years looked after her frail, impractical husband, the Good Old Man in the original tale. In *Sanetomo the Minister of the Right*, the assassin Kugyō is described as a nobleman who, "despite his carefree appearance, had something timid and subservient in his smile, the kind of smile one would expect to see in someone whose life since childhood had been wracked with care." In "Appeal to the Authorities," the "bad" man is no less than Judas Iscariot. He emerges as a sympathetic character who is trying to protect the charismatic but naïve Jesus from the pressures of the practical world. In order to keep his master pure amid the impurities of daily life, Judas himself sinks deeper into the mire. His struggle is threefold, for he has to fight with the ill will of the Pharisees, with the whims of his unpredictable master Jesus, and with his own introspective, and hence indecisive, mind. All those characters, as they appear in the stories rewritten by Dazai, have personalities that appear weak rather than evil. Indeed, it is because of their weakness that they have won Dazai's sympathy and are held up by him for the reader's sympathy as well.

For Dazai, then, weakness is a sign of goodness, not of evil. In his view, an evil person is a man who has no understanding of, and therefore no sympathy for, human weakness. He is like the Rabbit in "The Rabbit's Revenge," a beautiful maiden who tortures the ugly Badger to death, or like Hōjō Yoshitoki in *Sanetomo the Minister of the Right*, a master politician who takes advantage of the weak, impractical lord named in the title. Horiki, in *No Longer Human*, and Hirata, in "The Courtesy Call," are also of this type. So is Shiga Naoya, the only contemporary Japanese author to whom Dazai awarded this dubious honor. In "Thus Have I Heard," one of his last essays, Dazai savagely attacked Shiga, chiefly for having no understanding of human weakness; the beauty of weakness, Dazai argued, had passed Shiga by. As we saw in Chapter 4, Shiga thought that the basis of human nature was an instinctive animal wisdom, which he urged all men to follow with confidence. To Dazai, this belief of Shiga's seemed far too optimistic, far too self-indulgent, and far too inconsistent with man's sinful nature. "He does not understand the beauty of weakness," Dazai once wrote of Shiga. "He despises human weakness," he wrote elsewhere. In Dazai's opinion, the hero of *Voyage Through the Dark Night*, who struggles to reach a state of mind in which he can forgive his grandfather's incest and his wife's infidelity, is an intolerably arrogant person because he never stops to ask whether he really has the right to "forgive" either person, or whether indeed he himself is not as weak and sinful as they.

The same point is made in a short story by Dazai entitled "Seagulls." It includes a scene in which the hero, whose name is Dazai, is asked what he thinks is most important in literature. Is it love, humanism, beauty, social justice, or something else? His answer is instantaneous: he says it is regret. "A literary work devoid of regret is nothing," he says. "Modern literature—the very spirit of the modern age—was born of regrets, confessions, reflections, and things like that." He goes on to explain that all these self-incriminating thoughts are derived from one's "awareness that one is a dirty fellow." Dazai was nothing if not faithful to this principle. His very first work of creative writing, entitled "Recollections," resulted from his wish to "bare a record of my sins since childhood." In his last complete novel, *No Longer Human*, the hero's opening words are those of regret: "My past life is filled with shame." Other works by Dazai show the same characteristic. In "Villon's Wife," both husband and wife are aware that all men are criminals; the difference between them is that he always thinks of suicide, whereas she wants to live on even as a criminal. Naoji, a leading character in *The Setting Sun*, who eventually commits suicide, also suffers from the painful knowledge that there could be no man who is not depraved, while his sister Kazuko, who shares this belief, decides she can live with it. The reason why the heroes choose death over life and the heroines do the reverse (though both suffer equally from the knowledge of man's basic depravity) is related to Dazai's belief that women are more capable of withstanding the world's evil. Young, innocent women are an exception, however. In "Metamorphosis," for instance, the young daughter of a woodcutter flings herself over a waterfall when she is raped by her drunken father. Constance, in *A Women's Duel*, wants to die when she discovers her husband's infidelity; failing to die in a duel, she starves herself to death.

Dazai's ideas concerning the relationship between life and art can be summed up as follows. In his view, human reality was ultimately filthy and ugly, and human nature inherently depraved. He maintained, however, that literature should not concern itself wholly with that fact. The reason he gave was that it might be fact, but it was not truth. Truth, according to Dazai, lay with the "weak" people who were painfully aware that human reality is ugly and human nature foul. Their sufferings, their regrets, their remorseful reflections, their desperate attempts to ward off the ugliness and filth of life—all these were beautiful. The prime concern of literature was to depict that beauty.

Dazai expressed these views eloquently in a parable, which will serve as a fitting conclusion to this section:

The man was shipwrecked. Turbulent waves swallowed him up. Flung against the shore, he found himself desperately clinging to a window frame. It was the lighthouse keeper's cottage! Joyfully he peered into the room, intent on crying for help. The lighthouse keeper, his wife, and their little daughter were sitting happily at a modest dinner. "Oh, no!" he said to himself. "As soon as they hear my cry for help, the peace of their happy home will be shattered." For a moment he hesitated, suppressing his urge to yell out. The next instant, this timid-hearted man was attacked by a colossal wave and carried far out to sea. He was lost forever.

Now this man's behavior was admirable. But who was watching him? No one was. The lighthouse keeper's family, unaware of what had happened outside, went on with their happy dinner. Meanwhile, the shipwrecked man met a lonely death amid the angry waves. I rather fancy it was snowing; at any rate, neither moon nor stars witnessed the incident. And yet this man's admirable behavior is a fact that cannot be denied.

How do I know all this? I had a vision of it one night. But that doesn't mean I made it all up. The fact actually exists; somehow, it is now part of this world of ours. The wonder of the novelist's fantasy lies in precisely that. People say that fact is stranger than fiction. Yet there are facts to which there are no witnesses. And in many instances, such facts are all the more precious, shining like jewels in the dark. It is to present such facts that a novelist writes a story.*

Friend of the Weak

If the function of a novel is to depict a man painfully aware of his innate depravity, a novelist's prime qualification is to have a thorough and sympathetic understanding of basic human weakness. Dazai repeatedly emphasized this. On one occasion he remarked: "Artists have always been friends of the weak," and on another: "To be a friend of the weak—that is the artist's point of departure as well as his ultimate goal." He pleaded with Shiga,

---

* Dazai liked the episode well enough to write it twice, once in an essay called "A Promise," and again in the novel *Parting*. A similar incident is also described in *No Longer Human*. The shipwrecked man in the episode is to be interpreted figuratively—a man shipwrecked on the voyage of life.

who he thought was too "strong": "Become a little weaker. Be weak, if you are a man of letters. Be more flexible. Try to understand people who are different from you; try to understand their agonies." He wanted a novelist to understand the weakness of Constance, of Gertrude, of the Bad Badger. He criticized Shiga for not understanding Akutagawa's mental anguish. Just as strongly, he approved of Akutagawa as an artist well acquainted with the dark side of human nature.

All through his writings Dazai can be seen elaborating on this concept of human weakness. "Agony of a fugitive. Weakness. The Bible. Fear of life. Prayer of a loser." Such are the associations that it had for him. "A fugitive"—the word occurs frequently in Dazai's writings—is defined as "a wretched loser, a delinquent," in *No Longer Human*. The term evidently refers to a person like Ōba Yōzō, who, because of his awareness of "a lump of evil" lying deep within him, cannot be aggressive, and therefore cannot win a victory in the struggle for survival that is life. "Fear of life" is another favorite term of Dazai's; it denotes the fear of a man who lives a fugitive's life. For instance, the poet Ōtani in "Villon's Wife" says he is "always fighting with fear": he is afraid of God, who has seen through the "lump of evil" within him and who might punish him for it at any time. Dazai's reference to the Bible should be taken in the same context. In Christian terminology, all men are guilty of original sin; they are all depraved. The "prayer of a loser" is a prayer to Jesus, who was crucified to redeem humanity from original sin. Kazuko in *The Setting Sun*, when she realizes that becoming a sinner is the condition of being alive in this world, says: "Labeled a delinquent. That's the only kind of label I want to be crucified under." In "Appeal to the Authorities," Judas cannot convince himself of his absolute innocence, and he suffers painfully from it. "A leading characteristic of geniuses," says one of the letter-writers in "Letters in the Wind," "is that they are one and all convinced of their own sinfulness." In Dazai's opinion, this applies with peculiar force to geniuses who write novels.

But if a novelist is firmly convinced of his own depravity, will he not become a kind of holy man, and turn from literature to seek God and redemption? Dazai's answer is in the negative, unless "holy man" is interpreted in the broadest sense. Indeed, Yōzō in *No Longer Human* is "a good boy, like an angel"; Uehara in *The Setting Sun* is "a noble martyr"; and Ōtani in "Villon's Wife" is a poet who lives in fear of God. Yet they are all far from being saints or sages of any religion, Eastern or Western. In fact, they resemble Judas Iscariot more than the rest of the apostles. Dazai was too conscious of his own shortcomings to create a character in search of redemption. He was so sensitive on this score that it was difficult for him not to see a touch of pride (and hypocrisy) in the image projected by any religious leader. Convinced of basic human depravity, and moved by the nobility of men suffering from their awareness of it, he was too introverted, too self-conscious, and too timid to take any positive action. "A road leading to construction is a false road," he once wrote in a letter. "For today's young men, the only right road is the road to despair."

When Dazai said the novelist was a friend of the weak, he did not mean that he actually offered a helping hand to them. What he meant was that the novelist understood the weak and spoke on their behalf—bashfully, to be sure. Dazai once drew a portrait of the artist in an essay called "For Fifteen Years":

I am sure you all know about Böcklin, an artist who was fond of painting sea monsters. His paintings have an immature quality and may not be considered first-rate, but I cannot forget a work of his called "The Artist." It shows a huge tree covered with thick green leaves standing on a small island in the ocean, and in the tree's shade there is an ugly-looking, awkward creature with a little flute in his mouth. Hiding his hideous figure behind the tree, he is playing the flute. Lovely mermaids have gathered on the shore and are listening to the tune with ecstasy. No doubt they would faint with shock if only they could see the flute player. Knowing that, the latter has done his best to hide himself; he reveals nothing of himself but the sound of his flute. This is the wretched, lonely fate of the artist in a nutshell—and the true beauty and nobility of art. This doesn't quite say what I mean, but art is pretty much like that, I can tell you. A true artist is an ugly man.

The artist, then, is bashful, because he knows how ugly he is. He never preaches at a lectern; he never lectures from a dais. He conceals himself behind a tree and lets others hear his music. That is all.

Similar implications can be deduced from Dazai's better-known comparison of the artist with a pig. It appears in a dialogue that is part of a brief note called "A Faint Voice":

> "What is art?"
> "A violet."
> "Is that all?"
> . . . .
> "What is an artist?"
> "A pig's snout."
> "I protest!"
> "That snout can smell a violet."

Needless to say, the violet represents the beauty of human weakness, the beauty of those who, because they understand human nature, are harsh toward themselves and gentle toward others. Of these, some understand human weakness through conscious effort and others by instinct. Dazai was more attracted to the latter. He poured out his affection on those who were instinctively gentle and forgiving, those who could fully sympathize even with villains, criminals, and outcasts. In Dazai's stories they are mostly women; in his view, women were instinctively more gentle and forgiving. Sometimes, however, they fell prey to villains who took advantage of their innocence and gentleness. This happened to Yoshiko in *No Longer Human*, and to Mrs. Ōtani in "Villon's Wife." They were like violets trampled underfoot by callous men.

Most of Dazai's leading characters can be roughly classified as either "pigs" or "violets." In the former category are the two Japanese monkeys in "The Monkey Island," Tarō the Lazy, Jirōbei the Fighter, and Saburō the Liar in "Romanesque," the mental patient in "The Lost," Judas in "Appeal to the Authorities," the suicidal husband in "Osan," Tsuruta Keisuke in "The Criminal," Ōtani in "Villon's Wife," Naoji in *The Setting Sun*, Yōzō in "Recollections" and *No Longer Human*, and Dazai in "The Cherries" and many other stories. Among the violets are little Suwa in "Metamorphosis," the mother and daughter in "One

Hundred Views of Mount Fuji," Meros and his friend in "Run, Meros!," the heroine in "Mrs. Hospitality," Shūji in "The Courtesy Call,"* and Kazuko's mother and Mrs. Uehara in *The Setting Sun*, in addition to Yoshiko in *No Longer Human*. Mrs. Ōtani in "Villon's Wife" and Kazuko in *The Setting Sun* are violets at the outset, but they end up as pigs. Their stories are structured around their progress (or degradation, depending on how one looks at it) from the former to the latter.

From Dazai's point of view, then, all novelists must be pigs; those who are not are hypocrites, liars, or fakes. Dazai in his last years seemed to attack Shiga from this viewpoint. He charged that Shiga was self-indulgent in making himself to be a "good boy" in everything he wrote. "An athlete with his face made up," Dazai jeeringly called him. "A bully. An egotist. It looks as if he has muscles. I saw a photograph of him as an old man; he looked exactly like the decrepit foreman of a plant nursery." Shiga's works, Dazai pointed out, never descend into hell; all one sees is a storm in a teacup, like someone catching the flu. Dazai's attack on Shiga is often emotional and sometimes unfair, but there can be no doubt that Shiga was not a pig in Dazai's sense of the term; in fact, he tried hard to escape becoming a pig, and eventually succeeded. Dazai could not forgive him this.

If the novelist is a pig, it follows that the first principle in writing a novel is for the author to depict himself as a pig, that is, as an outcast and criminal and born loser. A Dazai-like narrator in "Spring Bandit" says:

Even in the *ich-Roman*, most writers depict themselves as "good boys." Has there ever been an autobiographical novel in which the hero is not a "good boy"? Akutagawa, as I recall, has said something to that effect somewhere in his writings. I was bothered by this question, and I therefore tried to describe my hero, "I," as a most ill-natured and monstrous person.

To Dazai's way of thinking, the heroes of autobiographical novels must be self-appointed pseudo-villains. They must be thieves, liber-

---

* Shūji was the given name of Dazai in real life. The English translation by Ivan Morris has changed it to Osamu, his pen name.

tines, prodigals, and scoundrels who have consciously become what they are. They must refuse to become happy, because it is wrong to want happiness in this world of men who, they know, are all depraved.

There is some question, however, as to whether Dazai's own heroes are cast exactly in this mold. The protagonists of "Villon's Wife," *The Setting Sun*, and *No Longer Human*—perhaps his three best works—are still "good boys" in some respects, and not without the author's knowledge. *No Longer Human* ends with the comment that its alcoholic hero, Yōzō, was "a good boy, like an angel." Uehara, in *The Setting Sun*, is a "noble martyr." Ōtani, in "Villon's Wife," is compared to the famous French poet. Dazai has often been criticized for being too indulgent toward his heroes, despite his promise to make them "most ill-natured and monstrous." His critics have a point. It should be remembered, however, that the characters Dazai attempted to create were pseudo-villains, not just plain villains. His heroes were ill-natured and monstrous, but they knew it—and suffered. If Dazai was overlenient toward them, it was because of his own good nature.

Tenderness, Sorrow, Humor—and a Touch of Nobility

Dazai's views on how a literary work should affect the reader have already been touched on. In a word, he liked the beauty of weakness. To him, this was the beauty that emerges from a confession by a sensitive person who knows the sinful nature of man, is pained by the knowledge, and refuses to be happy. The episode of the shipwrecked man is characteristic of Dazai's approach to literature. The episode in itself is too naïve: a good work of literature would be more complex, as life is complex. "What else does it [a novel] need," wrote Dazai in his comment on *The Declining Years*, "if it is tender, sorrowful, humorous, and noble?" The qualities imparted by a successful work of literature are tenderness, sorrow, humor, and nobility.

Of these four, sorrow is the one most closely connected with human weakness. The reader feels sorrow when he reads a novel describing human weakness, or when he reads about a man who suffers from his knowledge of the weakness that is in him. As an example of such sorrow, one can do no better than quote Dazai himself:

This happened five years ago, when I was living in Funabashi. One day I left home feeling depressed and somehow found myself in Ichikawa. There I sold some books I had brought with me, and used the money to see a movie. It was *Brother and Sister*. Watching it, I wept unabashedly. Mon's tearful protests made me unbearably sad. I kept crying aloud, until I could no longer stand it and took refuge in the washroom. It really was a powerful movie.

Brother and Sister is in fact a starkly realistic film that depicts a working-class family in rural Japan.* Mon, the sister in the title, is a young girl who falls in love with a college student; she is soon jilted by him and subsequently goes to the bad. One day the student, somewhat regretful of what he has done to her, visits her home and is beaten up by her rough, quick-tempered brother. Mon, who had been away at the time, hears about the beating upon her return and furiously remonstrates with her brother. Dazai was particularly touched by this scene; he found the girl's continuing love for the student "unbearably sad." Dazai's essay containing this episode is entitled "Food for the Weak." A movie becomes "food for the weak" when it conveys a forgiving attitude toward human nature rather than an indignant one. Goodness is weak, and is therefore always defeated. The fact that it nevertheless remains goodness is the source of Dazai's sorrow.

Dazai's own stories tend to lack the obvious emotional impact of *Brother and Sister*, but they are clearly in the same vein. His main characters may be weaklings in the conventional sense, but they are drawn in such a way as to inspire the reader's deepest sympathy. Here, for instance, is Uehara talking to Kazuko in *The Setting Sun*:

I don't care if I do drink myself to death. Life's too sad—I can't stand it. It's worse than just feeling lonely or depressed. I'm sad, I tell you. How can you be happy when the very walls are sighing all around you? How

---

* The original story by Murō Saisei (1889–1962) is available in English translation. See Ivan Morris, ed., *Modern Japanese Stories*.

would you feel if you discovered there was no way you could find happiness or fame during your lifetime? Work harder? Hungry beasts will eat it up, that's all. There are too many wretched people. Is that a snobbish thing to say?

Kazuko, herself a child of misfortune, allows him to make love to her. Uehara, as Kazuko has just realized, is dying of tuberculosis. And yet he apologizes for being too snobbish, and indulges in a great deal of amusing intellectual banter. With touches like these, Dazai evokes real sympathy not only for his characters but for all people caught in a situation they cannot control. This, he seems to say, is the fate of all of us, and we should pardon each other's weaknesses.

Hence the "tenderness" that Dazai spoke of as another important literary effect. Dazai defined it as "sensitivity to the loneliness, melancholy, and misery of others."

The ideogram *yū* makes me think. It is read as *sugureru* (to excel) and is used in such compounds as *yūshō* (championship) or *yū ryō ka* (excellent, good, fair). But there is another reading for it: *yasashii* (to be tender). If you take a close look at the ideogram, you will recognize its two components: "man" on the left and "to grieve" on the right. To grieve over men, to be sensitive to the loneliness, melancholy, and misery of others—this is "to be tender," to excel as a human being.*

A number of characters in Dazai's stories display this quality of tenderness. The hero of "Osan" is a married man who dies in a suicide pact with his mistress. Yet his widow remembers him as "a tender husband" and counts herself a happy woman to have loved such a man. The poet in "Villon's Wife" is a thief, drunkard, and libertine, yet his poor wife comes to conclude, toward the end of the story, that he is "more tenderhearted than most men around." A short story called "Mrs. Hospitality" describes a woman who, because of her innate "tenderness," cannot help offering the warmest hospitality to all and sundry, even though some of her visitors deliberately take advantage of her good nature. Her male counterpart is the narrator-hero of "The Courtesy Call," who finds himself

---

* The Japanese often amuse themselves by analyzing an ideogram in some fanciful way. Dazai's analysis of *yū* here is done in the same lighthearted mood and may or may not be correct in a scholarly sense.

unable to refrain from offering all his precious whiskey to a boorish guest whom he intensely dislikes; the story could be retitled "Mr. Hospitality." The adjective "tenderhearted" recurs many times in *The Setting Sun*, in most cases applied to Kazuko's mother. The epithet is not idly bestowed, as can be seen from this dialogue with her son Naoji, who is a drug addict. The pathos is heightened by the fact that it is Naoji who records this in his diary.

"Scold me, mother."
"How, Naoji?"
"Say I'm a weakling."
"You are a weakling. Are you satisfied now?"
Mother's goodness is unparalleled. When I think of her I feel like crying. I'm going to die in apology to her.

And Naoji does indeed commit suicide later in the book. He is not so much a depraved character as a weak one. Indeed, his weakness evokes so much sympathy that his depravity appears in a new light. "I wonder if depravity does not mean tenderness," says his sister Kazuko. By "depravity" she means one's own awareness that one is a "weakling," that is, a person who is too tenderhearted to take advantage of weakness in others. As Kazuko and her mother are kind to Naoji because he is a weakling, so are the female characters in *No Longer Human* kind to the unhappy Yōzō. Instinctively, they sense the goodness of heart that underlies his dissipated appearance. "My tender heart," Yōzō himself reflects, not without irony, "was so tender that it enchanted even myself." Of course, it also enchants the novel's readers, as Dazai intended.

We can see now why Dazai disapproved so much of "Ein Frauen-zweikampf": its author was entirely lacking in tenderness toward its three main characters. Dazai criticized Shiga on the same account, saying, "He does not even understand what tenderness is." Specifically assailed in this respect were two short stories by Shiga, "A Gray Moon" and "The Patron Saint." The former is a postwar story about a starving young workman being made fun of in a train by the other passengers; Dazai charged that nowhere in the story was any sympathy expressed toward the young workman. The latter story is about a wealthy man who, having by accident witnessed the wretched plight of a low-paid apprentice at a store, treats him to a feast at an expensive restaurant without revealing his identity. Dazai, referring to this story, wonders if the author "realizes how cruelly he is treating the poor." This may seem a little unfair of Dazai, but there can be no doubt that Shiga's realism, at least, is really an unconscious double standard that judges the poor far more severely than the rich.

"Nobility," the third of Dazai's array of desirable literary effects, is also related to tenderness. To be sympathetic and kind toward others presupposes a capacity for self-sacrifice, a capacity to keep selfish thoughts in check. An egotist can never be noble, because he is not sensitive to the suffering of others. A work of art, Dazai thought, should create an impression of nobility by describing sensitive, tenderhearted people. He implied as much when he made Naoji fall in love with the gentle wife of "a certain oil painter" and say: "If that painter's works breathe the noble fragrance of true art, it is because his wife has touched them with her tenderness." Elsewhere he declared: "Literature is always a *Tale of the Heike*." This rather eccentric definition of literature makes sense when *The Tale of the Heike* is understood as an epic eulogizing the fall of good but weak people, cultured to a fault, nobly meeting a tragic fate at the hands of their inferiors.

Many of Dazai's own works can be considered tales of this sort. The most obvious example, of course, is *The Setting Sun*, which may be considered an elegy mourning the death of the nobility in twentieth-century Japan. Kazuko's mother, with her extreme refinement and gentleness, best represents that nobility; she is "the last noblewoman in Japan." But Naoji also prides himself on his noble birth and concludes his suicide note by saying "I am a nobleman." The word "noble," in these instances, has at once social and moral implications, suggesting that a member of the nobility is likely to have a noble character, too. The commoners, on the other hand, are physically energetic, mentally robust, and aesthetically crude. They are the rough warriors who destroy the refined, gentlehearted courtiers. The sad inevitability of this outcome is narrated in a tone of Buddhist resignation in *The Tale of the Heike*, but Dazai

preferred to see it in the context of a Marxist view of history. He
seems to have thought that the people of noble birth, including
himself, would have no place in the utopian society that would
emerge after the forthcoming proletarian revolution. His pessimism is shared by Naoji, Yōzō, Ōtani, and other Dazai heroes, many
of whom are of aristocratic birth. They are of "the perishing class,"
as Dazai called them. "They get beaten, they perish, and their
mutterings become our literature," he explained; and elsewhere:
"Despair begets elegance." Presumably this "elegance" in literary
form is what Dazai meant by nobility.

There are occasions, however, when despair begets humor rather
than elegance. It is, of course, humor with a difference, a kind of
gallows humor. No doubt it is to humor of this kind that Ōtani,
in "Villon's Wife," is referring when he writes of "a great big
laugh at the end of the world." His wife uses these words to describe
the unexpected laughter that grips her when she learns that her
husband is not only a thief but hopelessly in debt. Her laughter is
directed at herself and her husband, who have long found life
without meaning but have nevertheless gone on living it. When
Dazai speaks of humor, then, it is of this kind of existentialist
laughter. In the very last line of *The Setting Sun*, Kazuko calls
Uehara "My Comedian." Kazuko herself, who was an elegant lady
of the nobility at the story's beginning, ends up as a comic rather
than a tragic figure, since she outlives both her mother and brother
and is determined to make some sort of life for herself and her
illegitimate child. The main character of *No Longer Human* is
a conscious comedian: Yōzō has always tried hard to make other
people laugh. When he is small his audience is his parents,
brothers, and sisters; when at school, his teachers and classmates;
as a grown-up, his friends and acquaintances. Appropriately, he
becomes a professional cartoonist.

Despair can be overcome by laughter. As Dazai observed: "Pain,
when there is too much of it, seems to transcend itself and turn
into humor." Ōtani's wife, who turns her plight into a transcenden-
tal joke, and Kazuko, who willingly makes a fool of herself, both
overcome pain and decide to live on. Yōzō becomes a mental pa-

tient, but he is not the "I" of the novel; there is a distance between him and the writer. In a postscript to his stories Dazai observed that he had written some of them out of pain and indignation, but that as he read them again he felt humor instead. That humor had arisen from the distance between Dazai the writer and Dazai the reader: the latter could look at the former with detachment and laugh at him. The haiku poet Bashō had a similar notion of humor; in order to distinguish it from the ordinary kind, he called it "lightness" (*karumi*). Apparently Dazai shared Bashō's view. In *Pandora's Box*, he wrote:

The spirit of the new age is certainly here with us. It is as light as a robe of feathers, as clean as the water of a shallow brook flowing over white sand. Mr. Fukuda, one of my middle-school teachers, once told me that Bashō in his last years advocated what he termed "lightness," placing it far above *wabi*, *sabi*, and *shiori*.* We can hardly contain our pride when we think that our age, simply by following the natural course of events, has now soared to spiritual heights so sublime that even a great genius like Bashō could not conceive of, far less attain them until his last years. "Lightness" does not mean levity. No one will understand that frame of mind until he reaches a point at which he is able to see his desires, his life itself, as nothing. It is a gentle breeze that comes after long hours of hard, agonizing labor. It is a light bird with transparent wings that was born of tense air amid the great chaos of the world. Those who do not understand it will be left behind the times, forever standing outside the current of history. Everything grows old with time. There can't be any argument about it. The peace and calm of a person who has lost everything: that is "lightness."

Pandora's Box was the first novel Dazai wrote after the Second World War. "The new age," therefore, refers to the chaotic period immediately following the war, when many Japanese felt as if they had lost everything that was dear to them. In Dazai's view, it was this sense of utter loss that led to the lightness of which he spoke. Lightness, then, comes very close to what he elsewhere called humor.

Dazai, however, was perhaps a bit too exuberant in *Pandora's*

* *Wabi, sabi,* and *shiori* are aesthetic-moral concepts Bashō advocated in his later years. Traditionally, they have been considered to represent his highest poetic ideals. *Wabi* and *sabi* imply the beauty of a simple life, while *shiori* refers to a capacity for empathy.

Box. His own works in the postwar period do not really express this "spirit of the new age." There is far more to *The Setting Sun* than lightness: it also has tenderness, sorrow, and nobility. The same can be said of *No Longer Human*, except, perhaps, that there is more sorrow and less nobility. If Dazai had come close to achieving lightness in his last years, this would surely be evident in his last novel, *Good-bye.* Indeed, this unfinished work, to judge from what there is of it, has more humor than any of Dazai's other desired effects. Its prose style is also more even than that of most other Dazai stories. Unfortunately, the novel is unfinished because Dazai killed himself. The reader is left wondering whether its hero, Tajima, will be able to say good-bye to the "tense air amid the great chaos of the world." But Dazai's suicide was probably his answer to that question. In the end he found himself unable to transcend the world's chaos. He chose to hurl himself into the muddy turbulence of the Tama River rather than to patiently seek out a shallow brook flowing over white sand.

Thoughts after Thoughts after Thoughts

In general, the formal elements of a literary work do not seem to have occupied Dazai overmuch. He was so deeply concerned with the novelist's moral attitudes that questions of plot and style appeared to him rather trivial in comparison. Consequently, he seldom discussed structural or stylistic questions in his writings. On the rare occasions when he did, he tended to minimize their importance.

Once, on one of those rare occasions, Dazai hinted at his ideas on the subject of plot. This was in a letter in which he revealed his feelings about his own story "Metamorphosis." The story describes the sad destiny of Suwa, a young girl who, after being raped by her own father, flings herself into a waterfall and becomes a carp. Recalling his frame of mind when he wrote the tale, Dazai said:

Even before I began writing the story, I had the concluding sentence in mind. It was, "Three days later Suwa's poor corpse was found under a bridge near the village." However, I cut it out after I finished the story. It was because I realized, to my despair, that my talent fell far short of elevating the story to the level of truth implied in that concluding sentence. I cleverly took an easy way out. I followed the dictum: "Aim at a sparrow on the eaves rather than at a hawk deep in the woods." When I discovered that I would have a well-constructed story but for the concluding sentence, I decided to remove the obstacle before anyone knew about it, even though I was aware that by doing so I would diminish the scale of the story. Now I know I did the wrong thing. The writer should voice his intent in his story until his voice becomes hoarse and his strength expires. He should do so even if he knows that, as a result, he will wreck his novel's structure and thereby expose himself to the attacks of the so-called critics. I am deeply regretful of what I did at that time.

At the opposite extreme, Dazai spared no pains in writing "Flowers of a Clown." This early work of his was initially an autobiographical story entitled "The Sea"; it described the aftermath of an attempted double suicide by its hero, Yōzō, and a barmaid he knew. Narrated from Yōzō's point of view, it told how he felt about the tragedy, and how he tried to rebuild his personal life after it happened. In Dazai's opinion, the story had a simple, straightforward, almost classical beauty. A few months after writing it, however, he came to dislike it so much that he drastically revised it, transposing it into the first person (with suitable monologues here and there) and cutting the original story apart, although Yōzō, not the author, is still the protagonist. "Flowers of a Clown" was the title of this new version. Clearly Dazai had been unable to put all he wanted to say or think into the character of Yōzō in the original story, and therefore had to add a part for himself. The result is that the new story is more complex—perhaps overly complex—since the events described are viewed by both Yōzō and the author-narrator. The flow of the narrative is interrupted whenever "I" appears and makes comments on the writing of the story. The author himself is aware of this. "This story is confusing in many places," he writes. "I see myself tottering along. I don't quite know what to do with Yōzō or Hida. They are irritated at my clumsy pen and want to go their own way."

A typical Dazai novel is more like "Flowers of a Clown" than "Metamorphosis" or "The Sea." Rarely does it have a plot that unravels by a single thread; rather, the flow of the story is interrupted here and there, sometimes for a disproportionate length of time. The reason for the interruption is usually for the sake of making the author's intention crystal-clear; the author has sacrificed a well-knit plot in his eagerness to clarify his theme. The interruption is usually caused by one of two factors: a multiple viewpoint or a long monologue. Conspicuous intrusion of the authorial "I" occurs in *A Women's Duel*, "Spring Bandit," "Revolving Lantern of Romance," and *Nursery Tales*, not to mention "Flowers of a Clown." In such works as "Schoolgirl," "On Clothes," and "On Keeping a Dog," "I" cannot be said to intrude into the story because he is the protagonist. Nevertheless, he gives the impression of figuring a bit too prominently for the purpose of the story. "I" is not quite so obtrusive in *No Longer Human*, but one still wonders whether the epilogue, which is written in the first person, could not have been shortened or even cut out altogether. Instances of a long monologue clogging up the flow of the story are seen in "Das Gemeine," *The New Hamlet, Parting*, and "Villon's Wife." In *The Setting Sun*, the narrative is interrupted by a lengthy quotation from Naoji's diary as well as by his suicide note. Whereas these constitute an integral part of the story, a writer more plot-conscious than Dazai would have made Naoji participate more in the action of the story instead of recording his confessions in the form of diaries and notes.

Even though he paid relatively little attention to plot construction, Dazai was exceptionally careful about one element of plot, the beginning. He seemed to believe that a good story must begin in an interesting way. "The fact that the story has an interesting beginning implies the writer's kindness," he wrote. The novelist, a humble outcast of society, should be kind to the reader, entertaining him as a clown does. To this end, a novel should begin with a sentence by which the reader will feel irresistibly drawn.

To show what he meant by "an interesting beginning," Dazai cited the opening lines of eight German short stories that he considered exemplary in this respect. Here are three of them:*

---

* These passages have been retranslated from the Japanese in order to approximate the way Dazai read them. The original stories were "Sara Malcolm" by Jacob Wassermann; "The Death of a Bachelor" by Arthur Schnitzler; and "The Earthquake in Chile" by Heinrich von Kleist.

It was toward the end of 1732. England was under the reign of George II. A London nightwatchman was making his round one night, when he came upon a young maiden lying collapsed on a road near Temple Bar.

Someone knocked at the door. Very gently.

It was when the great earthquake of 1647 was about to strike Santiago, the capital of Chile. A young boy was standing against a prison pillar. This native of Spain, named Jeronimo Rugera, had given up all hope in this world and was about to hang himself.

An interesting beginning, as conceived by Dazai, is a suspenseful beginning, one that whets the reader's appetite for more. "How about those?" Dazai asked his readers. "Aren't they well written? They make you want to read more, don't they? If I were to write a story, I'd certainly like to open it with sentences like these."

Although all storytellers wish to seize their readers' attention from the outset, Dazai's wish seems more fervent than most. In "Flowers of a Clown," for example, the author-narrator stresses the importance of its opening line ("A City of Sorrow beyond this point . . .") and says he would not erase it even if its presence ruined the entire story. The hero of "Monkey-Faced Youngster" is a novelist who believes that "the opening line determines the fate of the entire novel, no matter how lengthy it may turn out to be." As for Dazai himself, the works that are generally considered his best have the following beginnings:[*]

The mountain range at the northernmost edge of the main island of Japan is called Bonju. It is not shown on an ordinary map, because it is just a stretch of low hills less than one thousand feet long.

Please let me speak to you, sir. Please. He is an awful man. Awful! Yes, sir, he is a disgusting fellow. A rascal. I can't stand him. I just can't let him live on.

With a loud clatter the front door sprang open. The noise woke me up. But I remained in bed without saying a word, because I knew it was only my husband, arriving home dead drunk in the middle of the night.

"Oh!"
Mother uttered a faint cry as she sipped a spoonful of soup at breakfast in our dining room.

[*] These passages are from "Metamorphosis," "Appeal to the Authorities," "Villon's Wife," *The Setting Sun*, and *No Longer Human*, in that order.

I have seen three photographs of him.

One was a portrait of him in what seemed to be his childhood, for he looked about ten years old. Surrounded by many women (presumably his sisters and cousins), the child stood at the edge of a garden pond dressed in a broadly striped garment and showing an unpleasant smile on his face, his head slanted about thirty degrees to the left.

There is no doubt that these beginnings show more ingenuity than is found in the corresponding passages of most Japanese novels. The same quality is seen more clearly in some of Dazai's less famous stories. The first few paragraphs of "The Monkey Island" are tantalizingly ambiguous, paving the way for the big shock that is to follow a little later. The first couple of pages in "One Hundred Views of Mount Fuji" are devoted to discussion of Mount Fuji's vertical angles as depicted by great artists of the past, and the reader is left wondering what the story is all about. "The Criminal" tells of an attempted murder and suicide in the manner of a detective story; it certainly invites Shiga's criticism that a story should not deliberately keep the reader in suspense, that the reader should be given the same information the author has.

Dazai's concept of structure, then, must be said to be a peculiarly calculated one. In his opinion, a novel should begin with a very intriguing passage, involving the reader in the world of fiction as soon as he reads it. Once the reader is hooked, the writer can pay less attention to him and move on to what he wants to say. He need not weave an interesting plot; he may even break up the story to insert a long monologue here and there. The reader will stay with him to the end of the novel as long as he has something important to say, whether the plot is interesting or not. A good novel will grip the reader at the very beginning and never let him go until he has heard everything the novelist has to say.

Dazai's idea that the novel should above all express the author's intent is also reflected in his concept of style. He once said that "a good piece of prose is one in which 'words, charged with emotion, pour forth singing out what truly lies within the heart.' "* Dazai,

* The quotation is from the writings of Ueda Bin (1874–1916), a scholar famous for his translations of Western symbolist poetry into Japanese.

in other words, favored a style that was more expansive than deliberate. More than anything else, he wanted to say what he wanted to say; he did not particularly care about how it was said. He thought that the right words would naturally come pouring out of one's mouth if one's heart was brimming with intense emotion.

Dazai's prose style, then, can be characterized as expansive, emotional, and spontaneous. These adjectives are, of course, relative terms; no style can be completely devoid of intellectual restraint. But Dazai's style is far more spontaneous than that of any other modern Japanese writer of the first rank. Even compared with the style of Tanizaki, who termed his own style a "flowing" one, Dazai's style seems less strained, more artless. In a description of his own working habits, Dazai showed why this was so.

Hateful, hateful. Thoughts after thoughts after thoughts after thoughts. They spring up in an endless succession, filling the space all around me, till I wonder where to begin. My method in the past was to let this flood of mushy liquid congeal around my desk, cut it up into various sizes, and then patch the parts together into a piece of composition. But today I have decided to scoop up this overflowing liquid and put it down on paper just as it is, in all its shapelessness. I'm sure this will work.

Dazai is being disingenuous here: the truth is that to "scoop up this overflowing liquid" was his usual method of composition. And many of his works create the impression that this liquid had not congealed. This is particularly true of such works as "Appeal to the Authorities," "Schoolgirl," and "The Lost." It is also true of such famous passages as the restaurateur's long complaint in "Villon's Wife," Naoji's notes and Kazuko's letters in *The Setting Sun*, and Yōzō's second and third notebooks in *No Longer Human*. It is less true elsewhere in his writings, but it is always true to some extent. His sentences tend to be extra long or extra short, their subjects changing capriciously from clause to clause. The narrative logic shows unexpected leaps from time to time. His syntax is often whimsical, his grammar strained. His tempo is quick, his rhythm uneven, his tone informal if not colloquial. His paragraphs vary a great deal in length; some of the long ones last for several pages, while short ones consisting of only one word are not uncommon.

Altogether the style approaches the "stream-of-consciousness" technique, giving the impression that the writer wrote down whatever thoughts and impressions came into his mind just as they were, without paying much attention to the formal elements of prose style.

It is, of course, doubtful that Dazai's style really stemmed from artlessness. Many "stream-of-consciousness" writers have been self-conscious artists, and Dazai had plenty of models to choose from. Yet it is true that Dazai's style, more than that of any other Japanese writer, gives the impression of being spontaneous, of being spoken directly by the author. The reader can almost hear him breathing. The effect is particularly marked in his adaptations of other stories. Eulenberg, Hamlet, the Bad Badger—all speak in the Dazai fashion, once his pen has taken them over. The leading characters in his novels—Naoji, Yōzō, and many others—are as uninhibited, emotional, and moody as Dazai himself. If one likes Dazai and what he has to say, one will find his style most engaging because it is so intensely personal. If not, then reading Dazai can seem like being buttonholed by a lunatic.

Food for Losers

Dazai's ideas on the function of literature are most clearly suggested in "An Owl's Letter," a largely factual account of his lecture tour to Niigata in November 1940. Toward the end of the story the hero, a novelist named Dazai, goes to a local restaurant for dinner with a group of high school students. As dinner proceeds, the students' questions become faster and more direct:

"Do you feel guilty at all, sir, for having succeeded in becoming a novelist and living your life as such? I'm sure there are lots of people who aspire to be writers but can't be, for various reasons, and have to keep wasting their talents on other pursuits."

"You've got it the wrong way round. I became a writer precisely because I had failed at everything else."

"There's hope for me, then. I've failed at everything."

"You haven't done anything yet, young man. You can't say you've failed until you've actually tried, until you've fallen flat and hurt yourself. You say you've failed even before you try. That's laziness."

The dinner was over, and I said good-bye to the students.

"When you're in college and have personal problems, look me up," I said. "A writer can be a bum and still be able to help a bit in such cases."

In Dazai's view, then, literature is basically of little practical use and the novelist is a good-for-nothing. And yet it may be helpful to people with serious problems. But it is clear that the circumstances under which it is helpful are always exceptional ones. Dazai repeatedly stressed the uselessness of both art and artist in the practical domain. When he compared art to a violet he implied, at least in part, that art was beautiful but impractical. Similar metaphors abound in Dazai's writings: art is "an airplane that does not fly," "a steed that does not gallop," "an exploding firework," "a small box made of colored paper," etc. In *A Women's Duel*, Dazai has the medical student (that is, a practical person) jeer at her artist boyfriend as "a big idiot" and as "a dummy who has stopped growing." In a postscript to *The Declining Years* he warns his readers: "Reading my stories would not help you earn your living, nor would it help you rise in the world. It wouldn't help you in anything. Therefore, I can't much recommend these stories to you."

The reason why art and artist seemed useless is self-evident. For him, the artist was a criminal who was aware of his guilt, and a work of art was the song of a criminal on his way to the guillotine. The artist, because of his awareness of guilt, is passive toward others; he can never be aggressive. He is a social outcast because he chooses to be. He is too tenderhearted and sympathetic toward others to be a successful businessman. He would rather be Mr. Hospitality; he cannot stand to have other people pay for his drink— or even for their own drinks, when he is present. The artist is a nobleman. The rough seas of ordinary living are too much for him; he is always in danger of drowning. Even when he is fortunate enough to drift to a lighthouse, he is so timid that he cannot cry for help.

Why, then, did Dazai advise the students to come and see him if they had personal problems? Because the artist was a friend of the weak and suffering. Literature was a kind of food for losers. When a person who had failed at everything in life read a novel, he would find in it a character who exactly resembled him. He would then know that he had a friend, that, in fact, all of nature's noblemen and noblewomen were losers like him.

This being the case, the help that literature supplies is by way of understanding, sympathy, and consolation. But it is not a positive kind of help; it is not of the kind that actively stirs up the reader's courage and gives him renewed hope for life. Literature can never offer that kind of help as long as it rests on the premise that life is evil, that man is born to sin. On the contrary, it is possible that literature may cause the reader to wish for death, rather than for a new life. The reader, convinced that to live is to suffer, may choose to follow in the footsteps of Suwa, Constance, Tsuruta, and Naoji, all of whom killed themselves. So did Dazai, and the woman who died with him was someone who had come to consult him about her personal problems. The same thing might have happened to any of the students in Niigata, if they had turned to Dazai for help as he suggested. Some of his characters, of course, like Kazuko and Ōtani's wife, choose to live on. But they do so after losing all hope in life, and thereby arriving at some kind of existentialist affirmation of it. Can a literary work provide consolation to a despairing mind when its implications are nihilistic, or, at best, existentialist? For some it can, and for others it cannot; it all depends on the reader's age, temperament, and philosophy of life (Dazai would have wanted to add sex, too). For that reason, Dazai's works are balm for some and poison for others. All literature is like that to a certain extent; Dazai's case is an extreme.

CHAPTER SEVEN

Kawabata Yasunari

D URING HIS long and distinguished literary career, Kawabata
Yasunari (1899–1972) produced an immense number of theoretical and critical writings. Some of them, like *An Introduction
to the Novel, Studies in the Novel,* and *The New Composition
Reader,* dealt directly with the nature of literature. Others, like
his literary columns for newspapers and magazines, discussed individual writers and their works. For a student of Kawabata the
latter are far more interesting. His theoretical works borrowed a
great deal from Western scholars, critics, and theorists. But his
reviews show his own instinctive capacity to distinguish good
writing from mediocre. Characteristically, he looked at the work
rather than its creator; he never hesitated to praise a good story
no matter how obscure the writer, or to condemn a bad novel no
matter how famous the novelist. In consequence, he came to be
considered the foremost discoverer of new literary talent in modern
Japan. Writers whose debuts he helped include such well-known
names as Okamoto Kanoko (1889–1939), Ibuse Masuji (b. 1898),
Ishizaka Yōjirō (b. 1900), Kajii Motojirō (1901–32), Funabashi
Seiichi (b. 1904), Hōjō Tamio (1914–37), Toyoda Masako (b. 1922),
and Mishima Yukio.* This fact alone is enough to convince one

* Okamoto Kanoko, one of modern Japan's leading women writers, was
especially skilled in depicting young women reared in old, traditional families.
Ibuse Masuji, known for such tragicomic works as "The Salamander," *No
Consultations Today,* and *Lieutenant Lookeast,* is a highly respected contemporary novelist. Ishizaka Yōjirō, initially a schoolteacher, distinguished
himself by his novels vividly portraying girls of school age. Kajii Motojirō,
a meticulous stylist in the fashion of Shiga, was at his best in sketches of nature
and human life viewed through the eyes of a sensitive young man. Funabashi

that Kawabata had a very clear view of what literature is and should be, even though his novels may appear incidental in form and casual in intent. On close examination, one discovers that the novels themselves also have something to say about the nature of literature.

Reflections in a Window

One such scene appears near the opening of *Snow Country*. Shimamura, a rich Tokyo dilettante, is aboard a train going to the snow country in the north of Japan. Sitting diagonally opposite him is a beautiful girl. Her name is Yōko, though he does not yet know this. As dusk falls on the dreary landscape outside, the carriage window begins to mirror things inside the train, though in its depth it continues to show the darkening countryside. Shimamura is startled when, suddenly, a light out in the mountains shines in Yōko's eye, reflected in the window. He is deeply moved by its beauty.

Snow Country is narrated from Shimamura's point of view. The novelist, here at the outset of the novel, is suggesting to the reader what that point of view represents. Shimamura is a typically jaded modern intellectual. He is tired of living a monotonous life, like a passenger in a train tired of watching the monotonous landscape passing by. Such boredom can be broken only by the sight of some extraordinary beauty, like that of Yōko's eye sparkling in the train window. Shimamura is interested in that beauty, and in that beauty alone. *Snow Country* covers Shimamura's life over a span of nearly three years, yet he does not narrate all the events that happen during that time. He picks out only the ones that have this special beauty. All the others are not worth recounting.

Kawabata repeatedly made the same point in his critical essays. An obvious example is one of his lectures at the University of Hawaii in 1969, appropriately entitled "The Existence and Dis-

Seiichi is like Kawabata in his effort to capture the beauty of traditional Japanese women, but his heroines seem more earthy, sensual, and urbane than Kawabata's. Hōjō Tamio wrote some moving stories based on his experience at a hospital for lepers. Toyoda Masako was for a time an idol for all grade-school students interested in creative writing.

covery of Beauty." The main theme of the lecture is succinctly expressed in a little incident he describes at the beginning of the lecture, an incident he himself experienced in Hawaii. Kawabata was staying at the Kahala Hilton Hotel, which has a dining area on the terrace. As he went out there in the morning, he would see several hundred glasses placed upside down on the tables. The glasses shone brightly in the tropical sun, their bases glittering like diamonds and their sides gleaming more softly and delicately. Kawabata, who had never seen anything like it, was delighted with the spectacle. In his lecture, he suggested that literature recorded nothing but such encounters with beauty.

The parallel between this episode and the opening scene of *Snow Country* is unmistakable. To Kawabata, an artist was a seeker and discoverer of beauty. More specifically, a writer was a person who recorded his encounters with beauty. *Snow Country* is a record of such encounters.

What sort of beauty did Kawabata have in mind? He did not consider the mundane life of an average citizen good material for literature. He was opposed to the Japanese version of naturalism. "No work of art is born from observation of sufferings alone," he said, and concluded: "New 'realism' does not make good sense, whether it means a realistic representation of rural life or of urban life. If the new 'realist' stand is right, it would only indicate that the writers who take that stand today are leading a deprived existence." Life in the real world was a mixture of things true and untrue, pure and impure, sincere and insincere. A novelist leading a spiritually rich life would be able to pick out only those things in life that were true, pure, and sincere, and then rearrange them to produce an order of reality more beautiful than the everyday kind. A man living a spiritually deprived existence would not be capable of doing so.

This explains Kawabata's generally unfavorable attitude not only toward most Japanese naturalists but also toward Dazai, whose life and works he thought were "covered by gloomy clouds." It also accounts for his low appraisal of both Kafū's *During the Rains*, which he thought revealed the author's "infirmity," and

Tanizaki's *A Blind Man's Tale*, about which he said "the blind man is devoid of life and only the [Tanizaki] style is alive." Kafū and Tanizaki were not among his favorite writers, presumably because their life-styles seemed to him seriously lacking in vital qualities. Such a stand would place him closer to Shiga, and sure enough, he had a lifelong regard for him. Once, in an article entitled "Pippa Passes," he explained why:

> In literary writings and in writers' circles, we hear a lot of loud noise that disturbs the mind. Today, an average writer's view of life is generally passive, and when we come in contact with his work we feel the loneliness of a man living in a spiritually sterile world and in a humanistically barren society. Even when his view of life is more positive, that merely helps to make the noise louder. To those weary of the noise, literature debases character and discolors life. A sentimentally optimistic view of literature is apt to confuse this noise with pure sound. Shiga, however, is a person who listens to pure sound and nothing else.

Kawabata liked Shiga's works because they reflected a positive view of life, and indeed a positive kind of life. Upon reading Shiga's short story "Tree Frogs," Kawabata was reminded of Robert Browning's poem "Pippa Passes." It had the same joie de vivre, the same delight in natural beauty.

In general, then, it can be said that, for Kawabata, the best literary material was a life that was vital, positive, and pure. He praised such a life in various terms throughout his writings. Borrowing a phrase from a fellow writer, he once called it "an object aflame—the beauty of vitality," and observed that all great art is like that. Elsewhere he termed it "pure life," "genuine vitality," "purity of the wild," and "sturdy vitality." It served as one of the basic criteria in his literary reviews; he praised stories that displayed this sort of life and condemned those that did not.

Kawabata, however, differed from Shiga in one significant way: he did not idealize wild animals. For Shiga, the life of a sturdy animal in its natural setting was the ultimate model for human life. For Kawabata this was not so; animals in the wild might be living a more genuine life than men, but they were not conscious of it nor did they strive to perfect themselves. Human beings could help an animal to realize its potential because they could conceive an ideal image of it. Human beings could dream; animals could not. In "Of Birds and Beasts," Kawabata describes a young bachelor who lives with many pet animals and birds and constantly tries to improve the breed of each according to an ideal image of it. No such character ever appears in Shiga's animal stories.

"Pure life" as conceived by Kawabata, then, is dynamic. It is energy generated by striving after an ideal. To use his favorite word, it is a "longing." Deploring the fact that critics frequently called him a decadent writer or a nihilist, he once explained: "I have never written a story that has decadence or nihilism for its main theme. What seems so is in truth a kind of longing for vitality." A typical Kawabata hero longs for something so distant that it seems unattainable. Consequently, uninitiated readers took it for labor in vain or (to use another of Kawabata's favorite terms) "a waste of effort," and saw him as a man who had lost all faith in life. But life burns more purely, more beautifully, when it longs for a distant ideal. The ideal may not be attainable, but the effort to attain it is beautiful. This kind of effort is the very source of "pure life" as conceived by Kawabata. His comparison of it to fire ("an object aflame") is appropriate: it is a life that keeps burning until it either attains its ideal or burns itself out.

In this connection it is interesting to look through Kawabata's numerous book reviews and discover which books earned his warmest praise. The book that seems most deserving of that honor is a little-known work of nonfiction called *The Records of My Love*, by Yamaguchi Sato. The author was a young nurse who fell in love with a patient, a soldier wounded and crippled in the war. Against the advice of many who knew her, and in the face of hesitation by the soldier himself, who felt he was not fit to marry, she went ahead and married him. The book was her diary recording the joys and agonies of her life with him. In an extraordinarily long and enthusiastic review, Kawabata wrote:

Their love and marriage were neither unusual nor unhealthy. In our society there are countless married men and women who are physically healthy but otherwise malaised. The most bizarre domestic tragedies have become commonplace. Love not only is locked out but lies ableeding. The Yamaguchis, by comparison, appear simple, healthy, and wholesome.

They may not be termed the perfect couple, and their relationship may not plumb the depths of sensual love. But virginal, nonphysical love is not in the least unnatural. Such love is not confined to the relationship between a crippled soldier and his nurse, or even between husband and wife. The love transcends sexual union. Loving devotion exists even in things inanimate or formless; they, too, experience bliss. But Mrs. Yamaguchi does not want to be a model of devotion or self-sacrifice; she just wants to be a wife. Therein lies her agony, as well as the beauty of *The Records of My Love*.

Kawabata concludes the review by wondering if the kind of married life Mrs. Yamaguchi is leading could last. "I am sure she will do her very best to make it last," he says. "But it would not matter even if she should eventually fail. She has loved as much as is humanly possible and has found happiness as a woman in her life with her handicapped soldier-husband. If the marriage should some day break up, that would be an act of God, occurring after everything humanly possible had been done. Mrs. Yamaguchi will have lived her life to the full. And a beautiful life it is. Already, *The Records of My Love* stands as testimony to that."

There is a striking resemblance between Mrs. Yamaguchi and Yōko in *Snow Country*. Yōko is a "nurse" tending her lover, Yukio, who has been ill a long time and will soon die. She loves him intensely, all the more so because he is sexually impotent; in this way, her love keeps its maidenly purity. Because of Yukio's illness, there is an unbridgeable distance between him and Yōko. The harder she tries to bridge the distance through her love, the more intense her life becomes. She is a woman living a "pure life." That is why Kawabata makes her eyes shine so beautifully.

Yōko has a similar relationship with her younger brother Saichirō, virtually the only other person at whom her affection is directed. There is no question of a physical relationship, but he means a great deal to her. Saichirō is not sick, but he works on the railroad and always lives far away from her. She can only give him a message through a station master, or stand by the railroad and call out to him as the train passes by. Her sisterly love is all the more pure and clean because its object is far away.

The heroine of *Snow Country* is not Yōko but Komako, a young geisha who entertains hotel guests with song and dance. Although her way of life differs greatly from Yōko's, she is a variation of Yōko in the sense that her love is always directed toward some object that is unattainable. She has no brother (or if she has one, it is not mentioned in the novel), but she and Yukio were brought up together like brother and sister. As Yōko and her brother live far apart after they reach adolescence, so do the grown-up Komako and Yukio; she moves to Tokyo and he remains behind. Therefore, her love for Yukio must have had the same kind of purity as Yōko's love for Saichirō. Komako's diary, which begins with her separation from Yukio, is a record of her love, a love that cannot be consummated. In that respect, it is like *The Records of My Love*, by Mrs. Yamaguchi.

At first Komako loves Shimamura in the same pure way she loved Yukio; that is why she looks so attractive to him. She considers Shimamura a man from far away, a man as unattainable as a kabuki actor. Unfortunately, Shimamura is only too attainable, and Komako, though she tries to resist temptation, finally surrenders. The moment the unattainable becomes attainable, her love begins to lose its purity. The rest of *Snow Country* traces her steady degradation, until at last she herself realizes that painful reality and begins to repent.

Many other novels and stories by Kawabata center on this type of love, an impossible love that is pure and without stain because of its impossibility. In "The Moon in the Water," for instance, the heroine loves her husband all the more intensely because he is ill and dying; when she remarries after his death, she is puzzled and saddened—even becomes neurotic—to discover that she cannot give the same kind of love to her second husband, who is healthy. In "The Mole," the heroine faces the same problem in her first marriage, which she views romantically, while her husband just wants her to be a normal wife. The heroine of *Dandelions* is so lost in adoration of her fiancé, a rather normal young man, that she cannot bear the thought of making love to him, and ends up in a mental hospital. These heroines would have fared better if their husbands had been ill. They are as pure as Yōko, but un-fortunately they are married or engaged to normal, healthy men and are destined to lose their purity, as Komako did.

The same theme is given more dramatic expression in *The Sound of the Mountain*. Here the heroine, Kikuko, is a young woman whose affections waver between those of a Yōko and a Komako. On the one hand, she is like Yōko inasmuch as she is an eternal virgin to Shingo, her aged father-in-law, who hears the sound of his approaching death. Her feeling toward him is pure because his age and the familial relation create an insurmountable distance between them. On the other hand, Kikuko is like Komako inasmuch as she is a wife to Shūichi, a man of normal appetites who seeks to awaken her sexuality. She has yielded herself to him, as Komako yielded to Shimamura, and so is becoming less capable of the pure love she feels for Shingo. Experiencing this as a process of moral degradation, she tries hard to resist it, thereby creating tension in the novel.

In *Thousand Cranes*, Yukiko is the Yōko figure, and Fumiko the Komako figure. The former, a young woman whose beauty is sym-bolized by a thousand-crane pattern,* is a pure-hearted virgin who lives beyond the reach of Kikuji, the novel's guilt-ridden hero. Her love, however, is not to be depicted until the novel ends and its unfinished sequel, *Plovers on the Waves*, begins. More emphasis is placed on Fumiko, who yields her virginity and then disappears before undergoing further degradation. By her sacrifice, Kikuji is relieved of the guilt from which he suffered because of his father's many loves.

The heroine of *Beauty and Sadness* is yet another version of Komako. As a schoolgirl of sixteen Otoko falls romantically in love with a middle-aged novelist, who is already married. Pregnancy, only a worry for Komako, becomes a reality for Otoko, and she has a mental breakdown. Distance in time and space between her

---

* The thousand-crane pattern is a centuries-old art motif in Japan. Basically it is a stylized depiction of many cranes soaring in the sky, but there is also a variation that represents paper cranes rather than real ones. Yukiko is carry-ing a kerchief with this pattern on it when Kikuji first meets her. He always associates her with the pattern from that time on.

and her lover slowly soothes the pain, but her love itself seems to grow purer because of that distance.

The same kind of barrier between two lovers takes a rather unusual form in both *The Old Capital* and *The House of the Sleeping Beauties*. In *The Old Capital*, the barrier is created by the fact that the two central figures are twins brought up in two entirely different environments. One is a simple country girl working in a mountain village north of Kyoto. The other is a graceful young woman lovingly reared by her foster parents, who operate an old, established fabric store in the ancient capital. By its very nature their love for each other is sisterly, like Yōko's love for Saichirō, and it burns all the more passionately because of their difference in upbringing.

In *The House of the Sleeping Beauties*, physical love is ruled out by the fact that its hero, Eguchi, is a nearly impotent old man. The house in question is actually a brothel of a very strange and unusual kind: young girls are drugged to sleep throughout the night so that old men can gaze on and fondle their naked bodies. Thanks to the drug, the old men can enjoy the illusion that the girls find them desirable, though there is no lovemaking in the normal sense. What the old men are really paying for is a chance to recapture their youth. For old Eguchi, this takes the form of reminiscing to himself about his past associations with women. All we learn of these women and their love is what he remembers about them. Since memory beautifies all things, because of the long distance between the things recalled and the person who remembers them, Eguchi's past love affairs are all purified as they come back to him.

In all these instances, Kawabata used the character of a young woman to embody his concept of ideal love, a longing pure and without stain, impossible to consummate. Obviously this was because he felt that a young woman, more than anyone else, was capable of this type of love. She could love a man, no matter how far away he might be, no matter how unattainable he might be. Toward the end of *Snow Country* Komako observes, "Nowadays, only women have a capacity for real love." "Nowadays, yes," Shimamura feebly agrees. "But that's how it's always been," she replies. "Didn't you know that?" In a story called "Even Though They Fell," the narrator, who is a famous novelist, is moved to tears on reading some amateurish stories written by Takiko, a young girl who wants to be a novelist herself. "How nice a woman can be!" he says to himself, and then ponders:

Even though Takiko's four stories were little more than records of her actual life, they overflowed with the love she gave out unconditionally and limitlessly to her relatives, friends, and lovers. This fact deeply moved me. Of course, such love had been given more lofty, more profound, or more beautiful expression in many masterpieces of literature old and new, Eastern and Western. Still, Takiko's stories differed from all those in some definite way. If this sort of love existed in actual life, I thought, I would feel too embarrassed to look at it straight. As works of literature they were lacking in proper form and style, and under normal circumstances I might not have taken them seriously. But it seemed to me in my fatigued state, which made me less critical, that I could actually feel the author's naked warmth.

Takiko's love, unconditionally and limitlessly given, is like that of Komako, Yōko, and all the other Kawabata heroines discussed here. Kawabata liked to place a young woman in the center of his novel not only because she symbolized his ideal, but because she was capable of living intensely in her selfless efforts to fulfill that ideal.

There are some Kawabata stories without young heroines, though the number is small. Yet even in those instances love, or Kawabata's idea of it, is at work. One beautiful instance is a brief story called "The Moon," in which the youthful hero wants to give up his virginity to the moon. The object of his love is so distant that he cannot hope for fulfillment. And so he keeps his virginity and lives on with the kind of moral intensity that Kawabata so admired. Likewise the central character of "The Youth" is a fifteen-year-old boy who loves the narrator—admittedly young Kawabata himself—with a passion so pure and wholesome that it has a purifying effect on others. His "brotherly" love is later directed toward the Creator, a divine figure central to a nature-oriented religion of which he and his family are followers. This young man, who has handsome, almost feminine features, is in fact compared by the author to a maiden. A teenage schoolboy is also the central character of "The Diary of a Sixteen-Year-Old," the short story with which Kawabata made his literary debut. The boy's affection, almost invisible but ever-present under the surface, is directed toward his ailing grandfather, the only kin he has. The young man is a "nurse" to the dying man, and his love is all the more sincere because he knows the dying man is incapable of returning it.

Neither a maiden nor a youngster appears in *The Master of Go*, yet a similar type of love is present in it, too. Hon'inbō Shūsai, the master in the book's title, plays the game of go with the passion of an artist creating a masterpiece of art. Like a maiden who adores a man from a distance, he thinks of the game as existing on a higher plane of reality, and devotes his whole personality to attaining it, thereby living the purest, intensest kind of life. "Even when he played mahjong or pool, he took the same attitude as in playing go and entered a state of trance . . . ," the narrator says of Shūsai. "One could therefore say that the master was always true and pure. Unlike an ordinary person in a distracted state, the master seemed actually to have lost himself somewhere in the far distance." Shūsai does everything he can to attain his ideal; he dares a chronic heart ailment, and even death. The beauty of that devotion constitutes the main impact of *The Master of Go*.

To generalize, then, it can be said that Kawabata's ideas on the relationship between life and art are characterized by his concern with the pure beauty generated from the impossible longing of a romantic mind. In his view, the artist's task is to depict the beauty of a person pursuing a high ideal and living his—or more usually her—life to the full because of that pursuit. A young woman, Kawabata thought, was the most likely person to do this, although a young man or an artist was not incapable of such a pursuit if his ideal was a high one and his heart was pure.

Living for an ideal, while beautiful and pure, is also extremely dangerous; a person, in attempting to attain the unattainable, is risking his life. That person cannot live life to the full without being prepared to die at any time. Death, therefore, looms everywhere in the lives of Kawabata's heroes and heroines; it is a price they have to pay for living intensely. Thus Yōko dies a spiritual, if not physical, death at the end of *Snow Country*. Fumiko apparently commits suicide, as far as *Thousand Cranes* is concerned.* Takiko in "Even Though They Fell" is brutally murdered. The "dark girl" (she is never named) dies at the end of *The House of the Sleeping Beauties*. *The Master of Go* begins and ends with a reference to the master's death, which happened shortly after the important game described in the novel. Pure beauty, as conceived by Kawabata, is also perishable, fragile beauty. The beautiful ones die early and the ugly ones live forever, as Kikuji observes at the end of *Thousand Cranes*.

We can see now why Kawabata was so impressed by the sparkling glasses at the Kahala Hilton Hotel. Their beauty was evanescent; it would disappear the moment the sun rose higher or the observer moved a little. The glasses themselves were transparent (an adjective, incidentally, used by Kawabata to describe the clean beauty of a young woman) and breakable. Furthermore, they were described by Kawabata as sparkling like stars, which are located at an unattainable distance. Of course the inanimate glasses were not capable of longing for an ideal, but the person who looked at them was. Kawabata said he had been thinking about *The Tale of Genji* all the while he talked about the beauty of shining glasses. He did not volunteer to explain the relationship between the classical Japanese romance and modern American glasses. But at Hilo, in a sequel to that lecture delivered at the University of Hawaii, he did make clear that he and the authoress of *The Tale of Genji* shared an admiration for *A Tale of a Bamboo-Cutter*, an ancient Japanese tale about a beautiful maiden who came from the moon. In his youth he read the tale as an expression of the author's longing for the eternal virgin, as Lady Murasaki had also done centuries earlier. He felt reassured, he said, when he recently came upon the theories of today's Japanese scholars who interpreted the tale as an

---

* *Thousand Cranes* ends with Fumiko's disappearance from everyone's sight. Kikuji is sure of her suicide, as he remembers her words of the previous night that one's death lies close to one's feet. The fact that she is alive is not revealed until after the novel's sequel, *Plovers on the Waves*, begins.

embodiment of man's "longing for the infinite, the eternal, the pure." The eternal virgin of *A Tale of a Bamboo-Cutter* is named the Shining Princess, and the hero of *The Tale of Genji* is called the Shining Prince. It would have been quite natural for Kawabata, gazing at the glasses shining in the sun, to think of those old Japanese romances.

The people in Kawabata's stories, then, are purified by their longing for the infinite, which gives them a particular kind of beauty. For them, everyday life is transfigured; it has both the simplicity and the profundity of a fairy tale. "I have produced only a few works that stay close to facts," Kawabata wrote. The same applies to his well-known revelation that "Komako existed in reality, but Yōko did not." Yōko was a product of his imagination; she was his Shining Princess. Komako, on the other hand, was an idealized portrait of a real person, a young geisha he met in Yuzawa. Perhaps that is why, in the book, she is the one who loses her purity. Just how much Kawabata did idealize his real-life models can be seen from his essay about the making of "The Izu Dancer." The story, one of the most lyrical of all Kawabata's works, describes a chance encounter between a lonely high school student (the author, as he himself admits) and a troupe of traveling entertainers, a young dancer of innocent beauty among them. As he confides in the essay, written years later, the real entertainers were far less charming. The dancer's elder brother and his wife suffered from malignant tumors, apparently caused by venereal disease. The brother often changed his bandages at the public bath, right before Kawabata's eyes. The dancer's mother looked as if she never bathed at all. The dancer herself had a disproportionately small nose. Kawabata idealized them all by deliberately omitting information about their imperfections. He was like Shimamura in *Snow Country*: he selected only those events and personal characteristics capable of exemplifying the kind of ethereal beauty that never ceased to fascinate him.

A Composition Teacher, a Ghost Writer, and a Eulogist

In Kawabata's view, then, the proper function of the literary artist was to discover and reproduce the pure beauty generated by an intense life, a life lived to the full. The artist combined two abilities: an ability to see pure beauty, and an ability to represent it in literary form. Let us examine these two abilities and their likely possessors one by one.

What types of persons are best qualified to discover pure beauty? Kawabata seemed to think of three groups: little children, young women, and dying men.

It is no surprise to hear that small children have eyes to see pure beauty. Many romantic thinkers, Eastern and Western, have said something of the sort. A child's mind is fresh, genuine, innocent. Its eyes are not clouded by conventional modes of perception, and its sensitivity is not dulled by repeated exposure to the ways of the world. Everything a young child sees is a new wonder. Thus when a little child expresses itself in a piece of composition, the reader sees nature beautifully reflected in a clear mirror. "The prime value of a child's composition lies in its 'simple heart,' " Kawabata explained. "Despite the fact that a child lives a fairly egocentric life, its writing emits rays of innocent wisdom because it has a simple heart. By children's composition we are reminded that people are by nature good and beautiful, that our language is primarily for expressing human goodness and beauty."

Kawabata showed an unusual interest in children's composition. He helped to promote nationwide contests in creative writing among grade-school children, and often served on the screening committees himself. He also helped to compile *A Compendium of Model Composition* and contributed a preface to it. In the opening paragraph of that preface he declared: "A child's composition is the truest of all creative writings. It shows us literature's starting point no less than its destination." He went on to urge that the collection be read not only by students and teachers but also by adults who were neither. "All adults," he wrote, "should be reeducated by reading children's composition; they should contemplate the budding of the simple, pure life expressed therein."

Kawabata's predilection for amateur authors, as well as his passion for discovering new writers, can also be attributed to the high value he placed on the "simple, pure life." Amateur writers have more innocent eyes and fresher sensibilities than professional novelists, who tend to suffer unconsciously from affectation in both perception and expression. "I hate a professional," Kawabata once snapped, "in whom an amateur has stopped living." His literary reviews were filled with rebukes aimed at writers who had fallen into professionalism. In contrast, he always had warm praise for an amateur writer's work as yet unspoiled by affectation. It was on account of this sympathetic attitude toward amateurs that he eventually came to be considered the foremost discoverer of new literary talent in modern Japan. He took delight in reading unestablished writers' works, which many critics would have considered a waste of time. He was always willing to serve on committees that selected literary prizes; no one served longer, for instance, on the selection committee that biannually gave the Akutagawa Prize to a promising writer. At one point he even ventured to say that many writers fail to surpass their maiden works no matter how long their literary careers might last thereafter. This was so because they started off as amateurs; a maiden work was valuable because the writer was still an amateur, because he could still see with a child's eyes. Kawabata gave such lavish praise to *The Records of My Love* because of its childlike quality. Referring to that book, he remarked: "This is less an amateur writer's work than a classroom composition by an adult"—and he intended that remark to be high praise. To follow Kawabata's logic: a professional writer's work was seldom as good as an amateur's, which in turn was seldom as good as a child's.

It was no wonder that Kawabata was envious of Satō Hachirō (1903–73), who in his opinion was the only writer in contemporary Japan who could write a story from a child's point of view.* "Most works of juvenile literature written by adults are disgusting," wrote Kawabata. "If we ignore them as we should, we will be left with only one writer capable of writing a story touching on the reality of young people's lives. That is Satō Hachirō." Only Satō was able

---

* Satō Hachirō, son of a bestselling novelist, produced a voluminous amount of poems and stories for children. He was also very successful as a writer of popular songs.

to see reality through a child's eyes. What about Kawabata himself? "I don't seem to have much talent for writing juvenile literature," was his answer. "But," he continued, "I have always been ready to try my hand at it, not only because this helps me to earn a living, but because I have always felt that work of this kind might help restore vitality to my art as a novelist." He published two collections of stories for boys and girls, *Kawabata's Collected Juvenile Literature* in 1950, and *A Collection of Kawabata's Stories for Boys and Girls* in 1968. But many of the other stories that he published in various juvenile magazines still remain uncollected.

However, with all his enthusiasm for juvenile literature, Kawabata always seemed to draw a line between it and literature proper. As is apparent from his aforementioned remark, he considered writing for children a *means* to restore vitality to his art of fiction, not an end in itself. Not a single story for children is included in the latest edition of his collected works, which he edited himself.* A child's "simple heart" was important in creative writing, indeed; but that alone was not enough for writing a mature, full-fledged work of art. Juvenile literature was lacking in something that adult literature must have.

The fundamental difference between juvenile literature and literature proper was clearly explained by Kawabata when he discussed the writings of Toyoda Masako, a young girl who showed extraordinary ability in school composition:

The excellence of this schoolgirl's writings is so obvious that no one needs to have it explained. And yet in one respect her work puzzles me. In brief, her composition leaves the reader with a strangely "hollow" impression. He is filled with admiration while reading it, and yet when he finishes reading he finds almost no trace of it in his mind. Theoretically, a superior work of literature should not be like this. I begin to get frightened when I contemplate the meaning of that hollow impression. But perhaps I am taking it in the wrong way. Her book gives the reader an impression qualitatively different from that of literature proper, precisely because it is a child's composition. That qualitative difference is perhaps what

---

* Kawabata died before the entire edition was published, but he had by then finished selecting all the volumes of prose fiction. Only the essays and critical reviews were left unedited by himself.

puzzles me and gives me a hollow impression. If Toyoda is a genius, she is a genius of a rare kind: she has no aspiration. For a literary genius must of necessity be impregnated with a spiritual heightening. Little of that, however, can be recognized in her composition.

The key words here are "aspiration" and "spiritual heightening." An adult writer, being himself buried in the mire, must aspire for purity; that aspiration generates a spiritual heightening within him. A child (or a writer with a childlike mind) has that purity already and has no need to long for it. A child's composition therefore expresses no longing, and an adult reader like Kawabata, who expects to find spiritual aspiration in a literary work, is puzzled by its absence and feels dissatisfied after reading it.

It follows, then, that a writer of adult literature should ideally have not only a child's pure heart but also an adult's yearning for purity. In Kawabata's opinion, one of the persons most likely to have these qualifications was a young woman. This is not surprising when we recall his contention that maidens and young women were equipped with a capacity to love without the least expectation of receiving a reward in return. A maiden had a pure heart, which grew even purer as she loved a dying man or a brother. When such a person produced a literary work, it would reflect not only the writer's pure heart but also her aspiration, her longing, to become purer. As a result, the reader of such a work would not find it hollow; instead, he would be moved by its aspiration and longing.

Kawabata utilized this idea as a literary device in some of his works. In "The Mole," for example, the narrator is a young woman who longs to give her husband "pure love," the same kind of love she gave her mother and sisters as a little girl. The husband refuses to accept that love, which thereupon grows even more intense and pure. The same mechanism is at work in "Lyric Poem," except that the man whom the young female narrator loves not only refuses to accept her love but marries another woman and then dies, forever cutting off all hope that her love will be fulfilled. Again, in "Morning Clouds" the narrator is a teenage girl who nurtures a secret love for her teacher of Japanese, a beautiful young woman who tells her, among other things, of the impossible love embodied in *A Tale of a Bamboo-Cutter*. Appropriately the story ends with the young narrator seeing a vision of her teacher signaling good-bye in the morning clouds. In all these instances Kawabata used a young woman as his narrator because, in his view, a young woman was potentially an ideal storyteller, an ideal writer of fiction.

Some other stories by Kawabata, such as "The Moon in the Water" and "The Sister in a Dream," are not narrated by a young woman, but all the events that happen in them are told from a young woman's point of view. It was as if Kawabata tried to assume an ideal writer's position by placing himself in the position of a young woman, through whom he told the story. The reader sees, from within, a young woman pouring out her maidenly affection on a dying man, or on a man already married to her best friend. Though not so apparent, a similar device can also be observed in several of Kawabata's novels, such as *The Old Capital* and *The Waltz of the Flowers*.

A variation of the same device is seen in *Snow Country*. Shima-mura, from whose point of view all the novel's actions are told, is not a young woman; yet he can be termed a "maiden" since the quality of his aspiration resembles a maiden's. As a young man he had loved the kabuki dance. But when this "love affair" proceeded to the point at which he had to have a physical relationship with the kabuki (he felt he had to throw himself actively into the dance movement), he shrank back and gave it all up. He then acquired a new sweetheart: Western ballet. This time he was more careful: he saw to it that he never actually witnessed a ballet performed on the stage. He just dreamed of the ballet like a maiden dreaming of a distant lover. This maidenly quality within him is the main reason why Komako loves him. Kawabata, by using Shimamura as his mouthpiece, was able to let the reader see that quality early in the novel.

A similar quality is present in Kikuji, a young man who provides the author's point of view in *Thousand Cranes*. He aspires for an object that seems too beautiful and distant for him to attain: he longs for Yukiko, an eternal maiden whose beauty is symbolized by a thousand-crane pattern. Kawabata himself explained that the novel was an embodiment of his longing for the beauty of a thousand cranes soaring in the morning or evening sky. In January 1953, a few months after the first publication of the novel in book form, he also wrote a haiku:

> In the New Year's sky
> thousands of cranes hover—
> or so it seems to me.

Undoubtedly this longing is expressed through the person of Kikuji, who aspires for purity all the more because he feels he is hopelessly enmeshed in the evils of the past. His virginal quality is made even clearer in *Plovers on the Waves*, in which he marries Yukiko but shies away from physically touching her. He is a maiden even after marriage.

Kawabata's predilection for the maidenly quality in a writer is also reflected in his work as critic and reviewer. By and large, he appears to have been partial to female writers. We have seen how enthusiastically he reviewed *The Records of My Love*, by Mrs. Yamaguchi. At committee meetings to select Akutagawa Prize stories he sometimes recommended such obscure authoresses as Kawakami Kikuko, Ikeda Michiko, Oka Yōko, and Saitō Masako, and in each instance he was overruled by other committee members. This was in sharp contrast with his recommendations of male novelists, in which case other members generally agreed with him. In addition to Okamoto Kanoko and Toyoda Masako, he helped such women writers as Ōtani Fujiko, Yamakawa Yachie, and Chūjo Fumiko to get published. A passage that appears in his essay recommending Mrs. Okamoto is especially revealing of the reason why he so enjoyed authoresses like her:

Needless to say, all the beautiful women conjured up by Mrs. Okamoto are crystallizations of life and symbolize the eternal virgin and mother. They exude rays of almost religious light. This is what I meant when I once said "Her flowers, while rooted deep in the ground, bloom as radiantly as if they belonged to the water or the clouds." Those women, somewhat resembling the Virgin Mary or the Mona Lisa, are products of the Western tradition that idolized women. Japanese literature has had no such tradition—or, if one argues it had one in *The Record of*

Ancient Matters or *A Tale of a Bamboo-Cutter* or *The Tale of Genji,* it is a tradition that has long since withered away.* But without it, no art can boast true youthfulness.

The reason why Mrs. Okamoto was able to create such women in her stories was that she was a woman herself, a woman who always aspired after pure beauty. Kawabata concluded the essay by saying that he, as a novelist, wished to follow her footsteps. "In Mrs. Okamoto," he wrote, "I see a realm that I have always been seeking—in vain."

The maidenly quality, a transparent, heartfelt longing for pure beauty, is not limited to young women, however. It can be found in men, too, especially in dying men. Kawabata suggested this idea in a famous essay entitled "The Eyes of a Dying Man." The title is taken from a suicide note of Akutagawa's, which in part read: "Nature looks more beautiful to me now [after I have decided to kill myself]. You may laugh at the paradox: I am about to commit suicide when nature looks so tenderly beautiful. But nature looks beautiful precisely because it is seen through the eyes of a dying man." Kawabata heartily agreed with Akutagawa's observation. "I am convinced," he wrote, "that to the ears of an ascetic monk living in a world 'as transparent as ice,' burning incense may sound like a burning house, and a bit of ash falling from it may sound like thunder. The ultimate principle in all artistic activities lies in 'the eyes of a dying man.' "

Neither Akutagawa nor Kawabata volunteered to explain exactly why a dying man should be endowed with such an artistic gift. But the reason can be surmised, at least as far as Kawabata is concerned. It has to do with the fact that a dying person is physically inactive, if not incapacitated. He may be mentally normal and capable of forming a desire, yet he is lacking in the physical capacity to fulfill that desire. In other words, he is best qualified to be a dreamer, a person who harbors an impossible dream. His dream always remains a dream, since he cannot take

---

* A principal figure in the Japanese mythology as embodied in *The Record of Ancient Matters* is a female, the Sun Goddess. Reference has already been made to woman worship as portrayed in *The Tale of Genji* and *A Tale of a Bamboo-Cutter.*

physical action. Nature looks beautiful to him, because he cannot touch it. A young woman looks beautiful to him, all the more because he knows there is no chance of his marrying her. He can only beautify her in his imagination.

Kawabata depicted in his fiction some dying men who clearly fall in this category. In "The Moon in the Water," it is the dying husband who appreciates the beauty of nature, not only of the garden variety, but of his young, maidenly wife; he is a dreamer who longs to catch the image of the moon reflected in the water. In *Snow Country*, the dying Yukio seems to be the only person (except the narrator Shimamura) who appreciates the virginal beauty of Yōko; the villagers think of her as an odd person and not much more. In *The Sound of the Mountain*, the story is narrated from the point of view of Shingo, an aged man only too aware of his approaching death. The maidenly beauty of the heroine Kikuko is intensified, since it is seen through "the eyes of a dying man." The same can be said of *The House of the Sleeping Beauties*: the "beauties" are all the more beautiful because they are seen through the eyes of old Eguchi, who knows his days are numbered.

As a critic, too, Kawabata paid high respect to the works of dying writers. Thus he much admired Akutagawa's "Cogwheel," despite the fact that Akutagawa was not among his favorite writers, because he saw behind it "the eyes of a dying man." He called *Miniature*, by Tokuda Shūsei (1871–1948), "the greatest novel of modern Japan," though it was left unfinished at the author's death. Referring to "An Unpleasant Feeling" and "By the Abyss of Death," by Takami Jun (1907–65), he implied that these works were masterpieces because the author was dying of cancer, and that for him this fact could be considered a stroke of luck.* Kawabata also

---

* Tokuda Shūsei, one of the "four pillars" of Japanese naturalism, was a master artist at depicting the hard-pressed lives of middle- and lower-class people in a detached, realistic manner. Though generally averse to naturalism, Kawabata made an exception for Tokuda and paid the highest respect to him. Takami Jun, basically a writer of *ich-Roman*, produced a number of autobiographical stories full of his penetrating observations on the life around him. His friendship with Kawabata seems to have been through extraliterary activities in the main, such as the projects of the Japan PEN Club and the establishment of an institute in modern Japanese literature.

was an unwavering patron of Hōjō Tamio, a young writer dying of leprosy. "It is a wonder of literature," he wrote of Hōjō, "to make us see a man living a more vital life than ours, in spite of the fact that he has been effectively prevented from living in society." Hōjō was able to live a vital life because he knew he was dying; he had gained "the eyes of a dying man."

We have established that in Kawabata's view three classes of people—little children, young women, and dying men—were best qualified to see the "pure beauty" that comes of a life lived to the full. His writings, both in prose fiction and in literary criticism, substantiate that view. It does not necessarily follow, however, that he considered these classes of people to be the best writers; in fact, it would have been strange if he had, since they generally lack the literary skill to articulate what they see. They had to be helped out by those who possessed such skill. A little child had to be helped out by a composition teacher; a young woman, by a ghost writer; and a dying man, by a funeral orator.

That a little child must be assisted by a composition teacher needs little explanation. A child has clear eyes to see and a simple heart to feel, yet it has to learn how to express what it sees and feels. Language is man-made and social; written Japanese, in particular, has to be learned, since it is considerably different from conversational Japanese.* When a child produces a piece of composition, it consciously or unconsciously uses expressions it has learned from the teacher. "To be sure, composition is expressive of the child's life and sentiments," wrote Kawabata in his preface to *A Compendium of Model Composition*, "yet it is also a manifestation of the teacher's mind and character. That is the way I strongly feel as I read this collection. These pieces are not products of the children alone. Passages that seem to have come most naturally from a child's pen can also be said to have been co-authored by its teacher."

---

* The most conspicuous difference between written and spoken Japanese is that the former is lacking in a certain type of auxiliary verb, with which most sentences in the latter are concluded. Theoretically it is possible to write in conversational Japanese, and in fact some people do (Tanizaki called this the "conversational style," as we saw in Chapter 3), but it is far from common practice.

In regard to the deficiency of young women as writers, there is a famous passage by Kawabata in his essay "The Pure Voice":

In all the arts a maiden is a person to be sung of rather than a person to sing. In theatrical art, and in literary art in particular, a maiden's purity is delineated more capably by an adult woman or by a man than by the maiden herself. This is sad, but we will not grieve too much when we remind ourselves that all arts are a way of perfecting oneself.

A maiden, Kawabata seems to be saying, is no longer a child and therefore cannot write like one. On the other hand, she cannot produce a work of adult literature because she is too inexperienced as a literary artist. Within herself she has the longing, the aspiration, characteristic of a young maiden, yet she is too young to give it mature expression. Art is a process of self-perfection, and a maiden is just at its threshold. The maiden's predicament as writer lies in this paradox: being young, she has something invaluable in herself, but she cannot articulate it precisely because she is young. "Her childlike, sweet beauty is likely to fade if she approaches too close to literature," Kawabata once lamented. He made this dilemma the theme of "Even Though They Fell." One of its heroines, Takiko, has "beauty and goodness like eternal nature itself," but those qualities remain as precious ingredients for literature, without ever being made into a mature work of art. When she attempts to transform them into a work of literature, only "scribbles" emerge. Similar scribbles are produced by Komako in *Snow Country*, a diary-keeper and avid reader who takes notes as she reads novels and stories. As a young woman she possesses invaluable ingredients for literature, but she must wait until someone else comes along and transforms them into literature on her behalf.

Herein arises the need for a ghost writer. An older woman or man, who may not be living a life worthy of literary expression, but who understands literature well and has acquired the necessary powers of expression, should speak out on behalf of a young woman. This, however, is a rare talent. Kawabata once declared himself so disappointed with the professional women writers of his time that he dared to say: "I cannot help wondering whether all our women novelists' works have not been written by someone else." However, he did make some exceptions, notably for Okamoto Kanoko, who he thought had never lost a childlike quality even after growing up. Among male novelists he thought Ishizaka Yōjirō singularly gifted in this respect. Before becoming a professional writer, Ishizaka was a teacher of Japanese at a secondary school for girls and therefore had had an almost ideal preparation for becoming the type of novelist Kawabata admired most. Besides Ishizaka, Kawabata expressed his envy of the talent of Ryūtanji Yū (b. 1901), a writer who specialized in stories for young girls. It has already been mentioned that Kawabata himself posed as a ghost writer in such stories as "The Mole" and "Lyric Poem."

Kawabata's idea that a dying man must be helped to articulate his vision also seems logical enough. A person nearing death is usually unable to write, even when he is known to be an expert writer. The cases of Akutagawa and Tokuda are exceptional; few writers have such a persistent creative urge. Moreover, if a person acquires special powers of perception by virtue of his nearness to death, theoretically he will reach the height of his power at the very moment of death. But a dead person reports nothing. Here, then, is another paradox: nearness to death may give a person an extraordinary ability to see, but it takes away from him the ability to express what he sees. From this arises the need for a eulogist, a funeral orator who extolls the virtues of a dying or dead man.

It is true that a eulogist—or anyone else for that matter—cannot delve into a dead man's mind. Yet a dead man has no mind. A dead person lives only in the minds of his friends who outlive him and keep his image in their memories. A living man has a social identity, but he is the only one with direct knowledge of his own mind. When he dies, however, his identity is, as it were, dissolved into many pieces and enters the minds of those who knew him. In a sense, his mind becomes accessible to his friends for the first time when he dies. Kawabata even thought that the friends who witness the last moments of his life receive some kind of revelation about it. To Kawabata, the way one died was symbolic of the way one had lived. "It can be said," he wrote, "that the cause of one's death is one's entire career." The people who see a friend die are thus uniquely qualified to speak out on his behalf. And that was what a eulogy or funeral oration was all about.

Holding the views that he did, Kawabata wrote a number of eulogies and obituary essays himself. He was even nicknamed "the undertaker." His eulogy on Yokomitsu Riichi (1898–1947) remains one of the most celebrated of its kind in modern Japan. He also wrote eulogies or obituary essays on or shortly after the deaths of Iketani Shinzaburō (1900–1933), Naoki Sanjūgo (1891–1934), Hōjō Tamio, Jūichiya Gisaburō (1897–1937), Okamoto Kanoko, Tokuda Shūsei, Kataoka Teppei (1894–1944), Shimaki Kensaku (1903–45), Takeda Rintarō (1904–46), Nagai Kafū, Aono Suekichi (1890–1961), Takami Jun, Itō Sei (1905–69), Mishima Yukio, and Shiga Naoya.* These were writers of widely different schools and styles, some naturalistic and others romantic, and yet Kawabata praised them all for one virtue in the main, namely their devotion to their art. They were artists to their very fingertips and assiduously tried to improve their art to the very end of their lives. Many of them, in Kawabata's appraisal, had succeeded in doing so. Now that they were dead and no longer able to write, Kawabata took over; he wanted to record how they died and to suggest ways of reevaluating their works. In this sense, Kawabata's obituary essays resemble postscripts to the late authors' collected works. The authors themselves could not write the postscripts because they had died.

---

* Yokomitsu Riichi was a close literary ally of Kawabata's in the heyday of the Neo-Sensualist Movement, of which the two were the undisputed leaders. A tireless experimenter like Kawabata, he died before realizing his full potential as a novelist. Iketani Shinzaburō, who wrote both drama and prose fiction, was close to Kawabata as a member of the Neo-Sensualist group. Naoki Sanjūgo, known mainly for his popular samurai stories, shared with Kawabata an interest in the game of go. Jūichiya Gisaburō, another Neo-Sensualist, helped Kawabata in founding a new literary magazine. Kataoka Teppei was a Neo-Sensualist at first, but later joined the proletarian literary movement and then became a writer of popular fiction. Shimaki Kensaku, a novelist as well as an agrarian reformer, wrote essays and prose fiction that appealed especially to young readers because of their idealistic moralism. Takeda Rintarō was skilled in portraying oppressed plebeian life in Japan during the 1930's. Aono Suekichi, a critic and journalist, was one of the leading theorists in the later phases of the proletarian literary movement. Itō Sei led a versatile and productive career as a poet, novelist, essayist, social critic, literary theorist, professor of English, and translator of James Joyce and D. H. Lawrence.

Some of Kawabata's novels and short stories could be seen as eulogies. The most obvious is *The Master of Go,* which was written shortly after the death of the master, Hon'inbō Shūsai. It eulogizes Shūsai as an artist tirelessly trying to produce a masterpiece even when he was dying. In a more metaphorical sense, *Snow Country* is a eulogy for Yōko, an ethereal maiden whose beauty perishes at the novel's end, and for Komako, a more earthly maiden whose beauty dies a slow death in the second half of the novel. Likewise, *Thousand Cranes* eulogizes the womanly beauty of Mrs. Ōta, who commits suicide in the middle of the novel, and the virginal beauty of Fumiko, who fades out of sight at the end. *The Sound of the Mountain* could be read as a novel eulogizing Yasuko's sister, whom the hero could not marry because of her untimely death. Among Kawabata's short stories, "Memorial Poem" is quite obviously a eulogy, as the title indicates. To be included in this category also are "The Diary of a Sixteen-Year-Old," "An Undertaker," "The Death of a Knight," "Letters to My Father and Mother," "Even Though They Fell," "The Cold Wind," "The Year's End," "Tamayura," "Nature" . . . the list seems to go on forever.

Beauty, Sincerity, and Sadness

On January 9, 1968, Japan's leading long-distance runner, Tsuburaya Kōkichi, killed himself at the age of twenty-seven. He slashed his throat at his lodgings in Tokyo. His suicide notes were published in the newspapers. One of the notes was addressed to his parents and relatives, whom he had visited over the New Year's vacation. It was written in a simple, almost pedestrian style, beginning with "Father, Mother, I enjoyed your *tororo* rice.* I enjoyed your dried persimmons and rice cakes, too." The note went on to thank his many brothers and sisters and their spouses, one by one, for the hospitality they had given him during his last visit. It also named each of his seventeen young nephews and nieces, and urged them to become respectable people when they grew up. The

---

* *Tororo* is made of a kind of yam grown in Japan. The yam, grated and seasoned, is usually served on boiled rice or barley. In some areas of Japan it is one of the special dishes for the New Year's season, as it obviously is in Tsuburaya's hometown, Fukushima.

note concluded: "Father, Mother, I am far too tired to keep on running. Please forgive me. I don't know how to apologize to you for all the pain and trouble you went to on my behalf. I wish I had been living with you."

Kawabata was deeply moved upon reading this suicide note. After citing it in its entirety, he offered to explain why: "In the simple, plain style and in the context of the emotion-ridden note, the stereotyped phrase 'I enjoyed' is breathing with truly pure life. It creates a rhythm pervading the entire suicide note. It is beautiful, sincere, and sad." Kawabata then observed that this suicide note was not inferior to similar notes written by reputable writers, despite the fact that Tsuburaya was an athlete who boasted no special talent in composition. Kawabata even felt ashamed of his own writings, he said, when he compared them with this note.

Obviously, Kawabata saw the doomed Tsuburaya as an ideal writer. To him, Tsuburaya was both dying man and child. He was also a "maiden," in the sense that he was a dreamer always dreaming of a new athletic record. What is interesting here, however, is the language in which Kawabata described the suicide notes. An ideal work of art, he seemed to be saying, should impress the reader as being beautiful, sincere, and sad, just like Tsuburaya's notes. Let us take each of these terms in order.

It has already been noted that beauty, especially pure beauty, was conceived by Kawabata as an important literary effect. Both Yōko's shining eyes and the glasses sparkling in the Hawaiian sun have been mentioned as examples of things from which such beauty emanates. The beauty is "pure" in the sense that it is generated from an energy wastefully consumed, an energy used to reach out for an ideal far beyond its reach. It is like the beauty of a maiden, who is capable of loving a person with no expectation of having her love consummated. This kind of beauty necessarily has a dream-like quality, since it is based on an aspiration for the unattainable. A practical person interested only in the attainable would have nothing to do with it. Freshness, or naïveté, is also associated with it, for a person experienced in the ways of the world tends to lose his dreams; he knows his limitations and is prone to adjust his aim accordingly.

It is not difficult to see a relationship between this type of beauty and sincerity. Sincerity is an aesthetically beautiful but also moral manifestation of pure life-energy. A person living a pure life can be said to be living a sincere life from a more moralistic point of view, for he is trying to live his life to the full. He has set a very high ideal for himself and is doing his best to attain it, in disregard of his more mundane interests; he is an idealist, endeavoring to achieve his ideal at all costs. In Kawabata's view, this is what it means to be a man of sincerity, of integrity.

Kawabata at times used the word "goodness" in a similar sense. We have already cited his remark that "by children's composition we are reminded that people are by nature good and beautiful." We can now see how appropriate the parallel of "good" and "beautiful" is in that remark. In "The Izu Dancer," one of the few words uttered by the heroine in the entire story is that the hero is a "good" man; she repeats it three times. In *Snow Country* also, Komako calls Shimamura a "good, honest person" and offers to send her entire diary to him. And in the climactic scene of the novel, Shimamura calls Komako a "good" girl, and then a "good" woman, which she misunderstands momentarily, since she is, at this point, no longer a maiden physically or metaphorically.

Sadness, the third component of an effective literary style, also stems from a life lived in purity and sincerity. Kawabata took care to point out that the relationship was a natural one, even though it might not be apparent at first. "In the Japanese language," Kawabata once explained, "the word 'sadness' is related to the word 'beauty'. . ." Appropriately enough, the only major novel of his that presents a novelist for its hero has the title *Beauty and Sadness*. In this work he made frequent use of those two words, in both their substantive and their adjectival forms. Interestingly, when he used the word "sadness" (*kanashimi*) or "sad" (*kanashii*), it was always written with a Sino-Japanese character different from the one in standard use: the ideogram was *ai* (also *ai* in Chinese) instead of the usual *hi* (*pei* in Chinese). And another reading of the character *ai* is *aware*, meaning "pathos." Most likely, then, it was pathos that Kawabata meant.

In traditional Japanese aesthetics, "pathos" referred to an emotional impact that emerged when a person was confronted with an immense cosmic power and was sadly made aware of the mutability of human life. It manifested itself typically when a noblewoman of graceful beauty suffered a disaster by the hand of some mysterious superhuman force. Seen in this light, Kawabata's predilection for this type of literary impact is not hard to understand. A person living a "beautiful" and "sincere" life—that is, a person living his or her life to the full—is most likely to feel "pathos," if only the pathos of an unfulfilled (because unfulfillable) goal. The unattainability of his goal enables him to live with great intensity, but at the same time it makes him prone to frustrations and disasters on a superhuman scale. An intense life necessarily involves many risks, and the beauty of maidenhood is inevitably short-lived. Kawabata's favorite type of beauty was delicate, fragile, and perishable; when it perished, sadness ensued. Yōko's voice is "so beautiful that it sounds sad," Tsuburaya's suicide note is "beautiful, sincere, and sad." In short, anything truly beautiful is sad and anything truly sad is beautiful—as Dazai, too, observed.

The dominant emotional impact of a Kawabata novel can certainly be described as "beautiful, sincere, and sad," although the proportions in which these three components are present may differ from one work to another. The overall impact, however, necessarily remains the same, as long as the novel depicts a person who lives intensely. Most of Kawabata's novels could be retitled *Beauty and Sadness*—that is, if we assume that "sincerity" is partially implied by these other two qualities.

It is worth noting that Kawabata in his own works of fiction sometimes delineated a person touched by a combination of beauty and sadness. For instance, in *Beauty and Sadness* itself, there is a scene in which Taichirō, a young scholar in Japanese literature, tells of an episode concerning the recent excavation of the grave of Princess Kazu (1846–77), an unfortunate young noblewoman who was forced to marry a shogun for political reasons despite the fact that she loved another person. The excavators find, alongside the princess's skeleton, a wet photographic plate that faintly shows the figure of a young nobleman. Before anyone has had a chance to examine the photograph in broad daylight, the figure has faded away. While many assume that the figure must have been that of her husband, one museum staff member fancies that it might have been the portrait of the princess's lover, whom she was unable to marry. Taichirō, very much attracted to the latter fancy, terms the whole episode "beautiful, charming, and ephemeral." He also shares the museum employee's view that the episode, having such ephemeral beauty, would make a superb work of fiction if only some writer would take the pains to write it up. Doubtlessly Taichirō's feelings reflect Kawabata's view of literary and aesthetic impact. Princess Kazu, a young lady who bestows her maidenly love on a man beyond her reach, is a typical Kawabata heroine; in fact Otoko, the heroine of *Beauty and Sadness*, is very much like her. It seems reasonable to assume that through Taichirō Kawabata is explaining to the reader the nature of the emotional impact he is trying to create through *Beauty and Sadness*.

Kawabata did the same thing in a more subtle way in the concluding scene of "The Izu Dancer." There, the young hero has just bidden farewell to the heroine, a thirteen-year-old dancer with whose troupe he has enjoyed a brief tour through the Izu Peninsula. He has been deeply moved by the innocent beauty of the maiden, but he knows he has to leave her, and he does. As his boat embarks he weeps unashamedly, and when a fellow passenger asks him why he is so sad he replies, with simple honesty, that he has just parted with someone. He is in such a "beautiful and vacant" state of mind that he is able to accept any kindness offered to him by others. Beauty, honesty, sadness—they are all there and felt by the young hero, and it is on this emotional note that "The Izu Dancer" comes to a close. Kawabata clearly wanted the reader to experience the same kind of beauty, honesty, and sadness.

A similar scene concludes part one of *Snow Country*. Here again the hero has said good-bye to the heroine and is on a train back to Tokyo. Listening to the sound of the train wheels, Shimamura remembers some of Komako's words; they seem to indicate that she is living her life to the full. Among the few passengers aboard the train are a red-cheeked girl and a man in his fifties; they chat with each other—so much so, in fact, that they seem to be going on a distant journey together. When the train pulls in to a certain station, however, the man says to the girl: "Perhaps we'll have a chance to meet again some time," and hurriedly gets off. Shimamura, now realizing that the man and the girl were mere strangers who had happened to meet on the train, suddenly feels like weeping and recalls, once again, that he has himself parted with someone. This episode, which may seem unrelated to the main plot of *Snow Country*, is really Kawabata's way of suggesting how he wanted the novel to affect the reader. He wanted the reader to feel like weeping, as Shimamura did. He would have liked the reader to be moved, as Shimamura was, by the beauty, sincerity, and sadness that characterize the relationship between the hero and heroine. In other words, Shimamura himself is an ideal reader of a Kawabata novel.

Artlessness of a Child

In *An Introduction to the Novel*, Kawabata emphasized the importance of plot in prose fiction. Referring to the famous Akutagawa-Tanizaki controversy on the "plotless" novel, he expressed his agreement with Tanizaki, who favored a well-constructed plot. He likened Akutagawa's longing for the lyrical spirit to Walter Pater's contention that all arts would approach close to the condition of music if they were able. He repudiated this idea as being outdated:

Such an idea should be considered detrimental to the development of the novel, I think, because it proposes to use older, evaluative criteria for appraising the artistic value of the novel, a genre that had a late start and was not established in the present form until the nineteenth century. When one considers the fact that the unique kingdom of the novel emerged in response to the increasing complexity of human reality, one must conclude that the value of the novel lies heavily in its plot, by means of which complexities are brought to order. If the modern novel aims, as it should, at the interpretation and criticism of man's life, plot, which generates thoughts unique to the novel, must be said to participate in determining the value of the work in an especially significant way. The role of plot becomes even more important when one realizes that the substance of the novel is not so-called reality—factual reality consisting of coincidences—but condensed reality given a focus by means of plot.

This is a Western concept of plot. And, indeed, here as elsewhere in the book, Kawabata admitted to having resorted frequently to

Western authorities, especially to R. C. Moulton and E. M. Forster, in formulating this and other ideas on the art of the novel. Later, he bases his analysis of plot largely on Aristotle's idea of a beginning, a middle, and an end, all three being united by the law of causality. Starting from there, he goes on to discuss the structure of various novels by such Japanese writers as Sōseki, Shiga, and Akutagawa.

However, Kawabata's actual practice in writing fiction was generally in sharp contrast to the theories he voiced in *An Introduction to the Novel*. Many novels of his do not have tightly knit plots, as Tanizaki's novels do. They are lacking in a beginning, a middle, and an end—especially an end. Kawabata himself characterized his novels by that fact: "It can be said that my novel could end at any point," he once said, "and it can also be said that it never has an end." No other Japanese novelist has left so many works without an end. "Fire in the South," "Fire Festival on the Sea," "Crystal Fantasy," "Letters to My Father and Mother," "Memorial Poem," *Asakusa Festival*, "The Old Home," *The Waltz of the Flowers*, *Plovers on the Waves*, and *Dandelions* were all left unfinished, although, except for the last, the author had many more years to live after writing them. One is never certain whether *The Dancers* and *The Old Capital* have ended where they do. One is not sure, either, whether "The Bridge," "Wintry Rain," "Sumiyoshi," and "The Sumida River" were intended to be parts of a single novel or independent short stories. Even a reader as perceptive as Mishima Yukio thought, when the opening section of "One Arm" appeared in a magazine, that it was an independent short story; he was surprised, and ashamed of his misjudgment, when he found that the story was being continued.

Mishima need not have been ashamed, because Kawabata himself at times did not seem to know whether his own work had ended. When he finished serializing *The Lake* in a magazine, he wrote down the words "The end" at the finish of the last installment. But when he published it in book form four months later, he cut out what originally had been the last installment and chose to consider the novel unfinished. *The Master of Go* seems to have a fairly definite ending, but after its publication Kawabata thought he might later expand it to include more material on the hero's death. For whatever reasons, the expansion never took place. As for *Thousand Cranes* and *The Sound of the Mountain*, Kawabata reflected that they both should have ended with their first chapters; the remainder of these novels, he thought, was merely emotional overflow of these first chapters.

An even more extreme case is *Snow Country*. He had at first planned to write it as a short story. In a sense he did so, for the work could conceivably have ended with the scene where Shimamura, on a cold morning, watches Komako's bright red cheeks reflected in the mirror—a scene that echoes Yōko's evening mirror scene near the beginning of the novel. As if to prove that Kawabata had written it as a short story, the name Komako never appears throughout this part of the novel; she is nameless, merely a shadow of Yōko. But Kawabata kept on writing its sequel until he reached the departure scene, where Shimamura sees Komako's bright red cheeks through a shining windowpane at the railway station. Apparently deciding to end the novel at that point, Kawabata wrote down the words "The end" when he first published this part in a magazine. But he later reconsidered; again he went on to add more parts, and when *Snow Country* appeared for the first time as a novel in 1937, it ended with the celebrated scene where Komako misunderstands Shimamura's words "You are a good woman." After the publication, Kawabata was once again assailed with the feeling that the novel's conclusion did not harmonize with its beginning. He also wanted to create a fire scene. So he resumed writing and published the continuation in two parts, in 1940–41. These, however, did not satisfy him. He tried again, with better results, in 1946–47. Thus the 1948 edition of *Snow Country* ended with Komako holding the unconscious Yōko in her arms by the burning cocoon warehouse. This is the edition generally considered to be the standard one today. But Kawabata still did not seem absolutely certain that it had the right ending. "Perhaps," he wrote, "I should not have made those additions." A shortened version of *Snow Country*, written in his own hand, was found in his study after his suicide in 1972; this one ended, interestingly enough, with the morning mirror scene. It can therefore be said that *Snow Country* has at least four different endings. Kawabata himself once conceded that it was "the sort of work that can be cut off at any point."

Why did Kawabata, who advocated a novel that had a beginning, a middle, and an end, in practice write novels that could, by his own admission, end almost at any point? He attributed it to his "bad habit" of writing a novel part by part over a period of time and publishing it piecemeal in different magazines. He knew it was a bad habit, but he could not help it. "Having had it for so long, it has become second nature to me," he explained. "Very likely I shall never be able to change this habit, my inborn character being lazy and unmethodical. Nor shall I be able to gain the kind of financial security during my lifetime that will enable me to withhold publication of a novel until it is all finished. Perhaps I am going to die without ever having written a single work that I really wanted to write. All I shall have written will be works produced for expediency's sake." There is a sad note in these lines, and Kawabata was undoubtedly sincere when he wrote them. Yet the fact remains that many Kawabata novels, structureless though they tend to be, stand as fine works of literature. *Snow Country* does not seem to lose its artistic value because of its looseness in plot. *Thousand Cranes* reads like a sophisticated modern novel as it is, even though Kawabata considered it—or said he considered it—a first chapter expanded through dilution. Perhaps one should look beyond Kawabata's own words and seek further explanations, even if Kawabata (for whatever reason) would have rejected them. At least three such explanations will be offered here.

First, it seems quite likely that the structure of a typical Kawabata novel owes much to the stream-of-consciousness technique. There is plenty of evidence to prove that Kawabata, a tireless experimenter in his youth, was at one time interested in the newly emerging technique of the novel in the West. In *An Introduction to the Novel*, for instance, he referred to the writings of Joyce and Proust. Although he warned that a beginner in creative writing should adhere to a more conventional concept of plot, he defended these experiments by saying that they were an extension of plot rather than a negation of it. Largely following E. M. Forster, he also raised four questions that challenged the conventional definition of plot: (1) Can't a novel grow by itself, without any preconceived plan by the author? (2) Can't a novel have an "open" ending? (3) Can't the novelist follow wherever the work seems to beckon, so that the ending may surprise even himself? (4) Isn't the traditional concept of plot no more than a superstition, an idea conceived primarily for dramatic literature and misapplied to the novel? Kawabata thought Proust and some novelists of the younger generation had already answered each of these four questions in the affirmative. From the tone of his remarks one can see his own answers were all in the affirmative, too.

Kawabata produced several works in which the Western stream of consciousness is unmistakably present. The best known is "Crystal Fantasy," which includes several lengthy passages that record the chaotic progression of images through the heroine's mind. Another early Kawabata story, "Needles, Glass, and the Fog," is dotted with parentheses, giving the heroine's line of thought in the form of word lists. "The Footsteps" has a disproportionately long passage cataloging the images of people's feet as they pass through the hero's mind.

There are other examples in which Kawabata, while not using the Joycean technique, made the stream of consciousness define the structure of the story. Stories that consist entirely of monologues, such as "Lyric Poem," "Memorial Poem," and the Sumiyoshi tetralogy are good examples. Stories that consist entirely of letters, such as "The Mole," "A Letter," and "Letters to My Father and Mother," also fall in the same category. The flow of the protagonist's consciousness contributes much to the structure of the novel in *The House of the Sleeping Beauties,* in which most of the action takes place in Eguchi's mind.

Kawabata himself was generally reluctant to credit Western experimentalists with influencing the structure of his own works. In a well-known passage he explained his creative methods as follows:

I like to write with the flow of associations, which emerge one after another as I write on. Perhaps all writers are like that, but I suspect I am more addicted to the habit than most. I am probably lacking in ability to screen my associations. I could defend myself by saying, categorically, that the new "psychological" writers—the so-called stream-of-consciousness writers—like Joyce, Woolf, Proust, and even Faulkner have also produced a literature of associations and memories. But I have always felt that their kind of psychological novel reflects the infirmities, corruptions, and derangements of the modern age, in sharp contrast to the solid, well-balanced classics of older times.

As he made clear later in the same essay, Kawabata preferred to use an associational technique that was distinctively Japanese. In his view, *The Tale of Genji*, *The Pillow Book*, and linked verses all depended on association, and that associational structure had been nowhere so popular as in premodern Japan.

The difference between the Western stream of consciousness and Japanese associational structure is suggested in the passage cited above. As Kawabata saw it, the former reflected the loss of a coherent world-view in the modern age, whereas the latter did not. Associational technique in Japan was a result of not forcing a man-made pattern upon life; like Kawabata, the premodern Japanese were lacking in the ability—or the desire—to screen their associations. In *Studies in the Novel* Kawabata observed:

The Japanese have been said to be simple-minded and unable to devise too complex a plot, so that the literary works they produce are in the main simple and natural. But, in my opinion, this feature of Japanese literature is due less to national character than to the views of Japanese writers concerning the extent to which logic and artifice may be allowed in the novel. To be natural, to be true to nature—this has been the basic principle pervading all the arts in Japan, both past and present.

Here, then, is a second possible explanation for the apparent lack of structure in a Kawabata novel: following the Japanese literary tradition, he wanted to be natural, to be free of artifice, in devising a plot. His novels were relatively formless, as life is formless. Some of them have no real ending, since life flows on forever. A linked verse could end at any point in terms of plot—if it can ever be said to have a plot—and so could *The Pillow Book*. One can never be sure whether *The Tale of Genji* is really brought to a conclusion. A Kawabata novel is like all three in this respect.

Finally, the lack of plot in a Kawabata novel is probably connected with his interest in children's composition. We have already seen that Kawabata considered children's composition the beginning and end of literature. And a young child's composition is often lacking in a tightly knit structure. A child tends to jot down whatever comes to mind at the moment, without giving much thought to the overall structure of the piece. A child's associations are carefree, unpredictable, and unrestrained. It would be no wonder if Kawabata, consciously or unconsciously, saw an ideal type of literary structure as emerging from a child's mind.

Kawabata once quoted a child's composition that, he thought, had a good deal to suggest about the art of writing. It was written by a boy in the second grade on the occasion of a playmate's death:

Yesterday Ritsuko died. Ritsu died, though it was so cold. She was just four years old. Light snowflakes were coming down, hanging icicles were there, and it was cold, but she died. I was lonely when I thought of dead Ritsu going up to heaven and becoming a star. I made snowballs and threw them at the icicles. I threw again and again. The icicles fell.

Kawabata tried to analyze this composition and ran into a number of difficulties, such as whether the refrain "it was cold" was effective, and whether the second half of the composition went naturally with the first. He added: "All these speculations probably arise from my groundless suspicions, for a child writes with almost complete artlessness. We adults are therefore startled at the way sentences follow one after another in the first half of this composition. We also envy the little writer for giving no explanation about the dead girl." Ritsu's death, the cold weather, her age, snow and icicles, heaven and the star—the little writer wrote down everything just as it came to his mind. In this way, the composition came to have an associational structure without the writer's being aware of it.

Kawabata's fondness for children's composition also throws light on his concept of literary language. In brief, he both admired and tried to use a style that was simple in vocabulary and syntax but complex in meaning and connotation. Like the style of the second-grader quoted above, it was so artless as to raise insoluble questions. An uninitiated reader might read such prose, enjoy it, and even feel he had understood everything in it; a more sensitive reader, while understanding every word of it, would sense something indescribable hidden beneath the lucid surface.

Kawabata stressed the importance of simple language repeatedly in his essays and theoretical works. "The first principle of composition is simplicity and plainness," he wrote in *The New Composition Reader*. "A piece of writing, however beautiful it may sound, would be inferior to crude, mediocre writing if the reader finds it hard to understand." He witnessed the sentencing of Japanese war criminals at the Tokyo Trials and was chagrined by, among other things, the difficulty of the Japanese language; when the American judge said "death by hanging," for example, the interpreter translated it as the awesome-sounding *kōshukei* ("strangulation penalty"). In Kawabata's view, good composition should be so simple as to be readily understood when heard. "Modern written Japanese —at least as it is used in prose fiction—should aim at being understood perfectly when one hears it read aloud," he advised. To test whether the written language was simple enough, he proposed to try transcribing it in roman letters; if the composition was readily understandable in romanization, the language was simple and plain enough. As a young man, Kawabata was associated with a group promoting the romanization of Japanese.

Lying behind Kawabata's insistence on simple language was his belief that a verbal description, no matter how detailed it might be, would never be able to depict natural beauty at its most sublime. Words were always imperfect for a writer seeking to express the inexpressible. Once, in trying to describe a black lily, Kawabata measured the length of the flowers and leaves, counted the number of petals and pistils, and examined the color of the flowers in sunlight, lamplight, and other conditions. He wrote down all those details when he depicted the flower in a story.* After the story was published, however, he had second thoughts and wondered if he should not have written no more than "a black lily," omitting all the details and leaving the reader to visualize the flower as he

* The story, "Bells of Spring," was later incorporated into *The Sound of the Mountain*.

liked. Elsewhere he observed, again taking a lily as an example, "rather than trying to produce a beautifully composed piece describing a lily in thousands of words, it is perhaps purer and more beautiful to say just one word, 'lily.' " Description would encroach on the reader's imagination, and Kawabata did not like that. Since he saw beauty as subjective, he would rather invite the reader to fantasize; he would just say "a lily," and leave the reader to visualize the most beautiful lily he could imagine. Simple, common diction would function better in this respect. A widely used word, being less specific, would leave more to the reader's imagination. Tsuburaya's phrase "I enjoyed" might sound too general and commonplace, but the reader could imagine the most delicious taste because the writer did not specify what it was. The second-grader who wrote about his playmate's death never attempted to describe Ritsuko, but because of that very fact the reader could visualize the most enchanting four-year-old girl he knew.

In this connection there is a revealing scene in *Thousand Cranes* where Kikuji, on being informed of Yukiko's marriage, tries to recall the beautiful girl's face. To his surprise, he finds he cannot, despite the fact that he was deeply moved by its beauty when he met her; all he can recollect is the thousand-crane pattern on the kerchief she was carrying at the time. He then comes to think how clearly he can remember the ugly birthmark on Chikako's breast, though he saw it years ago. His conclusion is, naturally, that the more beautiful an object, the less easy it is to recall in detail. The scene can be interpreted as embodying Kawabata's concept of literary description. Certainly it explains why a description of Yukiko is almost totally lacking in the novel. Kawabata merely refers to Yukiko as "beautiful," or else brings out the image of the thousand cranes. "Beautiful" is a simple, plain—and one might say hackneyed—word for describing a girl, but now we know why Kawabata did what he did. Other Kawabata heroines are presented in the same way. The words depicting Yōko in *Snow Country* or Kikuko in *The Sound of the Mountain* are such simple, common ones as "beautiful," "lovely," "pure," and so on; in no case is there a minute description of their physical features.

Of course, a simple, plain word like "beautiful" would sound hopelessly stereotyped when used for such purposes by an inexpert writer. How, then, could a commonplace word be made imaginatively stimulating and expansive? By the context, Kawabata would answer. A hackneyed word suddenly assumes a fresh new meaning when placed in an appropriate setting. Tsuburaya's commonplace words "I enjoyed" had a powerful appeal because they appeared in his suicide note. The word "beautiful" is poignant when applied to Yukiko, because the reader knows, through her words and actions as presented in the novel, that she is a pure maiden. Kawabata explained this fact in "The Existence and Discovery of Beauty." He first quoted a haiku by Kobayashi Issa (1763–1827):

> How beautiful
> Is the night sky, on these closing
> Moments of the year!

He went on to observe that, while not knowing the exact location referred to in the composition, he could visualize the poet standing on a plateau near the snowy Echigo Mountains, where in fact Issa's home was. "As I imagine it," he continued, "the winter sky on that frosty night had never been so clear, with myriads of stars shining like a shower of sparkling rain. It was near midnight on the last day of the year. Under those circumstances, beauty was discovered, or created, in the commonplace words 'How beautiful.' " In Kawabata's view, then, the two hackneyed words of the first line were impregnated with a fresh new meaning when they were redefined by the second and third lines. The poet did not describe the nature of the beauty he saw; instead, he presented, or suggested, the particulars of the time and place that created the beauty. The reader who had been to the Echigo Mountains, who had seen the night sky in the snowy region of Japan in winter, and who had experienced the feeling of an eventful year coming to a close, could see the beauty in his mind's eye. To this type of reader, the poet needed only to give the proper setting and proper emotional stimulants; the reader took over from there, injecting his personal meaning into the commonest words.

While every novelist endeavors to create a proper setting for his novel, Kawabata seems to have been especially careful in preparing a cosmos uniquely his own. In the opening sentence of *Snow Country*, for instance, Kawabata takes the reader into a special world, the snow country, which is a world distinctly different either from Tokyo, where Shimamura grew up, or from the port town where Komako grew up. The world of *Thousand Cranes* is that of the tea ceremony, just as the world of *The Master of Go* is that of go players. *The House of the Sleeping Beauties* is about a strange world with strange rules; it is completely isolated from the rest of contemporary society. In these worlds of Kawabata's, some of the commonest words come to have special meanings, though they may vary somewhat from one reader to another. There emerges a tension between the generality of the word and the specifics of the context, and that tension becomes a source of stimulation for the reader's fancy.

Symbolism becomes important in this type of writing, for, when properly used, it can present a specific image without limiting its emotional connotations. Kawabata often made use of this fact. The thousand-crane symbol is a good example: one can clearly visualize it, because of its familiarity as a design in Japanese art; yet, while one can think of it as a beautiful image, the nature of that beauty remains undefined. When, therefore, Yukiko appears with a kerchief of the thousand-crane pattern, the reader instantly senses that she is a beautiful girl. Yet since the pattern is symbolic, not descriptive, of her beauty, each reader has the freedom to visualize her in the way he sees fit. One might say that Kawabata's picture of Yukiko both is and is not a picture of her kerchief, which symbolizes not only her beauty but the virginal purity of her life.

The ghost of a young woman who appears in "Memorial Poem" remarks: "We departed souls understand symbols better than spoken or written language." Kawabata, who was deeply concerned with the unearthly beauty of a soul, would have used nothing but symbols if he had been able to. In the use of language he was a symbolist, though Japanese literary historians have preferred to apply the misleading term "Neo-Sensualist" to him. His prose fiction could be considered a counterpart to Japanese symbolist poetry, which dominated the Japanese poetic scene during much of his lifetime. Yet, unlike most of those poets, he was a symbolist who used a simple vocabulary, easy diction, and common syntax. His prose style was deceptively lucid. Combining linguistic simplicity with literary ambiguity, Kawabata explored an area of modern Japanese prose that no other writer has come near.

Mask of a Smiling Man

Kawabata made a number of references, both in his prose fiction and in his essays, to his ideas on the use of literature and art. One of them appears in a scene toward the end of *Snow Country*. Shimamura, who is fond of antique kimonos, calls at a village renowned for its weavers of *chijimi*, an extraordinarily fine type of linen spun from locally grown flax. So difficult to weave is chijimi that the weavers, who are women, begin to learn their craft as children, and do their best work between the ages of 14 and 24. Walking through the wintry village, Shimamura muses on the hardships suffered by these maidens who toil to produce beautiful linen in the snow. The linen, because it is made into the luxurious kimonos that Shimamura and other dilettantes prize so highly, keeps living on even after the weaver who expended her loving care on it is dead and forgotten. Shimamura wonders whether such love and devotion, having materialized as the beautiful linen, will ever touch the heart of someone in some place at some time. He rather hopes that it might.

Shimamura's wish must have been Kawabata's, too. Just as young village maidens weave the chijimi with loving care, but without any assurance of being properly rewarded for it, Komako and Yōko weave a living fabric out of their capacity to love, with no expectation of being rewarded either. *Snow Country* is a kimono made of that fabric. Kawabata wrote the novel in the hope that it would inspire and move readers even after he was dead. That, in his opinion, was the prime function of literature and art.

Works of art actually inspire and move the main characters of *Thousand Cranes*. In particular, a pair of Shino tea cups, one formerly belonging to Kikuji's father and the other to Mrs. Ōta,

are so beautiful and so full of life that they have a powerfully purifying effect on Kikuji and Fumiko, who have both been tormented
by a sense of guilt. The artists who made the cups died several
centuries ago, yet their works remain to cast their spell. The symbolism is more complex, however: in a climactic scene, Fumiko
breaks one of the cups. Out of her maidenly love she has herself
become a prized work of art for Kikuji; she no longer needs such
an object. But the reader, not being Kikuji, does need one. That is
why Kawabata wrote *Thousand Cranes*, in the hope that other
readers, remote in time and place, would be inspired by her flaw-
less beauty.

Kawabata stated this function of art more directly in "The
Bridge." Through a narrator, he said: "As I watch an *objet d'art*,
especially an antique, I am struck with the feeling that now, and
only now, am I really alive. When I have no work of art to rest my
eyes on, I feel as if I were a man who, after suffering through a life
of shame, malice, and pain, is on the verge of death and is hardly
making any attempt to resist death." Gazing at a beautiful work of
art, people sense the pure, selfless love expended by the artist, the
beauty mixed with sincerity and sadness. They have the rare moments of witnessing the beauty of humanity and gaining renewed
strength to live on; for a moment, they feel they are "really alive."
The reader may recall Kawabata's remark, "Our language is primarily for expressing human goodness and beauty." To know the
goodness and beauty of a Yōko or Fumiko is to have reason for
living on, no matter how wretched one's own life.

Unfortunately, however, Kawabata did not seem capable of believing unwaveringly in this function of literature and art. He had
moments of doubt and ambivalence, when he wondered whether
artists, with their faith in the beauty and goodness of people, were
not self-deluded sentimentalists. For instance, he sometimes wondered if the ending of "The Izu Dancer," which symbolizes the
purifying effect of literature, was not too pleasant. "This narrator
has indulged himself in both sorrow and happiness," he said. "He
is grieved to part with the dancer, but the grief is not that of eternal
parting since at this point he expects to see her again in Habu, her

hometown. His is a temporary parting, a pleasant one." The young narrator did not know that he was destined not to meet the girl again, that life was hard, fickle, and unpredictable. Kawabata, as he grew older, became more and more painfully aware of the harshness of life and, proportionately, more and more dissatisfied with the pleasant note on which "The Izu Dancer" ended.

Perhaps the same can be said of the parting scene in *Snow Country*. Shimamura, on the homebound train (he has a wife and children in Tokyo), sees the man in his fifties saying good-bye to the young, red-cheeked girl. It is a sad scene, but a pleasant one as well. It is comparable to the ending of "The Izu Dancer," in that the hero indulges himself in his sorrow. Kawabata never admitted as much, but the fact remains that he decided not to make it the last scene of *Snow Country*. He went on to write part two, which shows that life is not so sweet. In this part, the lovely Yōko apparently goes insane, and Komako is left alone with her. The ending of part two is far from pleasant.

Should a work of art focus on people's goodness and beauty—or their potential for goodness and beauty—and thereby try to give the reader a renewed courage to keep living on? Or should it honestly present the hard facts of life as well, though that may provide less solace to the reader? This dilemma is the theme of a short but complex story by Kawabata entitled "A Man Who Does Not Smile."

The story is largely autobiographical, as Kawabata himself confessed. The hero, a writer who lives in Tokyo, is in Kyoto to help a team of film makers shoot a movie based on one of his stories. One fine morning, lying in bed at his riverside inn, the writer is visited by a vision of an old mask showing the face of a smiling man. Inspired by the vision, he changes the last scene of the movie; by adding a scene that shows masks of smiling people all over the screen, he brightens the ending of this gloomy film, which is about patients in a mental hospital. With the revision, he feels pleased with the movie script for the first time, imagining the mental patients all wearing the masks of smiling men at its end. Following this revision, the film makers hunt for artistic masks suitable for the purpose. They finally manage to borrow five beautiful ones, made years ago for the traditional Japanese dance. The writer likes the masks, which seem to him to symbolize the bright future of mankind. Therefore, when one of them gets slightly spotted with yellow paint while in use for the movie, and therefore cannot be returned to its owner, he gladly buys it. The movie completed, he goes back to Tokyo and visits his ailing wife at a hospital, bringing the mask with him. His children jovially try it on. But when his turn comes and they try to force him to wear it, he refuses, almost overemphatically, even angrily. To save the situation, his sick wife snatches the mask and cheerfully puts it on, before he has time to stop her. A couple of minutes later she removes the mask, and he is shocked to discover ugliness, pain, and misery on her face, which he has never noticed before. The beautiful mask now frightens him. Art is to blame, he thinks. He writes a telegram to be sent to Kyoto: "Cut out the scene with the masks." Moments later he reconsiders and tears up the telegram.

The implications of the story are obvious. Everywhere life is gray and gloomy, filled with pain and suffering; all men, at least all grown-up men, are ailing, though not all are hospitalized. One solace for them—perhaps the only one—is art, which enables them, even for a fleeting moment, to recognize beauty in life and goodness in human nature. It can give suffering humankind a glorious vision of the future. Unfortunately, it may work in the reverse way, too. Some may be elated to see how beautiful life can be or how noble a person. But others, who know the hardships of life all too well, may consider art nothing more than an idealistic dream, and fall into an even deeper despair. Those fortunate (or unfortunate) people who do not recognize ugliness in life because they have never seen beauty are awakened to life's ugliness when art shows beauty to them. The effect of art is double-edged.*

The writer-hero of "A Man Who Does Not Smile," caught in

---

* Though somewhat more indirectly, the same theme is treated in "The Moon in the Water," in which the ailing husband's hand mirror, while enabling him to see his lovely wife working in the garden, also forces him to see his own haggard face.

this dilemma, eventually decides to keep the film's final scene intact, thereby allowing the audience to see the masks of smiling people—a pleasant vision created by the artist. That was Kawabata's decision, too. He kept writing novels and stories, creating visions of pure, unearthly beauty that he hoped would elate the reader, but that, he fully knew, might have a depressing effect as well. Such was the nature of art.

CHAPTER EIGHT

Mishima Yukio

✿

M ISHIMA YUKIO (1925–70) was less a novelist than a thinker who expressed himself not only through his writings but also through his entire way of life. Virtually everything he said, wrote, or did had a proper place in his personal cosmology, which he had evolved over the years and which eventually induced him to take his own life. Literature occupied a prominent position in that cosmos, and he found it difficult to speak of the one without the other. Thus his ideas on literature appear everywhere in his writings, sometimes expounded with compelling logic in essay form, sometimes suggested by means of highly individual metaphors. One cannot understand Mishima's philosophy of life apart from his attitude toward literature and the arts. Those who study his thoughts on literature suffer not from lack of supporting evidence but from overabundance of it. They also suffer from its clarity, brilliance, and comprehensiveness. The initial impact is overwhelming: it is hard not to feel that Mishima has said everything about literature that needs to be said—and that he has said it well. Critics of a Mishima novel are often in the same position: the novelist seems to have anticipated everything a critic could possibly say about the novel.

How to Conquer the World

The Temple of the Golden Pavilion, one of the most successful of Mishima's philosophical novels, has a scene in which a university student named Kashiwagi arranges flowers in a bowl. He is a very unusual young man, with great powers of intellect; he also happens to have a clubfoot. He has come to excel in the traditional Japanese art of flower arrangement; under his masterful hands, nature's plants, which have hitherto existed *as they are*, are transformed into plants *as they ought to be*. By cutting the plants to proper length, by spacing the leaves at adequate intervals, by bending the stems forcibly, and by placing the flowers in certain preconceived locations in the bowl, Kashiwagi creates a small artificial universe.

Obviously, the episode is designed to illustrate Kashiwagi's role in the novel, which is that of an existentialist philosopher who has built a formidable intellectual universe on the foundation of his physical handicap. Yet it also shows Mishima's ideas on the relationship between nature and art at the most basic level. In Mishima's view, the artist works on raw nature and creates an artificial order out of disorder. With a pair of clippers in his hand, he brings wild nature under human control, reshaping it according to a premeditated design. Nature as it is is made into nature as he thinks it ought to be.

While a floral artist has clippers for his tool, a literary artist has language. "In all ages," Mishima wrote in an essay, "literature aims at an interpretation of the universe and a deep perception of humanity by means of language." Language, he felt, was a human invention with which people brought form and order to wild nature. The well-ruled kingdom that resulted was human civilization. Mishima saw the ancient epic poets as having functioned in this capacity. He compared them to an architect who has built a majestic palace towering over primitive surroundings to show the monarch's supreme authority over all men, animals, and plants. A monarch conquered the world with his sword; a poet did so with his words.

Young Mishima set out to conquer the world with words. As a middle-school student he wrote poetry and took delight in reshaping the external world through his verbal art. He was interested more in the results of poetic transformation than in poetry per se. In an autobiographical story called "A Youth Who Writes Poetry," Mishima admitted as much: "The youth did not like to keep his gaze fixed for any length of time, either on the outer world or on himself. He soon tired and dropped his gaze unless its object changed on the spot into something else—for instance, unless the silvery gleam of young foliage in the sun of a May afternoon was transformed into full-blossoming cherry flowers seen at night." Young Mishima, an admirer of Novalis and Yeats, lived in and for this imaginary nocturnal world; to it he would bring objects from the outer world and thereby make them his. He was a Kashiwagi in the making.

Why Mishima was concerned with ordering the world with such fervor is a question difficult to answer in specific terms, though it obviously bore some relationship to his extraordinary gift of intellect and self-awareness. The celebrated beginning of his autobiographical novel, *Confessions of a Mask*, has it that he could even remember how he was born; his self-awareness began at birth! He seems to have felt an unusual amount of fear at anything his consciousness could not reach or his intellect could not penetrate. He was seldom at ease when his mind perceived something but could not grasp it firmly, and he could convince himself that he had a firm grasp only when he was able to express it verbally. His lifelong fear of music stemmed from the fact that its message lay beyond words. He once compared music to a ravening beast forcibly confined in a cage, an undependable cage that might break down at any minute. "I have an unusual fear," he confessed, "of this formless thing called sound." Language, on the other hand, had form and order. Literature, with language as its medium, was a strong cage for the beast known as life.

Life in contemporary Japan seemed like a ravening beast to Mishima because he found it both violent and irrational. He particularly feared its irrational, mysterious quality. "Of late, the factual world has been buried under agnosticism," he wrote, "and its mystery has deepened as human society has come to cover a wider territory. Usually, the statements of people who have witnessed the same incident contradict one another. An extraordinary incident that shocks the whole society always contains an eternal mystery." Mishima could not leave mystery as mystery. In some of his novels, he attempted to unravel the mystery surrounding various shocking incidents that actually took place. Three notable examples are *The Blue Period*, which traces the career of a scandalous student entrepreneur in Japan's postwar years, *The Temple of the Golden Pavilion*, which probes the mind of a Zen acolyte who set fire to the famous pavilion in Kyoto, and *After the Banquet*, which draws on the Tokyo gubernatorial election of 1959.

Probing such mysteries to the core, Mishima eventually came upon the psychological element. "At the heart of an incident, as long as it takes place in the world of men, there always lies the human mind," he said. In particular, there was the darkness of the subconscious mind. Thus Mishima, in his attempt to get a firm grip on the outer world, was forced to look inward. The artist in language had to be a psychologist, too. Indeed, *The Blue Period*, *The Temple of the Golden Pavilion*, and *After the Banquet* can be called psychological novels in the sense that in each work the author vigorously pursues the internal, psychic events in the protagonist's life that culminate in the catastrophic external event.

Closest to the novelist in this regard is the psychiatrist. The parallel is drawn with clarity and forcefulness in Mishima's novel *The Music*. The title of the book is a euphemism for orgasm, which the young heroine is unable to reach. The novel consists entirely of a psychiatrist's clinical reports on her condition. He traces the cause of her frigidity to the innermost reaches of her mind and finally succeeds in curing her. In Mishima's view, a novelist functioned in the same way, defying the dark, weird sector of human life, and trying to pierce it with the searchlight rays of intellect. With his help, a person who has been afraid of "the music" and has refused to listen to it comes to shed these fears.

Mishima's viewpoint here is not unlike that of Sōseki, who, as we have seen, recognized the chief function of literature as its ability to disperse fear of the chaotic and unknown. There was, however, a significant difference between the two writers. Sōseki was more concerned with the conscious mind and had more confidence in its capabilities. He believed that the conscious mind, when it was ethically disciplined, would finally impose its will on the chaos of life. Sōseki's concept of literary form was primarily moral: a novel had a moral message to convey through its form. Mishima, on the other hand, was acutely aware of the subconscious mind and its devastating power. Well read in Tanizaki's novels, he was at home in the post-Freudian world and thoroughly acquainted with the murky area beyond the borders of consciousness where moral sense cannot reach. Compared with Sōseki, he had less confidence in the power of intellect and language. He wanted to believe, and did believe when young, that literature was a life-molder and conqueror of chaos. Yet that was not enough to put him at ease; in fact, he soon came to realize the limitations of literature and was very much disturbed by the realization. This is clearly seen, for example, in the ending of "A Youth Who Writes Poetry." The young hero, hitherto fully content with his ability to internalize the external, has a rude awakening one day when he learns that an older friend of his, another "youth who writes poetry," is extremely distressed over a futile love affair. The hero believes that a poet should be capable of mastering anything in this world, love included. Yet here is a young poet, whom he highly admires, failing to win a girl's heart. Similar instances, in which a man of the inner world fails to cope with the outer world despite his confidence to do so, are numerous in Mishima's novels. Even Kashiwagi, one of the most formidable masters of the inner world, finds himself powerless before the hero of *The Temple of the Golden Pavilion*, who turns into a man of the external world toward the end of the novel. In fact, the novel could be analyzed in terms of a confrontation between people of the inner world (the Superior, Kashiwagi, most of the other acolytes) and people of the outer world (the Naval Engineering School student, Uiko, Tsurukawa, the American soldier), with the latter group eventually winning Mizoguchi, the novel's hero, to their side.

Mishima came to believe that a large part of the reason why poets and other spiritually inclined people failed in their attempt to master life lay in the ineffectiveness of their weapon, language. In ancient times words were powerful because they were used denotatively, expressing thoughts and feelings shared by the entire community. Epic poets sang of communal emotions, of heroes and heroines who had already been given their proper place in a society of which they were truly a part. Modern poets abused language. They would take pride in using words in a private, personal way, a way no one else in the community had thought of. In many modern theories of poetry, the more individual the use of language, the better poetry it was considered to be. The result was that the poem lost its power to inspire ordinary people. Literature in the modern age might conquer the private world of an individual, but it was powerless when faced with the society, because its medium, literary language, was personal and alienated. In *Sun and Steel*, Mishima compared the function of poetic language to that of gastric juices, the prime function of which is to digest food, but which sometimes eat the walls of the stomach itself. Language, according to Mishima, was intended to digest raw life and make it part of man's system, but in modern times it had turned inward and begun eroding his inner world.

Behind this corruption of language there lay, Mishima thought, a widening dichotomy between mind and body. In ancient Greece, for instance, mind and body existed in close organic correspondence. The sound mind was considered to lodge in, and be represented by, the sound body. But since the flesh decayed and the spirit was immortal, the Greeks tried to unite the two in visual art. Mishima explained:

The mind, by its very nature, persistently tries to live forever, resisting age and attempting to give itself a form. It is because of this propensity that the mind has served as "a substitute for life" throughout the history of mankind. When a person passes his prime and his life begins to lose true vigor and charm, his mind starts functioning as if it were another form of life; it imitates what life does, eventually doing what life cannot do. The Greeks, who were aware of this fact, felt it possible to symbolize, and thereby perpetuate, all aspects of man's mind by way of statues representing the bodies of young men; and they succeeded in proving that this was indeed possible.

With the arrival of Hebraic influences, however, the classical correlation between spirit and flesh began to break down. "Men had been living a proud life, having felt no need for the spirit—until

Christianity invented it," Mishima observed. In its eagerness to overcome the fear of death, Christian culture placed the mind, "a substitute for life," over and above the body. The spiritual was to be valued more highly than the corporal because it lasted longer. People began to scorn the body as ephemeral and insignificant. Modern science, which seemed to oppose the spiritualism of religion, did not help to turn the tide since it was merely another kind of spiritualism—or rationalism, or utilitarianism, or whatever. In place of muscles and fists it used guns, tanks, planes, and nuclear weapons—all products of the human spirit. It is no accident that Mishima's ideal revolutionaries, described in *Runaway Horses*, refuse to use guns.

Mishima's aim in pointing all this out was not to attack Judeo-Christian culture or modern science as such. He was merely stating the natural course of human history as he saw it. He considered it a natural course because he thought he had discovered, beneath religion and science, man's basic psychic force going its own irresistible way. The force existed as a potential before the arrival of Hebraism or modern science. Mishima explained:

Animals do not have the spirit. Only the human species has it, because it alone has succeeded in conquering nature. The human race, its males in particular, invented the spirit when they found they had no role left to play after they finished performing their part in procreation (females had to rear children and hence had a role to play); in one way or another men had to fill the hollow period of time between procreation and death. Probably the spirit, in its origin, was an exclusive possession of males and served as their weapon, but the weapon turned against its owners and came to hurt them. The spirit became isolated; sadly, it came to be disowned even by Mother Earth, that female territory.

Here Mishima was using the word "spirit" almost as an equivalent of "intellect." In his way of thinking, a woman could never be a completely intellectual being because of her physiological makeup. Elsewhere Mishima observed: "A woman's mind, since it is tied down by her womb, cannot leave the body as a man's mind can. ... A woman has two nerve centers controlling her mind, the brain and the womb. The two always function so close together that her mind, caught between them, cannot depart from the body."

Women, therefore, did not suffer as much as men from the modern dichotomy between mind and body, and neither Christianity nor modern science had them in thrall.

The young Mishima's fear of raw life and its formlessness, therefore, also meant fear of woman, a strange creature in whom mind and body inseparably coexisted. The hero of *Confessions of a Mask*, a man of the spirit, is irresistibly attracted to his opposite, the body, as represented by an athletic classmate named Ōmi. In contrast, he feels no deep-rooted attraction to the lovely Sonoko, who is a woman and therefore is a mixture of body and mind. Physiologically, a woman contains a dark, disorderly world within her that cannot be penetrated by intellect, and that frightens him. If intellect cannot control woman, who represents the chaos of the external world, is there anything that can? The answer found by Mishima was that woman and the external world can be controlled by the opposite of intellect, namely, the body.

What Mishima had to do, then, was to bring "the body" to a prominent place in his scheme of things. In order to do so, he first needed to build up his own body, for he had by now realized that the prime reason he wanted to be a poet in his youth lay in his strong (but subconscious) inferiority complex over his delicate constitution. He had instinctively turned to the internal world of literature when, as a child, he sensed the inadequacy of his physique to face and explore the outside world. His inner urge to start body-building was intensified during his tour of Greece in 1952. After his return to Japan, he began a new life. He took up weight lifting, gymnastics, boxing, track and field, running, horse riding, and *kendō* (Japanese fencing). In due course he became "a man with the chest measurement of one meter," a muscular athlete like Ōmi, who he had set out to become. In 1963 he was confident enough to publish a book of photographs proudly displaying himself in the nude.

This new posture of Mishima's considerably modified his cosmology, tipping the balance between literature and external nature in favor of the latter. Finding that literature was powerless in the outer world, he came to trust his muscles more than his words. He was so absorbed in his attempt to match body to mind that he saw the two as irreconcilable enemies. Literature and external nature were wide apart, the former being unable to relate itself meaningfully to the latter. In *Thirst for Love*, Etsuko, the woman of the inner world, cannot relate herself to Saburō, a muscular man of the outer world. In *The Sailor Who Fell from Grace with the Sea*, Ryūji, a romanticist, is about to marry Fusako, a woman of the flesh, when he is murdered by her son and his gang, a group of young romanticists who feel he has betrayed them. In *After the Banquet*, the union of male and female principles is attained when the hero Noguchi and the heroine Kazu are united in wedlock, but the marriage breaks up in no time as their incompatibility becomes apparent. All those novels have a tragic—or at least unhappy—ending, because they deal with two conflicting philosophical systems, one built around the flesh (the external world) and the other around the spirit (the internal world), neither of which is powerful enough to subjugate the other. Each novel's denouement is brought about, not by a resolution of the dichotomy, but by violence or separation. In short, literature and external nature are incompatible.

If this concept of literature seems to have unfavorable implications about its nature and function, it was so in Mishima's mind. Having held extravagant expectations for literature in his boyhood, he was all the more disappointed when he discovered its limitations. His reference to the nature of literature in his mature years inevitably assumed a negative tone. In *Sun and Steel*, he compared literary art to white ants eating a wooden pillar, to nitric acid corroding a copper plate, and, as we have already seen, to excess stomach fluids digesting the lining of the stomach. In another essay we see him comparing the artist to a radiologist who sees through other men but is himself contaminated by the radiation. In a more characteristic metaphor, art is also seen as a charming but unfaithful woman who through her femininity castrates her husband. The metaphor appears in *Forbidden Colors*, in an interesting passage discussing the relationship between nature and land-scape gardening. In another later essay, Mishima openly stated that "there is cowardice hidden in all literature."

It may seem strange that Mishima, holding the negative view of literature that he did, continued to produce a number of literary works. Realizing this, he tried to justify it:

> To seek a model life within the mind means, especially for the artist, an effort to cripple his life, to cut off its growth and flow. Works of art are often born out of such primordial, uncanny energy. I decided to structure my life around an attempt to remove that energy as much as possible from the sphere of daily life and seal it into my literary works, thereby leaving myself free to seek a model life in the noncreative part of art, the mimetic part that all works of art borrow from life (that is to say, to faithfully follow the flow and evolution of daily activities). I tried to lead a "life without a theme" and, as years went by, developed a passion for conformity.

At the most basic level, then, literature continued to function for him exactly as it had in his boyhood. It helped to sort out the chaotic, uncanny part of his inner world. But the inner world no longer seemed so important to him as it once did. He had more confidence in controlling the mind, even the subconscious mind, since he now had a weapon far more effective than language: the body. The subconscious belonged to the body, and he had proved to be a master of his body, changing it at his will by the use of "sun and steel." His skin beautifully suntanned, and his muscles highly developed by dumbbells, he no longer had an inferiority complex over his physique. He felt no need to be a dreamer who, because of his delicate constitution, has to conjure up a romantic theme for his life. Mishima was now more interested in the physical world, a world where he coexisted with all kinds of people. He did not want to be an alienated poet; he wanted to be part of a community, part of life's daily ebb and flow. It was thus that he came to develop a "passion for conformity."

This changing attitude of Mishima's toward literature can be seen as a logical development of his initial concept of art. As a boy he wanted to structure chaos by means of literature, but soon discovered that literature depended on language, which was itself in chaos, during the modern period. He therefore proceeded to seek a greater principle of order by which literature itself could be overcome. He spent his mature years searching for it, producing novels in which the mind and the body, or the inner and the outer world, fail to unite themselves in one. At last, he found the principle he had been looking for. It was derived from *bunbu ryōdō*, the highest ethical principle for the Japanese samurai in the seventeenth and eighteenth centuries. Bunbu ryōdō advocated that a samurai should vigorously discipline himself in both the military and the literary arts; a perfect samurai had to be an expert poet as well as an expert swordsman. Mishima studied the origins of this idea and discovered death at the root of both arts. An ideal warrior trained his body, built up his muscles, and polished his swordsmanship, all in preparation for the ultimate combat, when death would await him. A perfect soldier was a man perfectly prepared for death. On the other hand, a poet trained his imaginative faculty, built up an intellectual universe, and polished his art of expression, also in preparation for death. He endeavored to overcome death by believing in the immortality of his mind, which would live on in his poetry after his physical death. A perfect poet, too, was a man perfectly prepared for death.

Such being the case, Mishima speculated that if he pursued death at once as a soldier and as a literary artist, he would be able to see the point of contact between the body and the mind. As described in the epilogue of *Sun and Steel*, he carried out the experiment by exploring outer space in a jet plane. The planet Earth was enveloped with death, and in order to go out there one had to be a scientist, a man of the mind who could operate the spacecraft, as well as a soldier, a man of the body who was physically able to withstand high altitudes. One winter day in 1967 Mishima flew to a height of 43,000 feet in an F-104 supersonic fighter. In a moment of almost sexual ecstasy he saw a huge white snake encircling the globe and "biting its own tail." High up in the sky, surrounded by death, he had glimpsed a union of mind and body.

As Mishima well knew, however, this resolution of the dichotomy concealed an element of tragedy at its root. An ideal warrior who

dies a heroic death in combat moves from the world of action to
that of literature, becoming the hero of an epic poem. But as a
man of action who refuses to dream, he has to die without grandiose
illusions; if he had any, he would no longer be a man of action.
On the other hand, a poet can never be the hero he eulogizes in
his poems, for he has to live on in order to eulogize. And when he
dies, his death would not be heroic; he has never been a hero. In
other words, an ideal man who has solved the dichotomy by way
of bunbu ryōdō can expect a dreadful death, with no solace from
either the military or the literary art. A soldier who has never read
an epic, or a poet who has never seen a real hero, can die more
happily. Fortunately, men who attain bunbu ryōdō are rare, and
even they are often betrayed by one or the other of their arts at
the last minute.

What about Mishima's own death? One is tempted to answer
that he died as a soldier. He seems to have become more and more
a warrior in his last years, especially since he founded the Shield
Society, a small private army committed to defending the emperor
at any sacrifice. It was as the leader of that "soldier" group that
Mishima, together with four other members, raided the eastern
headquarters of Japan's Self-Defense Force and, when the attempted coup failed, killed himself. Indeed, he performed a ritual
suicide in the traditional samurai manner. On the surface, then, it
was a happy death of a heroic soldier who died for the cause he
believed in.

There was another aspect to that, however. On the morning
of the day of his suicide, Mishima delivered the last installment
of his last novel, *The Decay of the Angel,* which describes anything
but heroic death. The novel has two principal characters: Honda,
an aged lawyer who has seen three people of action heroically
following their destiny (described in the three books that preceded
the novel in the tetralogy), and Tōru (a name literally meaning
"perception"), a young signal-station attendant whose duty it is
to watch the horizon for the first sign of an incoming boat. The
novel traces Honda's attempt to convert Tōru from a seer to "a
man to be seen"—from a man of inaction to a man of action—
since Honda is convinced that Tōru was born to be the latter. The

attempted conversion fails disastrously. Tōru tries to kill himself, but he turns out to be woefully lacking in the qualifications of a tragic hero. He ends up blind. The born seer, in failing to become a man to be seen, now loses even his natural gift of seeing. The novel closes with Honda, already a sickly old man of eighty-one, casting grave doubt on people's capacity to see. Throughout the tetralogy, he has functioned as an epic poet. His death is now imminent.

Mishima's death, therefore, was a poet's as well as a soldier's. Just as Honda died after the completion of *The Decay of the Angel*, so did Mishima the novelist. Mishima the soldier's death was sensationally reported in the newspapers, while Mishima the novelist's death was not even mentioned in his last novel. But this was as it should be. Mishima's death was happy as a soldier's, but meaningless as a novelist's. A novelist's happiness lies in living a long enough life to see his novels gain immortality. But old age would mean deterioration of the body, the decay of a soldier. Mishima wanted to live both as a man of the mind and as a man of the body; he could continue to do so only while his body kept its youthful vitality. When he knew he could no longer be both, he chose to die, fully aware that his choice was doubly tragic.

In summing up, then, we must say that Mishima's concept of the relationship between literature and external reality changed drastically with time. As years went by, he felt more and more strongly that literature was powerless to reshape life, since literary language had become too personal. He therefore brought in action, or physical strength, to perform that function; it was the body, not the mind, that had the potential to reshape nature into an ideal order. The role of literature changed from a life-shaper's to a life-recorder's. A literary artist was to observe and describe the external world, the world not as it was but as it changed into an ideal order through the efforts of a man of action. Literature, which had lost its power to reshape nature, regained it when supplemented by action, which had that power.

We conclude this part of the discussion by going back to the scene in *The Temple of the Golden Pavilion* with which we started. Kashiwagi, with just a pair of hand clippers, created an orderly little universe in a flower bowl. As an artist and creator, he reigned supreme over that cosmos. Yet in the scene immediately following, we see his girl friend in a fit of temper upturn the bowl and tear the flowers to shreds. The artist's universe is fragile indeed in the face of physical violence. To overcome that violence, Kashiwagi has to transform himself from an artist to a soldier: he grasps the young woman's hair and slaps her across the cheek. Mishima's concept of the ideal artist is represented, not by Kashiwagi the floral artist, but by the omniscient narrator, who watches and records the transformation of Kashiwagi from an artist into a soldier.*

Traveler with a Timetable

What is he like, then, this omniscient narrator of *The Temple of the Golden Pavilion*? Of all the characters appearing in the novel, the one who comes closest to the narrator makes only a very brief appearance, near the end. He is Father Zenkai, the head of a Zen temple in a northern prefecture, who by coincidence is paying a visit to the Temple of the Golden Pavilion on the very night it is set afire. A Buddhist priest, he belongs to the world of the spirit. Yet he has an outstandingly masculine physique: he is almost six feet tall, has dark skin and bushy eyebrows, and talks in a thunderous voice. Mizoguchi, the novel's hero, feels that he, and only he, has the eyes to see through everything and everyone, including Mizoguchi himself. He is omniscient, like the novel's narrator.

It can be surmised, then, that the ideal novelist, as conceived by Mishima in his mature years, has to enjoy a happy combination of both spiritual and physical power. The writer needs access to the worlds of both the mind and the body; he must therefore have the qualifications of both a poet and a soldier. Mishima implied this when he wrote in an essay: "In the ideal world where I wish to live, Boxing and Art would shake hands without being forced,

---

* Kashiwagi approaches the image of the ideal artist here, but only temporarily. Clubfooted, he can never be a full-fledged soldier. Yet the episode cited here illustrates the point well enough.

Physical Strength and Intellectual Vigor would run hand in hand, and Life and Art would smile at each other." This combination of an athlete's qualifications with a poet's is a distinguishing feature of Mishima's thought; no other major novelist of modern Japan held such a view, though Shiga was moving in that direction. The typical modern Japanese novelist, Mishima thought, was "an ugly cripple whose exterior has been deformed by the mind's poison." Ugliest of all was Dazai, an ailing man who never wanted his ailment to be cured. Akutagawa was a weak-willed invalid who allowed his fragile physique to affect his mind. Tanizaki was a clever writer who surrendered to defeatism (Tanizaki would call it masochism) without fighting, and then enjoyed plenty of good food and lived a long life. Kawabata was a calculatingly lazy man who made little or no effort to structure the chaos of life. Shiga alone was awakened to the importance of the body, but he was a complacent athlete who, once he had established a new athletic record, abandoned all effort to break it.*

As is suggested by this last instance, Mishima regarded the dichotomy of mind and body not only as the leading feature of the novelist's character but as the source from which his creative impulse sprang. Shiga stopped writing when he became too much of an athlete. Mishima's utopia, in which the boxer and the artist would shake hands, had better remain a utopia forever, because the artist created a work of art out of his frustration at not being a boxer.

For an artist to do creative work, he needs at once physical health and some physiomental ill health. He needs both serenity and gloom, both relief from distress and addiction to melancholy, both quiet happiness and smoldering anger, both joy on one level and grief on another level. Is such a delicate concoction humanly possible? Possible or impossible, one should keep trying at it, and the effort would be valuable in itself. If one completely abandons that effort, one would turn into a sloth, that animal which, hanging upside down from a tree, forever keeps sleeping while waiting for an inspiration.

* Mishima wrote extensively on these writers. This brief summary of his remarks on them is inevitably oversimplified. Despite these differences between him and other writers, he was seldom blind to their virtues and expressed high respect for their works. The only exception seems to have been Dazai, whom he was never able to like.

When one has perfect physical health and thereby secures serenity, ease, and happiness (as Shiga did), one feels no need for creating a work of fiction. On the other hand, if one's mental health is such that one feels nothing but gloom, melancholy, and anger, the result is likely to be complete withdrawal from the physical world and escape into a private world of fantasy. In this state, one would feel no need for others and therefore no need to express one's feelings for others to understand. For Mishima a novelist has within himself two mutually incompatible elements, an athlete and a dreamer, each striving to become the other, but in conflict for all that. Out of this strife comes energy for the novelist to create a work of fiction.

It is not easy to imagine exactly what sort of life such a novelist would live in contemporary Japan. Mishima, however, once drew up a model life-style for himself and then carried it out to a degree. "My ultimate aim is to stop associating [with writers and journalists] altogether," he said. "From now on I am going to divide each day neatly into three separate periods: time for sleep, time for work, and time for exercise." By "work" he meant creative writing, his work as a man of the mind. By "exercise" he meant boxing, gymnastics, horse riding, and kendō, his work as a man of the body. The main obstacle that hindered him from leading this ideal life came from journalists, who kept disturbing him for most of each day. Somewhat in jest (but only somewhat), he once suggested that the best way to escape from all this would be to go and live abroad.

In this connection it is interesting to take a glance at the "writers' paradise" that Mishima dreamed of in a lighthearted mood. In an essay called "Gymnasium for Individuality," he pictures a writers' colony in a wooded area some distance from Tokyo. It is a kind of abbey, where each writer lives and works in a soundproofed cell. The switchboard operator at the abbey refuses to take any call for any writer at work. Yet if a writer longs for a red-light district in the evening, Tokyo is within commuting distance and he is free to go there. As might be expected, the colony is well equipped for physical training: there are vaulting horses, Swedish bars, skipping ropes, mats, sandbags, etc. As for food, beefsteaks and tomato juice are plentifully supplied, while such delicacies as sea slugs and trepangs are severely rationed because of their low nutritive value. For mental exercise, there is an agora where writers gather for literary debates; there are also weekly lectures on ancient languages by professors of classics. The most distinctive feature of the writers' colony is a Japanese Reality Room, where each resident writer is required to spend at least five hours a week. The room has facilities to project films on the screen, reproduce sounds, emit smells, change the temperature and humidity, and so on—all at a push of the proper button. For example, when a writer pushes a button labeled "Precipitation over Japan," the air-tight room at once grows hot and humid, and the disgustingly sentimental melody of a popular song begins to be heard, followed by prolonged sobbing in a feeble voice, which gradually becomes louder and is joined by other sobbing voices. Each tearful voice is then translated into a visual scene projected on the screen; sorrowful partings between mother and child, between man and wife, between sweethearts, between blood brothers, and so forth are shown in an increasingly heart-rending sequence of scenes, finally reaching a climax in which all members of the family commit suicide. The spectator must sit through all this no matter how unbearable he may find it. There are many other similar buttons, labeled "Asian Stagnation," "Japanese Poverty," "Victims of Atomic Bombs," "The Demimonde," "An Introduction to Vaudeville," and so on. Although much of this is caricature, Mishima's underlying theme is a serious one: the novelist should stay in training, both physically and mentally. A Dazai or an Akutagawa would not kill himself after going through a training program like the one described.

For a novelist who has trained himself in this way, the creative process becomes a much more predictable affair. In an essay called "My Art of Writing," Mishima analyzed and explained his methods of composition to a degree few Japanese writers had cared to do. The outstanding feature of his approach to writing a novel was, as might have been expected, its deliberate, conscious orderliness. He compared it to his Mexican tour of 1957, a tour for which he prepared a detailed timetable in advance and followed it through, despite a friend's warning that the real Mexico would show herself only to a casual wanderer. Mishima called his way of writing a classicist's mode of traveling—that is, he preferred to impose a predetermined form on his creative imagination. In general, the process by which he wrote a novel went through four stages: search for a theme, survey of the milieu, construction of a plot, and actual writing. Mishima explained each stage in some detail. In so doing, he revealed much else about his working methods that seems entirely characteristic of him.

Mishima's first stage was itself practically unique among Japanese writers who were his contemporaries. Many of them would begin a novel without any clear identification or analysis of its theme; like Tanizaki, they would rather let the creative urge take possession of them, themselves becoming passive. Mishima did not deny the presence of the creative urge; indeed, he admitted that he himself could feel it in the presence of certain objects or incidents. Yet he would not be passive; he went out of his own free will to search for such objects or incidents. He compared himself to a man walking along a dark road with a flashlight in his hand. Suddenly, the light caught something that glittered with dazzling brilliance. On closer inspection, it turned out to be a splinter from a beer bottle. He had found both theme and material for his novel! He came back to his laboratory and examined the bottle fragment under a bright lamp:

I seldom begin writing a novel while leaving my newly discovered theme in the same state in which I found it. I examine the material, filter it, and try to extract its essence. I give it a complete analysis to find out why I was subconsciously attracted to it; I bring everything out into the light of the conscious mind. I rid the material of its specifics and reduce it to abstraction.

Mishima estimated that it took him from half a year to several years to complete the first stage. When it was done there followed the second stage, in which he studied the milieu. The abstract theme deduced at the conclusion of the first stage had to be given specific details to grow into a novel, and the milieu was what provided the details. In the second stage, then, he followed a procedure that was the reverse of the first. He now concentrated on studying all the material, such as police records, trial transcripts, newspaper reports, technical terms, dialects, and slang, that might be needed to give the story a sense of reality. What Mishima studied most intensively was the locale that was to provide the novel's setting. As a rule he traveled to the place in question and strolled around it in a leisurely fashion, paying attention to the smallest particulars. He tried to find out how a stranger would feel on visiting the place, for he wanted to create that impression when he came to describe it in the novel. In his opinion, nature as depicted in a novel had always to be "fictional" in the sense that the local inhabitants never saw it in that way, because they were too accustomed to the place. The more fictional the description of nature, the more readily the novel's reader would feel as if he were there. Once again, Mishima was untypical; most Japanese novelists depicted (or thought they depicted) a locale through the eyes of their characters.

In passing we might also note Mishima's confession that on such a field trip he was always moved more by external nature than by the people he saw. He attributed this to the fact that objects in nature were merely physical, while people consisted of both mind and body. Nature could not be reduced to abstractions. Mishima did not offer further explanations, but it is obvious that he was more at ease with external nature because it was all visible. A person brought to his notice had to be analyzed at both the conscious and the subconscious levels before he could relax. At all events, his observation that descriptions of nature always occupy an important part in his novels should be taken as good advice for anyone who reads them.

The third stage in Mishima's art of writing is plot construction, a topic we shall reserve for a later section. It would suffice here to note that he did more advance planning on his plots than most of his contemporaries; he was a classical plot maker just as he was a classical tourist in Mexico. He was especially careful in setting up the novel's climax; he might modify some particulars of the plot while he wrote, but he would never change the climax that he had planned for at the beginning. It has been reported that he wrote the concluding scene of *The Decay of the Angel* before writing the middle sections. While such a practice is inconceivable for a writer like Kawabata, it is quite characteristic of Mishima.

The fourth and final stage in the creation of a Mishima novel was the actual writing. At this stage, he temporarily cleared his mind of all the preparations he had made in the previous three stages. He would let his theme, which he had grasped so firmly at the first stage, slip out of his mind and wander where it would, like rainwater, until it was lost in the ground. He would forget about methodology and the creative process; all that would occupy his mind would be the part of the novel he was working on at that moment. He was, however, always aware of his hidden theme keeping a watchful eye on him from under the ground where it had sunk. When he felt that his writing passed inspection by this watchman, all would go smoothly. But if he felt that a particular detail did not match the theme, his pen stopped right there and would not budge. When this happened, he went back to the notes he had made during his visit to the locale and tried to relive the experiences he had had there. When he succeeded in regaining the "feel" of his initial experience, his pen came back to life and started moving again. The act of writing a novel consisted in a long sequence of such stops and starts, which would continue until the novel came to its proper conclusion.

The creative process, as described by Mishima, thus resembles a philosopher and a reporter teamed up together, trying to coordinate their different, and at times conflicting, propensities of mind. At the first stage it is the philosopher who is in charge. He meets with an actual happening that interests him; he tries to observe it, analyze it, and eventually reduce it to its abstract essence which is the theme. At the second stage the journalist takes over: he travels to the place of the happening, conducts interviews, reads necessary reports and documents, and otherwise takes note of the circumstantial details. The reporter remains in the forefront during the third stage, too, as he works out the most effective way of presenting the material that has been gathered. At the fourth stage he actually takes up his pen and starts writing the novel. But the philosopher is always looking over his shoulder. If the journalist swerves from the main theme, the philosopher taps him on the back, scolds him, and orders him to redo the work. This goes on until the novel reaches a successful conclusion.

Let Them Feel Strength Within

The effect of art on the spectator is explored at length by Mishima in *The Temple of the Golden Pavilion*. The Golden Pavilion is itself a celebrated work of art with a powerful appeal to everyone who sees it, especially the novel's hero, the young student Mizoguchi. The nature of its appeal is described in detail near the end of the novel, when Mizoguchi takes a last, lingering look at the pavilion before setting it afire. As before, the beauty of the towering structure almost overwhelms him, yet this time he begins to understand why. The essence of the Golden Pavilion's beauty, as he now perceives, lies in nothingness. The pavilion was built in the Dark Ages by people desperately trying to overcome nihilism, and it still retains traces of that effort. There are signs of uneasiness in the decoration: no detail is complete in itself, one detail seeking another to complete its beauty, in an endless and vain effort toward perfection. The whole structure, dreaming of a perfection that is never to be attained, trembles in anticipation of nothingness like a jeweled necklace trembling in the wind.

A beautiful work of art gives the spectator a feeling of nothingness. That is what Mishima seems to imply in *The Temple of the Golden Pavilion*. Indeed, the novel's narrator observes elsewhere: "Men inadvertently arrive at the darkest thoughts in the world when they pursue beauty, and beauty alone. Human beings seem to be made that way." Mishima might have added that beauty seems to be made that way, too. Underlying the observation is his idea that the artist creates a work of art in a desperate effort to diminish the chaos of the external and the internal worlds, chaos that fills him with unease, anxiety, and nihilism. In olden times, a work of art was a palace towering over the wilderness as a triumphant monument to the conqueror. In modern times, however, this rarely happened, because men became individualists and language and other artistic media lost their communal, unifying function. A work of art, created to overcome uneasiness, was uneasy in itself as it pined for its classical prototype that stood on firmer ground. It spread uneasiness to its onlookers, as the Golden Pavilion did to Mizoguchi.

Mishima made essentially the same point by quoting several poems from *The New Collection of Ancient and Modern Poems*, an anthology of poetry completed two centuries before the building of the Golden Pavilion. One was a celebrated poem by Fujiwara Teika (1161–1241):

> However far I gaze
> Neither cherry blossoms nor
>   Crimson leaves are in sight.
> Only a fisherman's hut on the shore
> In the autumnal evening.

Mishima could not accept the usual interpretation of the poem, which centers on the contrast between two types of beauty, the colorful and the austere, with the poet expressing a preference for the latter. According to Mishima, however, the poem is structured around the beauty of cherry blossoms and crimson leaves *that are not there*. The poet, standing on a desolate seashore as the autumn night fell, desperately longed for the colorful sight of cherry blossoms or bright leaves. When he realized the futility of that longing, he made it into a beautiful work of art, the poem. The poem's beauty, born of the poet's despair, conveys that despair to the reader—or at least to a reader like Mishima.

Mishima had an ambivalent feeling toward *The New Collection of Ancient and Modern Poems*, as Mizoguchi did toward the Golden Pavilion. While he was attracted to its colorful and delicate beauty, he did not like its implicit malaise, which he thought should be overcome. He saw the anthology as the first sign of a trend that was to dominate the poetry of the modern world.

Mishima recognized the same kind of beauty in some Western works of literature. For instance, he admired García Lorca for his skilled presentation of Spanish peasant life, but was disturbed

by the "uneasiness" that his work often created in the reader or
spectator. Mishima observed:

Such uneasiness is not unique to Lorca; we are familiar with it through
the symbolist plays of Maeterlinck and some Irish plays. The only difference is that Lorca's plays make us feel as though guitar music were
ceaselessly coming from behind the stage, its melody being that peculiarly
Spanish one—uneasy, nervous, like thin clouds shading the moon as they
pass its surface one after another in rapid succession. . . . In my opinion,
to produce such uneasiness in the spectator's mind is not a laudable theatrical technique. For this "unanalyzable uneasiness," conveyed through
simple characters in the drama, finds a ready audience in modern city
dwellers and in so doing expands itself within their minds in accordance
with their education and inner lives. It can balloon like bread with too
much yeast in it; it can be analogized, deduced, replaced, or used as a
metaphor for a higher type of anxiety.

The linking of uneasiness to music is characteristic of Mishima:
music, as we have seen, made him uneasy because it was invisible.
The plays he mentions were indeed very musical, not only in their
language but in their construction; powerful in mood but lacking
clearly expressible themes, they created the same kind of uneasiness
as music, an uneasiness that, since it was without shape, could expand forever in each reader's mind. As Teika's reader was free to
visualize any beautiful scene of cherry blossoms he might like,
the audience of a Lorca play was free to interpret it in a variety
of ways. Mishima did not like such freedom. He concluded that
Lorca, although undoubtedly a first-rate poet and playwright, was
also the "owner of an emaciated modern mentality."

Mishima felt the same way about the modern novel and its
readers. At the outset of *What Is a Novel?*, he observed that the
majority of people who seriously listened to the radio in today's
Japan were invalids who either did not have a television set or
were not allowed to see TV because of the nature of their illness.
He went on to assert that the modern novel was doomed to become
like the radio. In his opinion, the modern novel's readers were sick
men and women terrified of their own inner darkness, which nevertheless fascinated them. "Thanks to the fact that they have read a
novel," he said, "these people become awakened to the mystery of
human life, something of which they may never have become aware

otherwise. They are forced to discover the roots of that mystery in themselves and are led to confess it silently. Through their confession they are led forth into the wilderness lying outside society; they are made to gaze on themselves as outcasts of the society whose rules and manners they still want to observe. Thereupon 'uneasiness' emerges and forces itself upon them." A typical modern novel, being a record of the novelist's losing battle with anxiety, awakens its readers to the sense of anxiety; it makes them aware of the darkness within themselves. In short, the modern novel is a Golden Pavilion.

It logically follows, then, that the effect of an ideal literary work as conceived by Mishima should be the opposite of uneasiness, anxiety, and nihilism. It should be confidence, vigor, and courage. It should be like the impact of classical art rather than the baroque. Mishima gave this ideal clear expression toward the end of *A Short History of Japanese Literature,* a work left unfinished at his death. "When beauty emerges from the most rigorous discipline and still retains its power as beauty," he wrote, "we can call it classical beauty in the true sense of the word. Disciplined strength shows itself all too rarely in art. For art prefers to drift between a force too powerful to control and a force too feeble to need control." By "art" here he meant modern art. The uneasiness, anxiety, and despair characteristic of modern art stemmed from the unsettling position of the artist, who, in the process of trying to reduce the chaotic universe to some intelligible order, discovered either that his intellect was too feeble or that the universe was too unpredictable. The classical artist had no such trouble, since he lived in a harmonious world where order prevailed and people had firm confidence in that order. Classical beauty radiated from the sense of a harmonious world order reflected in a confident, well-disciplined mind.

Mishima found a perfect expression of such classical beauty in early Japanese court poetry, especially in *The Collection of Ancient and Modern Poems.* In his view, the authors of those poems lived in a world of classical beauty. "In the age of *The Collection of Ancient and Modern Poems,*" he observed, "a poet's conception of the moon, the snow, blossoms, love, spring, autumn, etc., were in perfect correspondence with the common notion of the external universe." The moon had become part of the man-made order and was given a proper place in human society. The sea was even awarded an official rank at court and made to serve the reigning emperor. A poem about the moon or the sea, therefore, had no element of mystery or uneasiness; the poet knew everything about the subject, and was able to predict all that it would do. The effect of such a poem upon the reader was that of a calm, assured beauty that Mishima called *miyabi*, or "courtly elegance."

Mishima demonstrated the point by citing examples from the anthology on several occasions. To take one of them:

> The spring night's darkness
> Is behaving senselessly
> Toward the plum blossoms.
> Though their color may be veiled
> How can their fragrance be hidden?

Here the darkness of a spring night is personified and made to become part of man's world. It is expected to behave reasonably, like a civilized man. Because it does not do so, the poet calmly proceeds to record his complaint. The basic assumption here is that there is a model pattern of thought and behavior for all people and all things, since all are part of an orderly universe. They may depart from good order at times, as the darkness did, but things become normal eventually—in this case, when the morning comes and shows both the color and fragrance of the blossoms. There is no element of mystery or uneasiness implied in the poem, hardly any room for the reader's imagination, even.*

One might argue that a poem like this is not very provocative or inspiring. *The Collection of Ancient and Modern Poems* as a whole has been attacked by some modern critics as being too intellectual, too lacking in imaginative power. Mishima, however, liked those

---

* A modern interpretation has it that the poem is allegorical, that the darkness of the spring night stands for a mother reluctant to let her daughter see the poet, who admires the young girl. But this interpretation does not seem right, in view of the poem's title, "Written on Plum Blossoms on a Spring Night." Moreover, the poem is categorized as a seasonal poem, not a love poem.

poems precisely for that quality. Inspirational poems seemed dangerous to him because, like modern novels or Lorca's plays, they encouraged introspection and anxiety. "The poems in *The Collection of Ancient and Modern Poems* do not easily move the reader's emotion," he observed. "They appeal only to those readers who, like the poets, feel strength within and know the meaning of self-control. These poems are expressly not designed to flatter the exhausted nerves, decadent desires, or caterwaulings of men gone soft."

It was no accident that Mishima found the same type of relationship between ancient Greek art and its audience. In fact, Mishima once put himself in that audience during his tour of Greece in 1952. Standing in the ruins at Olympia and meditating on the ancient city as it had stood there ages ago, he felt an ecstatic joy that he analyzed as follows. "When we visualize the original, complete form of the Parthenon or Erechtheum from its ruins, we do so by ratiocination, not by intuition. The joy of visualizing it lies not so much in the poetry of imaginative power as in the ecstasy of intellectual exercise. The emotion we feel is that of looking at a skeleton of the universal." Like the poets of *The Collection of Ancient and Modern Poems*, the ancient Greeks had "the universal," an image of a world order shared by all people in the community. Their artistic product, therefore, was a result not of a social misfit's whimsical imaginings but of a communal artist's vision in which the rest of the society participated. The people could predict what the work of art would be like, whoever the artist might be.

A typical Mishima novel, which aims at the beauty of strength, confidence, and self-control, all derived from a belief in a harmonious world order, is *The Sound of Waves*, in which the author tried to present "my Arcadia." Based on the story of Daphnis and Chloë, the novel describes the idyllic love affair of a sturdy young fisherman and a simple village girl on a rustic island off the coast of Japan. The island, largely untouched by modernization, retains a sense of order that is shared by all the islanders. There is a premodern type of community spirit, symbolized by a Shinto shrine that figures prominently in the novel's opening and concluding scenes. The hero and heroine have a high moral sense that matches their physical development. They can restrain their impulses even when they embrace each other in the nude, as they do in a controversial scene. This particular scene, along with several others, has often been attacked by some critics as unrealistic. Mishima never bothered to answer them, but if he had he would have said that the novel appeals only to those readers who know the meaning of self-control; it is not designed to flatter those who have no reserves of inner strength on which to draw.

Mishima, however, did not write another novel that produces the same type of happy combination of effects. Other novels of his may give an impression of vigor and self-control but not of classical harmony. The reason is obvious: they have neither an Arcadian setting nor a Daphnis and Chloë for their principal characters. The setting for most Mishima novels is contemporary Japan or, at any rate, the Japan of the last one hundred years. To Mishima, this was an impossible milieu for a sturdy, simple-hearted man of action; if he tried to be faithful to his nature, he would almost always meet a tragic end. Thus Saburō, the broad-shouldered servant in *Thirst for Love*, is murdered by a sophisticated modern woman bent on creating a small domestic monarchy for herself through her clever schemes and manipulations. The muscular navigator in *The Sailor Who Fell from Grace with the Sea* is killed, too, when he decides to forsake the seaman's life and become part of modern Japanese society. The young captain of a student kendō team in "The Sword" commits suicide upon discovering that the premodern community spirit that he had imagined his team to have is being violated by all his teammates. The young soldier in "Patriotism" also kills himself when he feels betrayed by his comrades in an attempted coup. The hero of *Runaway Horses*, another kendō expert, similarly commits ritual suicide after being betrayed by his own father (he does succeed, however, in assassinating one of the influential politicians he and his comrades had marked as their targets). These are all tragic characters, and the stories that feature them produce a basically tragic impact, with some minor variations among them. The reader sympathizes with the heroes and feels something akin to pity and fear as he watches them being destroyed by some colossal power, a power usually related to the modern age. In this respect the effect of a tragic Mishima novel is not unlike that of *Othello*, a drama of a sturdy soldier victimized by the schemes of a formidable intellect.

Mishima's tragic novels approach Greek tragedy, but there is an important difference. In a Greek tragedy, a restoration to order nearly always follows the catastrophe, in the spectator's mind if not in the play itself. The sense of harmony, or a fervent desire for it, is always present in such a play. Looking back on his trip to Greece, Mishima reflected:

In ancient Greece there was no such thing as "the spirit"; there had been just the body and intellect in perfect harmony, until "the spirit" was invented by Christianity. Of course the harmony had a propensity to break down, and the effort to prevent it created a beautiful tension. In my opinion, the lesson of Greek tragedy, where the proud human will always gets punished in the end, is that this harmony is all-important. In the Greek city-states, which were also religious communities of a kind, the gods always kept a watchful eye on the possible breakdown of harmony in the human world.

Contemporary Japan had no gods watching for a breakdown of harmony. Indeed, a happy harmony between body and mind had long vanished from the community, and without the help of Christian influence, too. What existed there was "the spirit," that is, imagination running riot. Japanese readers, after reading a tragic novel, would feel no sense of order being restored because they had no sense of order to share.

Mishima, then, faced an impossible task: to restore to a sense of order a reader who was lacking in discipline, self-control, and communal feeling. Mishima was living in an untragic age. In order to create a tragic effect as it existed in ancient Greece, he had first to educate his readers so that they could attain a sense of harmony or at least an aspiration for it. Yet literature was sadly unqualified to help that cause, since its medium, language, had a general tendency to promote disharmony in modern times. Mishima's tragic novels, though they powerfully evoke a longing for strength and communal order, are lacking in tragic effect because their principal characters are alienated from society. Mizoguchi, for example, is far from being a great tragic figure because few readers find him a representative one.

Understandably, Mishima became less and less optimistic about the usefulness of literature. Through literature he wanted to bring classical beauty, the beauty of strength, discipline, and harmony, to the minds of contemporary Japanese readers. Yet the current realities of Japan's culture, people, and language all went counter to his wishes. His readers were skeptics, hedonists, or weaklings, and the pleas contained in his literary works fell on deaf ears. Since they were generally hostile to *The Collection of Ancient and Modern Poems,* they were unreceptive to the message that Mishima wanted to convey; they accepted his works only on their terms, not his. To many Japanese readers, *After the Banquet* seemed just a topical novel; *Forbidden Colors,* a homosexual novel; *Modern Nō Plays,* avant-garde experiments. Though there were a few perceptive critics who saw a deeper meaning in those works, Mishima had wanted to reach the entire community. His stories sprang from his desire to create a sense of order that could be shared by the masses, but the masses were not receptive.

With such an objective, Mishima eventually had to, and did, go outside the realm of literature. He came to believe that classical beauty, disciplined strength, the mind-body harmony, and other related values could be more readily expressed in the realm of action through the medium of the body, especially of the male body. Action and the body could attain a physical effect that all people, including the illiterate, would be able to see. People differed widely in their idea of a beautiful art work, but they tended to agree on their idea of a beautiful body, as the ancient Greek sculptures showed. Physical beauty approached universality as it neared perfection, while imaginative beauty moved in the opposite direction. A muscular, fully developed male body signified strength, discipline, will power, harmony of mind and body, in a way that was visible and unmistakable to everyone. When such a man met a heroic death, everyone would see his death as a real tragedy, because everyone would be able to identify with his ideal physique.

Mishima's suicide could be interpreted as an attempt to accomplish in action what he had failed, or thought he had failed, to do in literature. He wanted to impress on the general public that his death was that of a heroic soldier. Whether he succeeded in that attempt is a question to be answered only by time. For the present, it does not seem he did. Few Japanese identified themselves with Mishima closely enough to feel a tragic sense of elation at his death. He perhaps overestimated the role of the body and action in contemporary Japanese life. An average Japanese could readily admire his sheer physical courage, but not the objective to which the courage was directed. The general public was more spiritually oriented than Mishima thought it was. To the modern sensibility, even the human body in action is equivocal.

Exactitude in Structure and Style

Mishima favored logically constructed plots. This is understandable in view of his ideas on the nature and function of literature: he held that a literary work should give form to life, and that it could do so only when it had a tight, artificial structure. He instinctively shunned works of art that, like music, had a loose or hidden form; they were too much like life. For him, the raison d'être of literature lay in its ability to structure life.

In this respect, it can be said that Mishima's liking for a tightly structured form preceded his theory of literature. Indeed, his inborn predilection for structure enticed him to become a writer. Already as a little child he was fond of playing with blocks. He tells us that he especially liked to pile them into a tower so perilously balanced that it would collapse if another piece were added to it. Young Mishima was also attracted to symmetry. He enjoyed gazing at a pair of stone pillars adorning the gateway to a mansion, or at a massive tree with its branches growing equally on both sides of the trunk. After mentioning these objects of his childhood fascination, Mishima reflected: "As a matter of fact, what I am trying to do as a novelist and playwright is to work on this childhood predilection of mine and develop it as much as possible."

Mishima's liking for the closely woven plot is best expressed in the concluding passage of his essay "On the Art of the Novel," where he describes his vision of an ideal novel:

In such a novel, the story would progress with all the predictability of a railway train running on schedule, so that the only surprise awaiting the reader would be the way in which the 1:05 train has arrived not a second earlier or later. All unforeseen, sudden happenings should be described in a manner so natural that the reader will feel as if he has been waiting for them all along; in this way, past and future will meet and kiss one another, like a magnet kissing a piece of iron, at every juncture in the novel. When a character dies, his coffin should fit his body perfectly, its size being not even a tiny bit too large or too small. In order for the novel as a whole to look like a fascinating coincidence on a large scale, all coincidences should be carefully removed from it; there should be no chance encounter, no unpredictable conduct, no casting of dice. Everything in the novel should move as the constellations do. A fastidious sense of balance should pervade the novel as it does the balance sheet of a commercial firm.

Mishima's ideal novel is artificial to the core, every little part of it controlled and manipulated by the author; there are no accidents and no coincidences. Such an ideal would seem to go directly counter to the traditional Japanese notion of loose, episodic construction. As we have seen, Akutagawa preferred a "plotless" novel, and Tanizaki suspected the Japanese might by nature be lacking in the ability to construct an elaborate plot. Mishima thought otherwise. Pointing out that some plays in the kabuki and the puppet theater had a highly dramatic structure, he maintained that Japanese novelists had merely been prejudiced against artificial plot construction because of their "realistic fallacy." They were quite mistaken, he thought, in presuming that in order to create a sense of reality they had to copy the capricious ways of life itself.

Mishima, however, did not like to emulate certain premodern Japanese novelists who, under the influence of the theater, devised a highly complex plot for its own sake. Instead, he sought out models in Western literature, and found the best one in *The Count's Ball* by Raymond Radiguet, which he had read in his teens.

Young Mishima adored the novel. One of its greatest attractions, as he recalled later, was its pure, abstract structure. The novel had to derive its main charm from its structure, he speculated, because the author was too young and too inexperienced to make profound remarks about life. For Mishima, *The Count's Ball* was the supreme type of pure, abstract novel. He termed its structure "optical," meaning that all its parts were made to converge on the final catastrophe just as rays of light converge through a lens. "This method of construction," he wrote, "which intensifies the novel's climax in a manner reminiscent of classical tragedy, was to become an indispensable element in my art of the novel."

Certainly, the method can be seen at work in his published fiction. It is not difficult to find a Mishima novel with a dramatic, "optical" plot. *Thirst for Love, The Temple of the Golden Pavilion, The Sound of Waves, The Sailor Who Fell from Grace with the Sea, Spring Snow*—each can be said to have an "optical" structure, with all the incidents presented in it converging on the final catastrophe. No other major author in modern Japan insisted so strongly on the importance of a logically unified plot or took so much pain in constructing one in an actual work of fiction. Tanizaki, indeed, stressed the importance of plot and wrote many tightly plotted works; yet in his instance the novel's unity was attained more through narrative than through discursive logic. He was more a storyteller than a philosopher.

Even so, Mishima was usually careful enough not to make his novel a thinly disguised treatise. He gave literary flesh to the philosophical skeleton in several ways. As a matter of strategy, he did plot construction in the third stage of the creative process, so that the bare plot line sank under the surface when the novel was actually written. He would temporarily forget about plot when he took up his pen and concentrated on the details of a particular scene. Mishima did this more deliberately than most writers, since he believed that Japanese readers were more fascinated with details than their counterparts in other nations. He speculated that American novels were unpopular in Japan because they were lacking in charming descriptions of minute details.

Another characteristic way in which Mishima adorned his plot was by the use of striking images and metaphors. Looking back to his days as an eighteen-year-old novelist, he recalled: "The most painstaking part of my creative writing was to find metaphors. When I found a good metaphor, I was happy all that day." Sixteen years later he stated he was rather tired of inventing striking metaphors but still continued to do so because it had become second nature to him. Indeed, Mishima's novels are aglow with brilliant metaphors. They are original, intellectual, and often ironic, as can be deduced from his views on the nature of literature. Mishima has been said to be one of the most quotable of writers; his metaphors are a large part of the reason. Aphoristic sentences strewn with metaphors help focus the reader's attention on the details rather than on the overall plot.

On the whole, however, it is not just images and metaphors but language and style in general that distinguish a Mishima novel and help attract the reader's attention to the particulars. Mishima was an extremely self-conscious stylist, a theorist who wrote *The Composition Reader*. One of the main points he made in that primer was that a modern Japanese reader should read a novel especially to enjoy the beauty of its language. He compared a novel to a roll of textile showing designs such as distant mountains, beautiful valleys, and evergreen hedges; he wanted the reader to take a close look at each design and appreciate its artistry. "Readers in the old days used to enjoy the textile designs," he wrote. "The novelist took delight, as an artisan does, in pleasing his readers through the beauty of the textile he wove."

What type of style did Mishima like best? In *The Composition Reader* he classified all prose styles into two broad categories, the Apollonian and the Dionysian. The former was a style that had clarity for its ultimate aim. It tried to present the subject with the utmost simplicity, refusing to be sidetracked by wayward imagination, subjective psychoanalysis, or flattery of the reader. And yet it was neither cold nor prosaic. "This is a lucid, logical, undecorative style that points directly to the subject," he explained, "and yet, in its watery transparency there lies poetry; like the chemical formula H₂O, the ultimate element of poetry is hidden in colorless, tasteless water." Mishima found the best examples of this style in the writings of Stendhal, who admired the Code Napoléon, and of Mori Ōgai, who, when asked to describe the characteristics of the ideal style, reportedly answered: "First, clarity; second, clarity; third, clarity."

In contrast, the Dionysian style had attributes far removed from watery transparency. It was colorful, imaginative, sensual. In Mishima's own words: "It creates an overflow of dazzling colors; it faithfully pursues the senses wherever they go. Instead of pointing bluntly at the subject, the passages invite the reader to enjoy a pure, sustained sensual experience. Once entrapped in this style, he has no time to examine the subject through a close look or touch; he drowns in the colorfulness of the language, and falls into a kind of intellectual trance." He considered Izumi Kyōka (1873–1939) the master of this style and placed Tanizaki in the same category.*

Not surprisingly, Mishima theorized that the origins of these two dominant styles in Japanese literature went back to the Heian Period, when there was a clear-cut distinction between the languages of men and women. The Apollonian style originated in classical Chinese, which men used in their public functions. The Dionysian style originated in classical Japanese, which court ladies employed in their private lives. Japanese literature developed along the lines of the latter, because writers found it easier to express themselves in their native language. Classical Chinese, which was more logical and intellectual, almost disappeared from the main current of Japanese literature. With it went the masculine type of literary work. The male protagonists in Japanese literature became more feminine than their counterparts in Western literature—a characteristic that, in Mishima's opinion, could be seen even in Shiga's *Voyage Through the Dark Night*. Naturally, the

---

* Izumi Kyōka was a leading modern novelist who specialized in the mystic, supernatural themes reminiscent of late Edo literature. His admirers among later generations of Japanese writers have been few but ardent. Tanizaki was one of them, as noted earlier.

dominant style of Japanese prose fiction became feminine and Dionysian.

Behind all this one can detect Mishima's preference for the Apollonian style over the Dionysian, even though, in all fairness, it must be said that his treatment of the two in *The Composition Reader* is admirably impartial. He liked the masculine style, since it had all the classical virtues. Mishima's *The Composition Reader* makes an interesting contrast with Tanizaki's book of the same title. Tanizaki, it will be remembered, seemed to favor the more feminine styles. Obviously, Mishima's primer of composition was intended to tip the balance the other way.

Predictably, Mishima tried to write in the Apollonian style, increasingly so as he grew older. Always a deliberate experimenter, he used many different styles, steadily moving toward a style like Ōgai's. He testified to it in "My Effort Toward Self-Reform," an essay written in 1956 that traces the vicissitudes of his prose style up to that time. With an openness that few writers have ever achieved, he conceded that most of his fiction had been written in stylistic imitation of a writer or writers he happened to admire at that particular time. By his own admission, "Stained Glass" (1940) was stylistically influenced by, among others, Paul Morand, Hori Tatsuo (1904–53), and the Neo-Sensualists;* "The Moon at Minomo" (1942) by Heian classics and Hori's modern translations of them; "The Medieval Age" (1945) by European fin-de-siècle literature; *Thieves* (1948) by *The Count's Ball*; "Sunday" (1950) by Ōgai; *The Blue Period* (1950) by Stendhal; *Forbidden Colors* (1953) and *The Sunken Waterfall* (1955) by Stendhal and Ōgai; and *The Temple of the Golden Pavilion* (1956) by Ōgai and Thomas Mann. Since Morand, Hori, and the Neo-Sensualists, not

* Hori Tatsuo, a friend and admirer of Akutagawa, was known for his delicate, sensitive use of modern Japanese prose. He wrote novels and stories under the influence of contemporary French literature as well as of Heian authoresses. As we have seen, the Neo-Sensualists were a group of young writers, led by Yokomitsu Riichi and Kawabata Yasunari, who, stimulated by Paul Morand and other contemporary Western writers, attempted to incorporate the techniques of symbolism, expressionism, and surrealism into modern Japanese fiction.

to mention the Heian writers, can all be said to have used some version of the Dionysian style, Mishima's progress from the feminine to the masculine style is evident. Thomas Mann may not be said to have a clearly Apollonian style, but Mishima sensed a masculinity that was inherent in the German language itself.

Mishima made no effort to trace his stylistic vicissitudes after 1956, but it is not difficult to see a continuation of the earlier trend toward the Apollonian style. Indeed, the style described as his ideal in *Sun and Steel* seems about as masculine as it could be. He now liked a formal style, a style that gave the impression of polished hardwood coldly gleaming in the entrance hall of a samurai mansion on a winter's day. He tried to make it his own style, even though it was not at all fashionable. His style became more and more old-fashioned, dignified, and ceremonious, stripped of all superfluous adornments. It became like a muscular athlete who through rigorous exercise got rid of all fat, just as Mishima himself became such a man.

If there was any change in Mishima's attitude in his later years, it was that he stopped trying to imitate other writers' styles. He no longer endeavored to make his style masculine by emulating Stendhal or Ōgai. Rather, he tried to attain the same end by becoming a man with a highly masculine body. He renovated his prose style by renovating his physique. In this respect he shared Tanizaki's view that one's style is rooted in one's physical constitution. Yet whereas Tanizaki believed that one's basic style of writing is physical and therefore cannot be changed, Mishima maintained that one's basic style is physical and therefore *can* be changed. This belief was the outstanding characteristic of Mishima's conception of prose style; there was no other Japanese writer who held such a view. In a passage most revealing of his ideas on style, Mishima observed:

Throughout my life I have believed that a writer's style represents his *Sollen*, and not his *Sein*. If the style of a literary work shows nothing but the author's *Sein*, it is merely a reflection of his sensibility and physique, and, as such, does not qualify to be called a style. . . . The style can be meaningfully related to the theme in a literary work only when it is expressive of the writer's *Sollen* and represents his intellectual effort to attain the unattained. For the theme of a literary work is always something not yet attained. Having held such a view, I have never intended my style to be expressive of what I am; rather, I have created my style out of my will, my aspiration, my effort toward self-reform.

Here Mishima is saying not only that style can be changed but that it should be changed. A writer, in particular, should be an idealist, always trying to attain an aim that has not been attained; he should always be trying to renovate his style and bring it closer to his ideal. A writer's style should be dynamic, not static.

Did Mishima as a literary artist eventually attain the kind of masculine style he had held as ideal? The question can be answered only in relative terms, but one is tempted to say he did. The styles used in, say, "The Sword," "Patriotism," and *Runaway Horses* do indeed have something like the cold gleam of polished hardwood in the hall of a samurai mansion. They are terse, subdued, unadorned. *Sun and Steel,* in which he describes his ideal style, is written in a similar style, too. In those works his styles came remarkably close to Ōgai's—more so than in "Sunday," *Forbidden Colors,* or *The Temple of the Golden Pavilion,* in which he was consciously imitating Ōgai.

However, when a writer pursues a masculine style to its logical conclusion, he will eventually have to leave the realm of literature. In *The Composition Reader,* Mishima already notes that Ōgai had written no long novel, and speculates that an Apollonian stylist aiming at clarity could not write a lengthy work because he knew the limitations of language all too well. Mishima, who became an athlete in order to be able to write in a masculine style, realized that athletics belonged to the world of action, not to the feminine world of literature. In this respect, one could argue that Mishima's masculine style culminated in the nonliterary writings of his last years, such as *In Defense of Japanese Culture* and other political essays. The style used in these writings is too masculine to be called literary. Those who spurned the prose style of his last appeal to the Japanese Self-Defense Force and said it was not worthy of a professional novelist were rather wide of the mark. From Mishima's point of view, a novelist's style would be totally unsuited to affairs of state, which were essentially masculine. The same reasoning can be applied to his seeming return, however cautious, toward stylistic femininity in *Spring Snow*, *The Temple of Dawn*, and *The Decay of the Angel*. Having firmly established himself as a man of action beyond the literary world, he was no longer afraid of using a style somewhat less than completely masculine.

Epic Poet in the Modern Age

As we see from the foregoing sections, Mishima held a pragmatic view of literature, always thinking of it in terms of its use either for himself or for society. To him, writing from impulse without a conscious aim was an act to be ashamed of. His ideas of what that aim should be, however, changed with time, as did his ideas on the scope of literature. In his boyhood he set a very ambitious goal for literature: he wanted it to create an orderly world. Bitterly disappointed in this venture, he came to expect far less from it. Thus his later writings about the use of literature often show a negative, even cynical attitude.

We have already seen Mishima picturing a professional writer as an invalid, a coward, and a criminal. In *Forbidden Colors* the novelist Shunsuke is described as one of the living dead. In *The Temple of the Golden Pavilion* Kashiwagi spurns art as "barren" and "inorganic," something no better than a pile of stones. Mishima's most devastating remark on the use of literature appears in his brilliantly satirical book *Lectures Promoting Immoral Education*. Claiming that the surest way to world peace would be for every youngster on this earth to become a weakling, Mishima recommended a number of ways in which a young man could impair his physical fitness. One of the most effective methods was to become an avid reader of books.

Reading will serve the purpose very well. If practiced simultaneously with coffee drinking, it will be even more effective in promoting your insomnia. It will help you to become more dreamy and unrealistic, while also serving to weaken your physical condition. Since constant reading bends your spine forward, you will be found unfit for military service. The more books you read, the less decisive your mind will become, until you lose your ability to act. Nothing could be more desirable than that.

For Mishima, then, literature was useful only in a negative sense; in his utopia, its role was essentially passive. In the main, he appears to have assigned it two functions. First, a literary artist could play the role of an epic poet. He could sing of heroes who fought and died for a worthy cause. Though a weakling himself, incapable of participating in the battle, he was also a seer, a visionary cursed with the truth. This involved being coward enough to live on after the battle was over. A true hero would not be able to see his own beauty; besides, his heroism would end in death. "By its very nature," Mishima wrote, "action presupposes one's entire strength dashing out toward one's aim at full speed. It cannot see its own beauty, just as a galloping deer cannot see its own beauty." It was here that the epic poet came into his own. He watched the hero's entire course of action from the sidelines, and recorded it as a valuable part of the human heritage. If *The Sea of Fertility* can be called an epic, as Mishima intended it to be, then Honda is an epic poet who records the lives of four heroes (or two heroes, one heroine, and one pseudo-hero). The fact that he is a Peeping Tom is symbolic of his function as a seer. In the same way Shunsuke in *Forbidden Colors* functions as an epic poet for the hero Yūichi. When the hero himself becomes a seer at the end of the novel, the poet loses his raison d'être and commits suicide.

The crucial factor here is that the poet should function on an epic scale. He should concern himself only with a hero sanctioned by society as such; in this way, he will speak for the entire community of which he is a member. It is therefore incumbent upon him, above all, to sense the cultural climate of his age, to have a firm grasp of it and be able to express it articulately. Mishima conceived culture as an active power operating invisibly within a community. He wrote: "Culture governs all the members of a community in regard to their modes of thinking, feeling, living, and artistic appreciation, even though they may not be aware of the fact. It is an absolute necessity for community life, like air or water. Under ordinary circumstances, people draw on culture without stint, not appreciating its value. But when, at some critical moment, they realize they are doomed without it, they allow themselves to be strictly bound by it and pattern their behavior accordingly." In Mishima's view, a hero is a person who tries, through his actions, to express contemporary culture in its highest form, even at the expense of his life, and who thereby gains the admiration of all his fellow men. A literary artist records such a hero's action, and bequeathes the record to posterity. It was from this point of view that Mishima wrote *A Short History of Japanese Literature*. His selection of masterpieces was therefore quite idiosyncratic. It included such works as *Records of the Legitimate Succession of the Divine Sovereigns* and *Hidden in the Leaves*, which would normally be excluded from a history of Japanese literature as compact as Mishima's, or at any rate only briefly alluded to.* Mishima held these works in high regard because their authors, he thought, were epic poets with a sound grasp of the culture governing their communities, a culture that they were able to express in literary form. Literature contributed to society by pointing to its "air" and "water," the invisible essentials without which it would collapse and die.

Second, a literary artist could use his powers of perception to defend activities that were wrongly condemned as antisocial. It is significant that Honda, in *Runaway Horses*, is a lawyer by profession and defends Isao at a trial. In ancient times the community produced universally admired heroes because it shared a common set of values. But in modern times, when individualism reigned, a hero, if there was one, was often misunderstood and mistreated, as Isao is. A man of letters, being a seer, should be able to recognize a true hero in a mistreated criminal, and present him in proper perspective.

Nothing stimulates the novelist's imagination more, challenges his ability more, and inspires his creative urge more, than a crime that seems in-

---

* *Records of the Legitimate Succession of the Divine Sovereigns* (1339) is a Japanese history written with the aim of clarifying and justifying the Japanese imperial lineage, which was in dispute at the time. Its author, Kitabatake Chikafusa, wrote the book while his castle was besieged by enemy forces. *Hidden in the Leaves* (1716) is a collection of talks given by Yamamoto Jōchō, a samurai serving in a clan government. Some authorities consider it the best textbook on samurai morals. Mishima wanted more people to read it, and wrote *Hidden in the Leaves: An Introduction* in 1967.

defensible in the light of ordinary morality. In such a case, the novelist takes pride in his courage to render a different verdict, though the rest of the world may condemn him. Perhaps the criminal, in his unrepentant pride, is the harbinger of hitherto unknown values. In any case, a novel reveals its uniquely ethical nature at a crisis like this one.

In other words, a novelist is a soothsayer who can see what lies ahead. Thus old Honda is able to predict the imminent death of Tōru at the age of twenty-one. Literature, especially modern literature, can and should depict heroes born too far ahead or too far behind the times.

If this second role of literature seems overly romantic, it seemed so to Mishima too. In the end he did not entirely subscribe to it. He made Honda defend a heroic criminal, but at the end of *Runaway Horses* we find that the lawyer did not succeed in saving Isao's life. In *The Decay of the Angel*, too, Honda fails as a soothsayer: Tōru does not die at the age of twenty-one. In a degenerate age like ours, a true hero is hard to find, as is a true artist. Ultimately, Mishima's pessimism on the function of literature in our time derived not so much from his views on the nature of literature as from his appraisal of the state of human civilization.

Source Notes

❁

This section is for those who read Japanese and who wish to consult the sources in the original texts. The present author is responsible for the translation of all quotations from Japanese sources in this book.

In the notes below, the numerals at the left refer to page and then to line numbers in this book. The two italicized words following the numerals are the end of the quotation or phrase that is being annotated.

CHAPTER ONE

The volume and page references are to *Sōseki zenshū*, 16 vols. (Tokyo: Iwanami Shoten, 1965–67).

2.8. *views nature."* XI, 577–78.
2.19. *other two.* II, 456–57.
3.34. *a demigod."* XI, 577–78.
4.14. *is painful."* X, 425–26.
4.26. *December 31.* X, 433.
4.29. *artistic freedom.* X, 284.
4.31. *actually existed.* X, 185.
5.4. *but consciousness."* XI, 36.
6.12. *so forth."* XI, 52.
6.23. *incites emotion.* IX, 27–29.
6.32. *the society."* X, 49.
6.37. *do so.* X, 365–71.
7.25. *second place.* XI, 174–80.
7.28. *people's behavior.* XVI, 517.
7.31. *proper viewpoint.* XVI, 539.
7.37. *this kind."* XI, 79.
10.16. *Japanese haiku.* XI, 56.
10.24. *beautiful effect,* XVI, 544–45.
11.8. *the moon.* II, 471–72.
11.41. *haiku form."* X, 56.
12.1. *aesthetic purpose.* XVI, 545.
12.5. *water wheel.* XII, 569.
12.8. *a dream.* XII, 639.
12.11. *of Heaven.* XII, 702.
12.18. *third one.* VIII, 285.
12.36. *at all.* X, 325.

13.14. *it himself.* XI, 57–58.
13.21. *or independence!"* XIII, 106.
13.25. *to death.* XII, 551.
14.11. *suffered unfairly.* XI, 74–75.
14.14. *conclusion depressing.* XI, 72.
14.27. *English literature.* XI, 58–60; IX, 53–91.
14.31. *this category."* IX, 77.
15.7. *leads us.* IX, 83.
16.23. *Zen meditation.* XI, 60–62.
16.33. *a Cat.* I, 346.
17.2. *Meiji Restoration."* XIV, 492.
17.16. *heroic characters.* XI, 240–42.
17.20. *contemporary literature.* XI, 66.
18.13. *organic structure.* X, 436–38.
19.7. *of interest.* X, 440–43.
19.8. *episodic structure.* XI, 201.
19.16. *shaseibun writers.* XI, 27–28.
19.19. *sluggish progression).* XII, 191.
19.24. *human reality."* XIII, 518.
19.27. *should study.* XI, 180.
20.10. *in literature.* IX, 256–381.
22.25. *artistically superior.* IX, 319.
22.29. *as natural?"* XI, 185.
23.11. *was entertaining?"* X, 294.

23.26. *unlikely place.* X, 297.
24.6. *future life.* X, 202.

24.28. *and naturalism.* XVI, 398.
25.12. *other individuals."* XI, 386.

CHAPTER TWO

The collection of Kafū's works referred to below is *Kafū zenshū,* 28 vols. (Tokyo: Iwanami Shoten, 1962–65).

27.9. *to be.* XXVI, 91–92.
27.17. *of it."* XXVI, 107.
27.19. *of men,"* XV, 152.
27.21. *such-and-such circumstances."* XVI, 388–89.
27.31. *about life.* XVIII, 384.
27.34. *on it.* XVIII, 549.
28.2. *and gardens.* XIV, 407.
28.4. *River Sumida.* XIII, 347.
30.32. *and society."* XVI, 388.
31.13. *and immoral.* V, 237.
31.24. *social justice.* XIII, 307–8.
32.18. *of imagination."* XIV, 404.
32.22. *and then.* XV, 111.
33.2. *be dressed."* XV, 72–75.
33.14. *from within."* XIV, 405.
33.20. *and sympathy."* XV, 78.
33.30. *with reality."* XVIII, 404.
33.35. *put it.* Hattori Dohō, *Sanzōshi. Nihon koten bungaku taikei,* LXVI (Tokyo: Iwanami Shoten, 1961), 398.
34.33. *of reference.* XIV, 276–77.
35.4. *him grow.* XIV, 406.
35.14. *his novels.* IV, 268.
35.22. *writer's personality."* XIV, 405.
35.29. *of today."* XXVI, 264–65.
36.21. *outstanding one."* XIV, 398–99.
36.23. *urgently needed."* XIV, 400.
36.28. *anything else."* XIV, 408.
37.6. *on it.* IV, 11–12.
37.9. *emotional excitement."* XIV, 398.
38.23. *of light.* XI, 318.
38.39. *being human.* IV, 328–29.
39.17. *Wagnerian opera.* IV, 397–98.
40.6. *deep sorrow.* XIII, 184.
40.12. *their rulers.* XIV, 6.

40.30. *momentary pleasure?"* IV, 116.
41.4. *more wrong."* IV, 116.
41.16. *Japanese literature.* XIV, 141.
42.19. *informed men's."* XIV, 396.
43.9. *the work."* XIV, 404.
44.3. *sneered at."* IX, 119.
44.7. *or acquaintances.* XIII, 177.
45.35. *in point.* XIV, 407.
46.5. *doing it."* XIV, 406.
46.26. *Japanese prints.* XIV, 24.
47.5. *I mean.* XXVI, 111.
47.19. *color sufficiently.* XXVI, 112.
47.23. *the subject."* XXVI, 112.
48.1. *nineteenth-century Japan.* XIII, 26–27.
48.31. *Chinese writings.* XIV, 317.
49.2. *of life."* XV, 187.
49.12. *prose style;* XXVI, 526.
50.11. *this earth.* XIV, 152–53.
50.17. *to Mozart?* XI, 428.
50.34. *a novel.* XXVI, 539–40.
51.1. *unacceptable elements.* XV, 151–52.
51.3. *from it.* XV, 95.
51.6. *and gamblers.* IV, 35.
51.14. *to write."* XIV, 397.
51.17. *his parents.* XVI, 435.
51.21. *a diversion."* XIV, 399.
51.23. *likes to.* XIV, 397.
51.36. *in me."* XV, 465.
52.6. *console myself."* IV, 17.
52.13. *than pleasure.* XV, 463.
52.19. *his views.* XVI, 356.
52.22. *to read.* XXVI, 56.
53.6. *only value.* XIV, 249.
53.15. *nonartistic terms.* XXVI, 96–97.

CHAPTER THREE

The references are to *Tanizaki Jun'ichirō zenshū,* 28 vols. (Tokyo: Chūō Kōron Sha, 1966–69).

55.11. *into truth.* XXIII, 39.
55.29. *abstract hypotheses?"* XXII, 67–68.

56.6. *imitates art."* VI, 273.
56.28. *serious ailment.* XIII, 214.
57.8. *to be."* XX, 6–7.

57.35. *inner world.* XX, 408–9.
58.20. *of art."* XX, 28.
58.23. *his work."* XX, 497.
58.35. *actually happened."* XX, 333.
59.4. *is realistic."* XX, 72.
59.9. *from Japan.* XX, 73.
59.19. *his imagination."* XXIII, 130.
60.6. *given date.* XXII, 364.
61.1. *by each."* XXII, 66.
61.23. *his mind.* XXII, 65–66.
62.8. *tight rope."* XX, 140.
62.21. *called dissipation.* XXII, 29.
62.23. *got married.* XXII, 27–28.
62.35. *married her.* XIX, 398.
63.10. *within her."* XIX, 402.
63.26. *a woman.* XIX, 406.
63.35. *a baby.* XXII, 24–31.
64.18. *winter came.* XXII, 41.
64.22. *in December.* XXII, 65.
64.29. *ten lines.* XIX, 422.
64.31. *the novel.* XXI, 253; XXIII, 289.
64.34. *in Yoshino."* XXI, 254.
64.37. *minor revisions.* XXIII, 238–39.
65.7. *in reality."* XX, 42.
65.13. *of creation.* XX, 43.
65.24. *gloomy complexion."* XXI, 170.
66.27. *Japanese-style washroom.* XX, 520.

66.29. *than eat.* XX, 531.
66.32. *a dream."* XX, 532.
66.35. *its reflections.* XX, 530.
67.17. *its web.* XX, 551.
68.10. *encourage dreamers."* XXII, 432.
69.20. *cunning woman."* XVII, 264.
69.24. *Simone Signoret.* XIX, 25–26.
69.29. *a devil."* XXIII, 116.
70.4. *beautiful woman.* XXII, 124.
70.9. *or loveliness."* VI, 214–15.
71.17. *complicated plots.* XX, 73.
71.30. *complicated plot.* XX, 26–27.
72.22. *to construct."* XX, 108.
72.33. *would collapse."* XX, 45–46.
74.8. *Japanese orthography.* XXII, 19–23.
74.11. *and journalists.* XXI, 463–79.
74.20. *artistic language."* XXI, 94.
74.28. *literary composition."* XXI, 97.
76.4. *same stimulant."* XXI, 147.
79.10. *happiness himself.* XVII, 246–47.
79.30. *private world.* XIX, 421.
80.7. *writing it.* XXIII, 238.
81.5. *popular literature."* XX, 79.
81.23. *thing exists."* XX, 154–55.
81.39. *important message.* XX, 155.
82.33. *is beauty."* XXII, 90–91.
83.26. *his death."* VII, 511–12.

CHAPTER FOUR

The latest edition of Shiga's collected works, *Shiga Naoya zenshū*, 14 vols. (Tokyo: Iwanami Shoten, 1973–74), is the text referred to below.

86.2. *they were,"* VIII, 11.
86.3. *actually happened."* VIII, 11.
86.6. *actually occurred."* VIII, 24.
86.14. *this work."* VIII, 109.
86.32. *in general.* VIII, 23.
86.36. *the title.* VIII, 43.
87.11. *given circumstances."* VIII, 20.
87.24. *his mind.* VIII, 12.
87.27. *same reason.* VIII, 38–39.
87.33. *a fact."* VIII, 7.
88.3. *same time.* VIII, 6, 93; X, 376.
88.6. *seriously injured.* VIII, 5.
88.14. *of literature."* VII, 3.
88.23. *most natural."* VII, 57–58.
88.30. *popular fiction.* VII, 57.
89.30. *noble family.* X, 523.
89.36. *of nature."* VII, 424.
90.22. *senseless tragedies."* IV, 433.

91.5. *on them."* II, 376.
91.14. *sensible people.* II, 377.
91.25. *Dark Night."* VIII, 86–87.
92.20. *human folly.* VIII, 86.
92.24. *about them.* VIII, 165.
92.26. *human life."* VII, 15.
92.28. *and frauds.* IV, 430.
92.35. *of misfortunes."* IV, 430.
95.8. *feels happy."* VII, 28.
95.23. *with murder.* I, 208–9.
95.28. *"Claudius' Diary."* VIII, 95–97.
96.13. *between them."* VII, 429.
96.18. *own misfortunes.* VII, 430.
96.22. *die alone?"* VII, 404.
97.6. *to it."* V, 236–38.
97.26. *and carefree.* X, 927.
98.28. *secondary importance."* IV, 613.

100.35. *by it.* VIII, 159.
102.5. *with joy.*" VII, 247.
102.7. *the paper.*" VII, 87.
102.10. *heart leap.* VII, 165.
102.16. *its vibrations.*" VII, 73.
102.19. *rotten fish.*" VII, 3.
102.25. *emulate Saikaku.* VII, 10.
102.27. *author's part.* VII, 3–4.
102.32. *foreign languages.* VII, 519–20.
102.33. *centuries passed.* X, 946.
103.8. *his part.* VII, 82–83.

103.23. *spiritual elation.* VIII, 260.
103.27. *total elation.*" VII, 17.
104.30. *he said.* III, 433.
105.5. *second reading.* VII, 402.
106.4. *the material.* VII, 3.
106.35. *the brain.* VII, 37.
108.32. *this way.*" VII, 457.
109.1. *consciously didactic.* VII, 337.
109.7. *work's effectiveness.*" XII, 340.
109.10. *a clown.* VIII, 210.
109.30. *to face.*" V, 113–14.

CHAPTER FIVE

Akutagawa Ryūnosuke zenshū, 8 vols. (Tokyo: Chikuma Shobō, 1971) is the edition used here.

111.25. *of ideograms.*" V, 285.
112.18. *he wrote.* V, 288.
112.35. *an Apollonian.* IV, 177.
113.22. *to narration.*" V, 3.
113.32. *a microcosm.*" IV, 136.
114.24. *becomes meaningful.* VII, 55.
115.15. *same monster.*" II, 39.
116.5. *am asleep?*" IV, 88.
116.10. *human animals.*" VIII, 116.
116.35. *or both.* IV, 149.
117.31. *writing haikai.* V, 189.
118.9. *Japanese composition.*" V, 423.
118.33. *that reason.* V, 15.
119.7. *the surface.* V, 104.
119.10. *Ages Ago.* V, 126.
120.11. *or biography.*" V, 188.
120.17. *Ihara Saikaku.*" V, 188.
120.34. *broadest sense.*" V, 141.
121.2. *moving way.*" V, 118.
121.6. *his mate.*" V, 143.
121.23. *for women.*" VIII, 116.
121.34. *animal life.* V, 189–90.
122.28. *a novelist.*" V, 189.
122.32. *endure harder!*" I, 236.
123.29. *Tahitian woman.*" V, 159.
123.34. *realistic schools.*" V, 160.
124.1. *Arles period.* V, 160.
124.4. *the sky.*" VII, 76.
124.20. *or delicate.*" V, 126.
125.9. *great poets.*" V, 270.
125.24. *this world.*" V, 134.
125.31. *has created.*" V, 136.
126.15. *"poetic spirit.*" V, 135.

126.34. *Greek gods.* V, 162.
128.3. *him laughing.*" V, 26.
128.22. *elegant beauty.*" V, 160.
128.25. *'Young Buddha.'* " V, 161.
129.24. *many angles.* V, 76.
131.23. *into being.*" V, 130.
132.2. *a plot.*" V, 123.
132.10. *to Andreev.* V, 123–24.
132.24. *leading examples.* V, 130–31.
134.16. *to tell.* V, 130.
134.18. *essay-like stories.* V, 133.
135.24. *and everything.*" V, 133.
136.16. *manner of writing.*" V, 137.
136.30. *type of writing.* V, 419.
137.16. *that green.* V, 348.
137.31. *like Shiga.* VI, 188.
138.1. *write clearly.*" IV, 177.
138.4. *of vagueness.*" IV, 177.
138.25. *than this.* V, 131.
139.6. *the word.*" V, 179.
139.9. *an instant.*" V, 193–94.
139.19. *read books.* III, 236.
139.40. *female animal.* III, 237.
140.17. *around me.*" VII, 100.
140.36. *some time.*" IV, 193.
141.3. *not destroy.*" IV, 193.
141.15. *other faiths.*" VII, 55–56.
141.26. *within him?*" V, 256.
142.5. *the romantics.*" V, 200.
142.10. *understand him.*" V, 199.
142.15. *similar characteristics.* V, 215.
142.26. *(Jesus) added.*" V, 215.

CHAPTER SIX

References are to *Dazai Osamu zenshū*, 12 vols. (Tokyo: Chikuma Shobō, 1971–72).

145.6. *his looks.* VI, 3.
145.8. *own work."* II, 50.
146.30. *read it?* III, 243.
146.32. *a crime.* III, 266.
146.35. *serious misgivings."* III, 243.
147.6. *isn't it?* III, 244–45.
147.10. *by day."* III, 245.
148.10. *his wife.* III, 275.
149.11. *as "truth."* III, 269.
149.31. *with care."* VI, 50.
150.26. *of Shiga.* X, 299.
150.27. *wrote elsewhere.* X, 318.
151.5. *like that."* III, 94.
151.7. *dirty fellow."* III, 95.
151.10. *since childhood."* IV, 58.
151.12. *with shame."* IX, 366.
152.27. *a story.* X, 258–59.
152.33. *the weak,"* III, 334.
152.35. *ultimate goal."* III, 44.
153.4. *their agonies."* X, 323.
153.6. *mental anguish.* X, 325.
153.11. *a loser."* X, 325.
153.14. *Longer Human.* IX, 396.
153.20. *with fear"* IX, 38.
153.29. *crucified under."* IX, 179.
153.33. *own sinfulness."* IV, 320.
154.5. *an angel"* IX, 470.
154.6. *noble martyr"* IX, 225.
154.18. *to despair."* XI, 61.
154.37. *ugly man.* VIII, 220.
155.14. *a violet."* X, 200.
156.16. *plant nursery."* X, 319.
156.32. *monstrous person.* III, 115.
157.30. *and noble?"* X, 84.
158.10. *powerful movie.* X, 205.
159.4. *to say?* IX, 224.
159.22. *human being.* XI, 293.

159.27. *a man.* IX, 247.
159.29. *men around."* IX, 39.
160.13. *to her.* IX, 154.
160.18. *sister Kazuko.* IX, 163.
160.25. *even myself."* IX, 396.
160.30. *tenderness is."* X, 299.
160.35. *young workman.* X, 320.
161.4. *the poor."* X, 318.
161.18. *her tenderness."* IX, 234.
161.19. *the Heike."* XI, 293.
161.28. *in Japan."* IX, 204.
161.29. *a nobleman."* IX, 238.
162.8. *our literature,"* XI, 293.
162.9. *begets elegance."* XII, 414.
162.34. *into humor."* X, 372.
163.4. *humor instead.* X, 372.
163.27. *is "lightness."* VIII, 119.
165.11. *that time.* XI, 15.
165.19. *classical beauty.* X, 26.
165.34. *own way."* I, 273.
166.27. *he wrote.* III, 235.
166.33. *this respect.* III, 236.
167.13. *like these."* III, 237.
167.19. *entire story.* I, 248–49.
167.21. *to be."* I, 113.
167.26. *feet long.* I, 61.
167.29. *live on.* III, 146.
167.32. *the night.* IX, 14.
167.35. *dining room.* IX, 98.
168.6. *the left.* IX, 364.
168.35. *the heart.' "* X, 37.
169.20. *will work.* X, 58.
171.2. *such cases."* IV, 82.
171.12. *paper,"* etc. X, 66–67.
171.15. *stopped growing."* III, 250.
171.18. *to you."* X, 84.

CHAPTER SEVEN

Volume and page numbers are those of *Kawabata Yasunari zenshū*, 19 vols. (Tokyo: Shinchō Sha, 1969–74), unless noted otherwise.

175.11. *with beauty.* XV, 203.
175.25. *deprived existence."* XVIII, 213.

175.34. *gloomy clouds."* XIX, 239.
176.2. *is alive."* XII, 320, 331.
176.16. *nothing else.* XVI, 159.

176.27. *like that.* XVIII, 50.
176.27. *"pure life,"* XIV, 385; XVIII, 55.
176.27. *"genuine vitality,"* XVIII, 123.
176.28. *the wild,"* XIII, 47.
176.28. *"sturdy vitality."* XIII, 54.
177.12. *for vitality."* XIX, 44.
178.9. *My Love.* XIX, 91.
178.19. *to that."* XIX, 101.
182.2. *know that?"* V, 354.
182.18. *naked warmth.* III, 301.
183.21. *far distance."* X, 76.
185.2. *the pure."* XV, 223.
185.11. *Kawabata wrote.* XIV, 40.
185.13. *did not."* XIV, 130.
185.24. *less charming.* XIV, 135–36.
186.21. *and beauty."* XIII, 338–39.
186.29. *its destination."* XIII, 331.
186.33. *expressed therein."* XIII, 332.
187.4. *stopped living."* XII, 293.
187.17. *last thereafter. Shin bunshō tokuhon* (Tokyo: Shinchō Sha, 1954), p. 104.
187.23. *an adult"* XIX, 76.
187.33. *Satō Hachirō."* XVIII, 50.
188.6. *a novelist."* XVIII, 51.
189.4. *her composition.* XIX, 23.
191.3. *evening sky.* XIV, 262, 266.
191.8. *to me.* XIV, 262.
192.3. *true youthfulness.* XIII, 198.
192.9. *in vain."* XIII, 200.
192.19. *dying man." Akutagawa Ryūnosuke zenshū,* VIII, 116.
192.24. *dying man.' "* XIII, 58.
193.26. *modern Japan,"* XIX, 112.
193.30. *of luck.* XIX, 218.
194.4. *in society."* XIII, 127.
194.32. *its teacher."* XIII, 334.
195.7. *perfecting oneself.* XIII, 112.
195.18. *once lamented.* XVIII, 184–85.

195.24. *"scribbles" emerge.* III, 304.
196.1. *someone else."* XVIII, 185.
197.1. *entire career."* XIII, 232.
199.4. *with you."* XIV, 384.
199.10. *and sad."* XIV, 385.
200.27. *word 'beauty' . . . "* XV, 196.
203.36. *of plot. Shōsetsu nyūmon* (Tokyo: Kōbundo Shobō, 1970), pp. 64–65.
204.15. *an end."* XIV, 242.
204.29. *being continued.* "Kaisetsu" in Kawabata Yasunari, *Nemureru bijo* (Tokyo: Shinchō Sha, 1967), p. 197.
205.3. *hero's death.* XIV, 246.
205.7. *first chapters.* XIV, 270.
205.35. *those additions."* XIV, 131.
206.5. *any point."* XIV, 131.
206.19. *expediency's sake."* XIV, 259–60.
207.14. *affirmative, too. Shōsetsu nyūmon,* p. 71.
208.10. *older times.* XII, 277.
208.30. *and present. Shōsetsu no kenkyū* (Tokyo: Kōbundo Shobō, 1970), p. 47.
209.18. *icicles fell.* XIII, 233.
209.27. *dead girl."* XIII, 235.
210.9. *to understand." Shin bunshō tokuhon,* p. 17.
210.14. *"strangulation penalty"*). XIII, 275.
210.17. *he advised.* XVII, 138–39.
211.1. *he liked.* XIII, 375–79.
211.4. *word 'lily.' "* XIII, 165.
212.24. *'How beautiful.' "* XV, 207–8.
213.31. *written language."* III, 100.
215.18. *resist death."* VII, 35.
216.1. *pleasant one."* XIV, 388.
216.6. *himself confessed.* XIV, 207.

CHAPTER EIGHT

References are to *Mishima Yukio hyōron zenshū* (Tokyo: Shinchō Sha, 1966), if no title is cited. The definitive edition of Mishima's complete works, *Mishima Yukio zenshū,* 36 vols. (Tokyo: Shinchō Sha, 1973–) is being published at present, and it is abbreviated as *MYZ* hereafter.

220.8. *artificial universe. MYZ,* X, 155.
220.22. *of language."* P. 864.
220.29. *and plants. Nihon bungaku*

shōshi (Tokyo: Kōdan Sha, 1972), pp. 61–63.
221.5. *at night." MYZ,* IX, 261.

221.24. *any minute.* P. 460.
221.25. *called sound."* P. 462.
221.36. *eternal mystery."* P. 499.
222.11. *he said.* P. 499.
224.14. *stomach itself.* Mushiaki Aromu, ed., *Mishima Yukio bungakuron shū* (Tokyo: Kōdan Sha, 1970), p. 12.
224.34. *indeed possible.* P. 1008.
225.1. *Mishima observed.* P. 691.
225.29. *female territory.* P. 1008.
225.37. *the body."* Mushiaki, p. 288.
226.22. *delicate constitution.* Mushiaki, pp. 149–50.
227.32. *the radiation.* P. 900.
228.2. *landscape gardening. MYZ*, V, 251–52.
228.3. *all literature."* Mushiaki, p. 439.
228. 16. *for conformity.* P. 544.
233.2. *each other."* P. 424.
233.7. *mind's poison." MYZ*, V, 548.
233.9. *be cured.* P. 461.
233.10. *his mind.* Pp. 134–35.
233.13. *long life.* P. 116.
233.14. *of life.* Pp. 87–89.
233.17. *break it.* P. 508.
233.34. *an inspiration.* Pp. 509–10.
234.19. *for exercise."* P. 427.
234.26. *live abroad.* P. 426.
235.25. *so on.* Pp. 312–14.
236.10. *of him.* Pp. 452–55.
236.31. *to abstraction.* P. 452.
239.23. *the wind. MYZ*, X, 265–67.
239.29. *that way." MYZ*, X, 55.
240.22. *not there.* P. 317.
241.15. *of anxiety.* P. 528.
241.27. *modern mentality."* P. 529.
242.6. *upon them." Shōsetsu to wa nani ka* (Tokyo: Shinchō Sha, 1972), p. 9.

242.21. *need control." Nihon bungaku shōshi,* pp. 146–47.
243.3. *external universe."* P. 491.
243.17. *be hidden?* Cited by Mishima in *Nihon bungaku shōshi,* pp. 134–35.
244.9. *gone soft." Ibid.,* p. 147.
244.20. *the universal."* P. 690.
244.31. *"my Arcadia."* P. 510.
246.19. *human world.* P. 404.
248.34. *as possible."* P. 908.
249.18. *commercial firm.* Pp. 281–82.
249.32. *life itself.* Pp. 481–82.
250.11. *the novel."* Mushiaki, p. 456.
250.36. *minute details.* P. 541.
251.5. *that day."* P. 434.
251.27. *he wove." Bunshō tokuhon* (*Fujin kōron* furoku. Tokyo: Chūō Kōron Sha, 1959), p. 37.
252.2. *tasteless water." Ibid.,* pp. 46–47.
252.6. *third, clarity." Ibid.,* pp. 45–46.
252.15. *intellectual trance." Ibid.,* pp. 47–48.
253.29. *Thomas Mann.* Pp. 419–21.
254.12. *winter's day.* Mushiaki, p. 32.
255.4. *toward self-reform.* P. 422.
255.26. *too well. Bunshō tokuhon,* p. 50.
256.20. *living dead. MYZ*, V, 108.
256.22. *of stones. MYZ*, X, 126.
256.36. *than that. Fudōtoku kyōiku kōza* (Kadokawa Bunko. Tokyo: Kadokawa Shoten, 1967), p. 97.
257.12. *own beauty." Kōdōgaku nyūmon* (Tokyo: Bungei Shunjū Sha, 1970), p. 53.
258.2. *behavior accordingly." Nihon bungaku shōshi,* p. 17.
259.5. *this one. Shōsetsu to wa nani ka,* p. 105.

Selected Bibliography

✿

I. IN ENGLISH

General Works

Fujino, Yukio. *Modern Japanese Literature in Western Translations: A Bibliography.* Tokyo, 1972.

Keene, Donald, ed. *Modern Japanese Literature: An Anthology.* New York, 1956.

Kimball, Arthur G. *Crisis in Identity and Contemporary Japanese Novels.* Tokyo, 1973.

Kokusai Bunka Shinkōkai, ed. *Introduction to Contemporary Japanese Literature.* 3 vols. Tokyo, 1939, 1959, 1972.

Miyoshi, Masao. *Accomplices of Silence: The Modern Japanese Novel.* Berkeley, Calif., 1974.

Morishige, Alyce H. K. "The Theme of the Self in Modern Japanese Fiction." Diss., Michigan State, 1970.

Morris, Ivan, ed. *Modern Japanese Stories: An Anthology.* Tokyo, 1962.

Nakamura, Mitsuo. *Contemporary Japanese Fiction, 1926–1968.* Tokyo, 1969.

———. *Modern Japanese Fiction, 1868–1926.* Tokyo, 1968.

Okazaki, Yoshie. *Japanese Literature in the Meiji Era,* tr. by V. H. Viglielmo. Tokyo, 1968.

Chapter One

Etō, Jun. "Natsume Sōseki: A Japanese Meiji Intellectual," *American Scholar,* XXXIV (1965), 603–19.

Flutsch, Maria. "The Novels of Natsume Sōseki's "Middle Road": A Critical Examination of the Development of Sōseki's Thought and Art in His Creative Writings from 1907 to 1910." Diss., Sydney, 1974.

Hibbett, Howard S. "Natsume Sōseki and the Psychological Novel." In Donald H. Shively, ed., *Tradition and Modernization in Japanese Culture* (Princeton, N.J., 1971), pp. 305–46.

Japanese National Commission for Unesco, ed. *Essays on Natsume Sōseki's Works.* Tokyo, 1972.

McClellan, Edwin. "An Introduction to Sōseki, a Japanese Novelist." Diss., Chicago, 1957.

———. *Two Japanese Novelists: Sōseki and Tōson.* Chicago, 1969.

Matsui, Sakuko. "Natsume Sōseki as a Critic of English Literature." Diss., Sydney, 1971.

Natsume, Sōseki. *Botchan,* tr. by Alan Turney. Tokyo, 1972.

———. *Grass on the Wayside,* tr. by Edwin McClellan. Chicago, 1969.

———. *I Am a Cat,* tr. by Katsue Shibata and Motonari Kai. Tokyo, 1961.

———. *Kokoro,* tr. by Edwin McClellan. Chicago, 1957.

———. *Light and Darkness,* tr. by V. H. Viglielmo. Honolulu, 1971.

———. *Mon,* tr. by Francis Mathy. London, 1972.

———. *The Three-Cornered World,* tr. by Alan Turney. London, 1965.

———. *The Wayfarer,* tr. by Beongcheon Yu. Detroit, 1967.

Sparling, Kathryn W. "Early Natsume Sōseki: Images and Patterns of the Absolute." Diss., Harvard, 1973.

Viglielmo, Valdo H. "An Introduction to the Later Novels of Natsume Sōseki," *Monumenta Nipponica,* XIX (1964), 1–36.

———. "The Later Natsume Sōseki: His Art and Thought." Diss., Harvard, 1957.

Yu, Beongcheon. *Natsume Sōseki.* New York, 1969.

Chapter Two

Cheng, Ching-mao. "Nagai Kafū and Chinese Tradition." Diss., Princeton, 1971.

Iriye, Mitsuko M. "Quest for Literary Resonance: Young Nagai Kafū and French Literature." Diss., Harvard, 1969.

Nagai, Kafū. *Geisha in Rivalry,* tr. by Kurt Meissner. Tokyo, 1963.

———. "Hydrangea," tr. by Edward Seidensticker. In Morris, ed., *Modern Japanese Stories,* pp. 65–80.

———. "The River Sumida," tr. by Donald Keene. In Keene, ed., *Modern Japanese Literature,* pp. 159–200.

Seidensticker, Edward. *Kafū the Scribbler.* Stanford, Calif., 1965.

Chapter Three

Chambers, Anthony H. "Tradition in the Works of Tanizaki Jun'ichirō." Diss., Michigan, 1974.

Hibbett, Howard S. "Fantasy in the Fiction of Tanizaki Jun'ichirō." Japan P.E.N. Club, ed., *Studies on Japanese Culture* (Tokyo, 1973), I, 252–56.

Hosillos, Lucila. "Tanizaki's *The Makioka Sisters* as a Reflection of the Dialectics of the Modernization of Japan," *ibid.,* I, 270–80.

Keene, Donald. "Tanizaki Jun'ichirō." In Keene, *Landscapes and Portraits* (Tokyo, 1971), pp. 171–85.

Seidensticker, Edward. "Kafū and Tanizaki," *Japan Quarterly,* XII (1965), 491–97.

Tanizaki, Jun'ichirō. *Ashikari and the Story of Shunkin,* tr. by Roy Humpherson and Hajime Okita. Tokyo, 1936.

——. *Diary of a Mad Old Man*, tr. by Howard S. Hibbett. New York, 1965.

——. "The House Where I Was Born," tr. by S. G. Brickley. In S. G. Brickley, *The Writing of Idiomatic English* (Tokyo, 1951), pp. 118–29.

——. "In Praise of Shadows," tr. by Edward Seidensticker. *Japan Quarterly*, 1 (1955): 46–52.

——. *The Key*, tr. by Howard S. Hibbett. New York, 1961.

——. *The Makioka Sisters*, tr. by Edward Seidensticker. New York, 1957.

——. "The Mother of Captain Shigemoto," tr. by Edward Seidensticker. In Keene, ed., *Modern Japanese Literature*, pp. 387–97.

——. *Seven Japanese Tales*, tr. by Howard S. Hibbett. New York, 1963.

——. *Some Prefer Nettles*, tr. by Edward Seidensticker. New York, 1955.

——. *A Spring Time Case*, tr. by Zenchi Iwado. Tokyo, 1927.

Chapter Four

Mathy, Francis. *Shiga Naoya*. New York, 1974.

Shiga, Naoya. "At Kinosaki," tr. by Edward Seidensticker. In Keene, ed., *Modern Japanese Literature*, pp. 272–77.

——. "Han's Crime," tr. by Ivan Morris, *ibid.*, pp. 261–71.

——. "The Patron Saint," tr. by Michael Y. Matsudaira. In Richard N. McKinnon, ed., *The Heart Is Alone* (Tokyo, 1957), pp. 74–85.

——. "The Razor," tr. by Francis Mathy. *Monumenta Nipponica*, XIII (1957), 165–76.

——. "Seibei's Gourds," tr. by Ivan Morris. In Morris, ed., *Modern Japanese Stories*, pp. 81–89.

Sibley, William F. "The Shiga Hero." Diss., Chicago, 1971.

Chapter Five

Akutagawa, Ryūnosuke. "Autumn Mountain," tr. by Ivan Morris. In Morris, ed., *Modern Japanese Stories*, pp. 173–84.

——. "A Clod of Earth" and "Flatcar," tr. by Richard N. McKinnon. In McKinnon, ed., *The Heart Is Alone*, pp. 3–9, 118–33.

——. "Cogwheel," "The Marshland," and "The Mirage," tr. by Beongcheon Yu. *Chicago Review*, XVIII (1965), No. 2, 31–62.

——. *Exotic Japanese Stories*, tr. by Takashi Kojima and John McVittie. New York, 1964.

——. *A Fool's Life*, tr. by Will Petersen. New York, 1970.

——. *Hell Screen and Other Stories*, tr. by W. H. H. Norman. Tokyo, 1948.

——. *Japanese Short Stories*, tr. by Takashi Kojima. New York, 1961.

——. *Kappa*, tr. by Geoffrey Bownas. London, 1970.

——. *Rashōmon and Other Stories*, tr. by Takashi Kojima. New York, 1952.

————. *Tales Grotesque and Curious*, tr. by Glenn W. Shaw. Tokyo, 1930.

————. *The Three Treasures and Other Stories for Children*, tr. by Takamasa Sasaki. Tokyo, 1944.

Arima, Tatsuo. "Akutagawa Ryūnosuke: The Literature of Defeatism." In Arima, *The Failure of Freedom: A Portrait of Modern Japanese Intellectuals* (Cambridge, Mass., 1969), pp. 152–72.

Hibbett, Howard S. "Akutagawa Ryūnosuke and the Negative Ideal." In Albert M. Craig and Donald H. Shively, eds., *Personality in Japanese History* (Berkeley, Calif., 1970), pp. 425–51.

Tsuruta, Kinya. "Akutagawa Ryūnosuke and I-Novelists," *Monumenta Nipponica*, XXV (1970), 13–27.

————. "Akutagawa Ryūnosuke: His Concept of Life and Art." Diss., Washington (Seattle), 1967.

Yu, Beongcheon. *Akutagawa: An Introduction*. Detroit, 1972.

Chapter Six

Brudnoy, David. "The Immutable Despair of Dazai Osamu," *Monumenta Nipponica*, XXIII (1968), 457–74.

Dazai, Osamu. "Cherries" and "Of Women," tr. by Edward Seidensticker. *Encounter*, I (1953), 23–28.

————. "The Courtesy Call," tr. by Ivan Morris. In Morris, *Modern Japanese Stories*, pp. 464–80.

————. "Metamorphosis," tr. by Thomas J. Harper. *Japan Quarterly*, XVII (1970), 285–88.

————. *No Longer Human*, tr. by Donald Keene. New York, 1958.

————. "Osan," tr. by Edward Seidensticker. *Japan Quarterly*, V (1958), 478–87.

————. "Romanesque," tr. by John Nathan, *ibid.*, XII (1965), 331–46.

————. *The Setting Sun*, tr. by Donald Keene. New York, 1956.

————. "Villon's Wife," tr. by Donald Keene. In Keene, *Modern Japanese Literature*, pp. 398–414.

Keene, Donald. "Dazai Osamu," in Keene, *Landscapes and Portraits* (Tokyo, 1971), pp. 186–203.

O'Brien, James A. "A Biographical and Literary Study of Dazai Osamu." Diss., Indiana, 1969.

————. *Dazai Osamu*. New York, 1975.

Chapter Seven

Araki, James T. "Kawabata: Achievements of the Nobel Laureate," *Books Abroad*, XLIII (1969), 319–23.

————. "Kawabata and His *Snow Country*," *Centennial Review*, VIII (1969), 331–49.

Fernandez, Jaime. "The Unreality of Love: Time and Death in Kawabata's 'Lyric Poem,'" *Monumenta Nipponica*, XXVI (1971), 267–85.

Kawabata, Yasunari. *Beauty and Sadness*, tr. by Howard S. Hibbett. New York, 1975.

——. *The Existence and Discovery of Beauty*, tr. by V. H. Viglielmo. Tokyo, 1969.

——. *The House of the Sleeping Beauties and Other Stories*, tr. by Edward Seidensticker. Tokyo, 1969.

——. "The Izu Dancer," tr. by Edward Seidensticker. *Atlantic Monthly*, January 1955, pp. 108–14.

——. *Japan the Beautiful and Myself*, tr. by Edward Seidensticker. Tokyo, 1969.

——. *The Lake*, tr. by Reiko Tsukimura. Tokyo, 1974.

——. "Lyric Poem," tr. by Francis Mathy. *Monumenta Nipponica*, XXVI (1971), 287–305.

——. *The Master of Go*, tr. by Edward Seidensticker. New York, 1972.

——. "The Mole," tr. by Edward Seidensticker. In Keene, ed., *Modern Japanese Literature*, pp. 366–74.

——. "The Moon on the Water," tr. by George Saitō. In Morris, ed., *Modern Japanese Stories*, pp. 245–57.

——. *Snow Country*, tr. by Edward Seidensticker. New York, 1956.

——. *The Sound of the Mountain*, tr. by Edward Seidensticker. New York, 1970.

——. *Thousand Cranes*, tr. by Edward Seidensticker. New York, 1958.

Liman, Anthony V. "Kawabata's Lyrical Mode in *Snow Country*," *Monumenta Nipponica*, XXVI (1971), 251–65.

Mathy, Francis. "Kawabata Yasunari, Bridge-Builder to the West," *ibid.*, XXIV (1969), 211–17.

Seidensticker, Edward. "Kawabata," *Hudson Review*, XXII (1969), 6–10.

Swann, Thomas E. "Thematic Structure in Kawabata Yasunari's *Kinjū*." In Japan P.E.N. Club, ed., *Studies on Japanese Culture*, I, 421–25.

Tsukimura, Reiko. "Theme and Technique in *Mizuumi*," *ibid.*, I, 433–39.

Tsuruta, Kinya. "The Flow-Dynamics in Kawabata Yasunari's *Snow Country*," *Monumenta Nipponica*, XXVI (1971), 251–65.

Chapter Eight

Duus, Louise. "The Novel as Kōan: Mishima Yukio's *The Temple of the Golden Pavilion*," *Critique: Studies in Modern Fiction*, X (1968), 120–29.

Keene, Donald. "Mishima Yukio." In Keene, *Landscapes and Portraits*, pp. 204–25.

Lebra, Joyce C. "Mishima's Last Act," *Literature East and West*, XV (1971), 279–98.

McCarthy, Paul F. "On *Confessions of a Mask*." In Japan P.E.N. Club, ed., *Studies on Japanese Culture*, I, 314–21.

Mishima, Yukio. "An Appeal," tr. by Harris I. Martin. *Solidarity*, August 1971, pp. 32–35.

——. *Confessions of a Mask*, tr. by Meredith Weatherby. New York, 1958.

——. *Death in Midsummer and Other Stories*, tr. by Edward Seidensticker et al. New York, 1966.

———. *The Decay of the Angel*, tr. by Edward Seidensticker. New York, 1974.

———. *Five Modern Nō Plays*, tr. by Donald Keene. New York, 1956.

———. *Forbidden Colors*, tr. by Alfred H. Marks. New York, 1968.

———. *Madame de Sade*, tr. by Donald Keene. New York, 1967.

———. *Runaway Horses*, tr. by Michael Gallagher. New York, 1973.

———. *The Sailor Who Fell from Grace with the Sea*, tr. by John Nathan. New York, 1965.

———. *The Sound of Waves*, tr. by Meredith Weatherby, New York, 1956.

———. *Spring Snow*, tr. by Michael Gallagher. New York, 1972.

———. *Sun and Steel*, tr. by John Bester. Tokyo, 1970.

———. *The Temple of Dawn*, tr. by E. Dale Saunders and Cecilia Segawa Seigle. New York, 1973.

———. *The Temple of the Golden Pavilion*, tr. by Ivan Morris. New York, 1958.

———. *Thirst for Love*, tr. by Alfred H. Marks. New York, 1969.

Nathan, John. "The Life and Works of Yukio Mishima." Diss., Harvard, 1973.

———. *Mishima: A Biography*. Boston, 1974.

Scott-Stokes, Henry. *The Life and Death of Yukio Mishima*. New York, 1974.

Seidensticker, Edward. "Mishima Yukio," *Hudson Review*, XXIV (1971), 272–82.

Viglielmo, Valdo H. "Mishima and Brazil: A Study of *Shiroari no su.*" In Japan P.E.N. Club, ed., *Studies on Japanese Culture*, I, 461–70.

II. IN JAPANESE

Primary sources can be found in the preceding section entitled "Source Notes." The place of publication for the works below is Tokyo unless indicated otherwise.

Chapter One

Etō, Jun. *Natsume Sōseki.* 1960.

Karaki, Junzō. *Natsume Sōseki.* Nishinomiya, 1966.

Kataoka, Ryōichi. *Natsume Sōseki no sakuhin.* 1962.

Komiya, Toyotaka. *Natsume Sōseki.* 3 vols. 1953.

Nihon Bungaku Kenkyū Shiryō Kankōkai, ed. *Natsume Sōseki.* 1970.

Senuma, Shigeki. *Natsume Sōseki.* 1968.

Yoshida, Seiichi, ed. *Natsume Sōseki hikkei.* 1967.

Chapter Two

Akiba, Tarō. *Kōshō Nagai Kafū.* 1966.

Hinatsu, Kōnosuke. *Kafū bungaku.* 1950.

Miyagi, Tatsurō, ed. *Nagai Kafū no bungaku.* 1973.

Nakamura, Shin'ichirō, ed. *Nagai Kafū kenkyū.* 1956.

Nihon Bungaku Kenkyū Shiryō Kankōkai, ed. *Nagai Kafū.* 1971.

Satō, Haruo. *Kafū zakkan*. 1947.
Yoshida, Seiichi. *Nagai Kafū*. 1953.

Chapter Three

Ara, Masahito, ed. *Tanizaki Jun'ichirō kenkyū*. 1972.
Itō, Sei. *Tanizaki Jun'ichirō no bungaku*. 1970.
Nihon Bungaku Kenkyū Shiryō Kankōkai, ed. *Tanizaki Jun'ichirō*. 1972.
Noguchi, Takehiko. *Tanizaki Jun'ichirō ron*. 1973.
Nomura, Shōgo. *Tanizaki Jun'ichirō*. 1973.
Saegusa, Yasutaka. *Tanizaki Jun'ichirō ronkō*. 1969.
Yoshida, Seiichi, ed. *Tanizaki Jun'ichirō* (Kindai bungaku kanshō kōza). 1959.

Chapter Four

Imamura, Tahei. *Shiga Naoya ron*. 1973.
Nakamura, Mitsuo. *Shiga Naoya ron*. 1966.
Nihon Bungaku Kenkyū Shiryō Kankōkai, ed. *Shiga Naoya*. 1970.
Nishio, Minoru, ed. *Shiga Naoya no tanpen*. 1968.
Shindō, Junkō. *Shiga Naoya ron*. 1970.
Sudō, Matsuo, ed. *Shiga Naoya* (Kindai bungaku kanshō kōza). 1967.
Yasuoka, Shōtarō. *Shiga Naoya shiron*. 1968.

Chapter Five

Akutagawa Ryūnosuke zenshū (Chikuma Shobō edition), bekkan, 1971.
Bungaku Hihyō no Kai, ed. *Hihyō to kenkyū: Akutagawa Ryūnosuke*. 1972.
Fukuda, Tsuneari, ed. *Akutagawa Ryūnosuke kenkyū*. 1957.
Nakamura, Shin'ichirō, ed. *Akutagawa Ryūnosuke annai*. 1955.
Nihon Bungaku Kenkyū Shiryō Kankōkai, ed. *Akutagawa Ryūnosuke*. 1970.
Yoshida, Seiichi. *Akutagawa Ryūnosuke*. 1942.
———— et al., eds. *Akutagawa bungaku: kaigai no hyōka*. 1972.

Chapter Six

Kamei, Katsuichirō, ed. *Dazai Osamu* (Kindai bungaku kanshō koza). 1959.
Koyama, Kiyoshi, ed. *Dazai Osamu kenkyū*. 1956.
Moriyasu, Masahiro, ed. *Dazai Osamu no kenkyū*. 1968.
Nihon Bungaku Kenkyū Shiryō Kankōkai, ed. *Dazai Osamu*. 1970.
Okuno, Takeo. *Dazai Osamu*. 1973.
Saeki, Shōichi, ed. *Dazai Osamu*. 1966.
Sako, Jun'ichirō. *Dazai Osamu ron*. 1963.

Chapter Seven

Hasegawa, Izumi. *Kawabata Yasunari ronkō*. 1969.
————, ed. *Kawabata Yasunari*. 1970.
Hasegawa, Izumi, and Takeda Katsuhiko, eds. *Kawabata bungaku: kaigai no hyōka*. 1969.

Kaishaku Gakkai, ed. *Kawabata Yasunari no bungaku.* 1972.
Kawabata Bungaku Kenkyūkai, ed. *Kawabata Yasunari no ningen to geijutsu.* 1971.
Nihon Bungaku Kenkyū Shiryō Kankōkai, ed. *Kawabata Yasunari.* 1973.
Yamamoto, Kenkichi, ed. *Kawabata Yasunari* (Kindai bungaku kanshō kōza). 1959.

Chapter Eight

Hasegawa, Izumi, ed. *Mishima Yukio.* 1971.
────── et al., eds. *Mishima Yukio kenkyū.* 1970.
Muramatsu, Takeshi. *Mishima Yukio: sono sei to shi.* 1971.
Nihon Bungaku Kenkyū Shiryō Kankōkai, ed. *Mishima Yukio.* 1972.
Saegusa, Yasutaka, ed. *Mishima Yukio: sono unmei to geijutsu.* 1971.
Sugawara, Kunitaka, ed. *Mishima Yukio tokuhon* (*Shinchō* rinji zōkan). 1971.
Yoshimura, Teiji. *Mishima Yukio no bi to haitoku.* 1966.

Index

*Containing both original titles
and translated titles*

Index 291

DAZAI

AKUTAGAWA

TANIZAKI

KAFŪ